The Cover Story

The cover photograph provides a **cohering image** for this book's title and contents. Wood and flesh are flowing upward. I helped my father plant the tree almost three-fourths of a century ago, and almost half of a century ago planted my hand on the tree and took the picture by self-timer — my hand below our firstborn's and above my mother's, whose hand is above her mother's.

Imagine a series of time-lapse photographs of that tree in one-year intervals: can you not see its wood flow upward, its branches reach out and up? Phenomenological photography is the art of taking a single frame in such a way that the subject seems to move, the impossible ideal being to take a picture of a tree's growing but not of the tree. In this photograph, I sought to convey a sense of the flow of *wood* by superimposing on the tree trunk a flow of *flesh,* four generations of my family. (Get out an old family album and peruse it rapidly enough so you can see the flesh flow.)

Do you see the metaphor in the paragraph immediately above? It's not **flow,** for wood as a plastic flows and flesh flows through genes. The metaphor is **reach** applied to tree branches, which can't really reach because they're not arms. We're like all of nature in that we flow, and we're unlike almost all of nature in having reaching arms ending in grasping hands.

And we are unlike all of nature in — here comes another metaphor — reaching for *invisibles.* We need a word for what in us does this peculiar, unique reaching. The most frequently encountered word for it is *spirit.*

Now you have the whole title: *Flow of Flesh, Reach of Spirit.*

In his *Four Quartets,* T. S. Eliot wove together, in four long dialog meditations, his thoughts on the essential human **tension** between our place in the space-time world (flow of flesh) and our striving to escape into transcendence (reach of spirit). While I was experiencing the play on Broadway, 1,700 miles away our middle son died, forever imbuing that play for me with poignancy and prayer. This book is about that tension, and its divinely intended resolution.

LOREE GANGWISH ELLIOTT

Chaplain and Director of Pastoral Services,
Hospice of Cape Cod

and

for a half century
my beloved wife, partner, and companion
on whom I have never looked
without
joy

Flow of Flesh, Reach of Spirit

THINKSHEETS OF A CONTRARIAN CHRISTIAN

Willis Elliott

WILLIAM B. EERDMANS PUBLISHING COMPANY
GRAND RAPIDS, MICHIGAN

© 1995 Wm. B. Eerdmans Publishing Co.

255 Jefferson Ave. S.E., Grand Rapids, Michigan 49503

Printed in the United States of America

00 99 98 97 96 95   7 6 5 4 3 2 1

Library of Congress Cataloging-in-Publication Data

Elliott, Willis, 1918-
Flow of flesh, reach of spirit: thinksheets of a contrarian
Christian / Willis Elliott.
p.   cm.
Includes bibliographical references and index.
ISBN 0-8028-0813-1 (paper: alk. paper)
1. Theology. 2. Christianity — 20th century.
3. Christian life — United Church of Christ (U.S.) authors.
4. Elliott, Willis, 1918-   . I. Title.
BR50.E55   1995
248.4'85834 — dc20   95-17636
CIP

Contents

III. THE WORLD AGAINST US: Evil

IV. THE WORLD WITHIN US: Interiority

Contents

Foreword

For several decades now, some of us have been trying to keep Willis Elliott a secret. Journalists in particular need not only their sources but also their trusted back-bench experts — experienced thinkers and thinking practitioners whom they can turn to, toss ideas around with, test hunches on. A good back-bencher is not a monologist. You have to know how to listen as well as talk. You have to be self-effacing, too: back-benchers don't get quoted much, that's how we keep them secret. The influence they enjoy is a subtler kind. They help others get things straight. Willis Elliott is one of my most dependable back-benchers, but he is not mine alone.

Two decades ago, Willis went public on his wide circle of friends and correspondents. Every few weeks he would send on his "Thinksheets," two- to eight-pages of reflections on whatever animated, intrigued, infuriated, delighted him, to a group he chose to call religious leaders. The voice was unmistakably his, and so was the format. By now, there are some 2,800 Thinksheets.

A Thinksheet of his is not another newsletter (thank God!) but a conversation in printed form. For Willis Elliott is not just a theologian but that rarer, more comprehensive figure: a superb conversationalist who, in the manner of Boswell's Dr. Johnson, takes all of culture and politics as grist for comment and reflection. Indeed, Elliott's most important achievement, amply demonstrated in the pages that follow, is to remind us that all really good theology is, or ought to be, good conversation.

Theology as conversation: the notion is as old as Paul's letters, as up-to-date as modern hermeneutics. David Tracy, the contemporary Roman Catholic theologian at the University of Chicago (where Elliott earned a doctorate), has identified three "publics" which theology must address: society, the church, and the academy. Willis Elliott has been doing that for more than half a century. He has been, among other things, a pastor and counselor, a university and college professor, a denominational bureaucrat, and a seminary professor and administrator. That's the short list. For the past fifteen years he has been the biblical scholar in residence at the United Church of Christ's Cape Cod retreat center in Craigville, Massachusetts. He also remains, at age seventy-seven, professor at large of New York Theological Seminary.

It's that "at large" that I want to stress. Even when he worked within ecclesiastical or academic structures, Elliott has always operated "at large" with that personal concern which makes all true conversation an exercise in conversion. (Like Kierkegaard, he is instinctively aware that the other party to a conversation is someone whom "God puts in our path.")

For example, when I first met Willis more than twenty-five years ago, he was dean of exploratory programs at New York Theological Seminary, which was then just three blocks east of the *Newsweek* building and only a few doors from my favorite after-hours bistro. George ("Bill") Webber had just taken over as president and wanted to bridge the gap between the seminary and the streets. Among other tasks, Elliott was assigned to entice scholars currently resident in New York City for other reasons (usually research) to teach courses at the seminary. I asked Willis how he screened candidates. "It's simple," he replied, "as simple as Psalm 84. I ask them what they sing about and what they long for. If they are singing without longing, they are too satisfied with the status quo. And if they are longing without singing, they lack the joy of the Lord and are too ready to sacrifice the present to the future. What I'm looking for are people with the right biblical balance."

It is characteristic of Elliott that he found the answer to an administrative task in the pages of the Bible. If there has been one constant in his long and variegated life, in addition to his dedication to Christ ("Jesus," he likes to say, "is my relative absolute") and his devotion to his wife Loree, it is the Christian Scriptures. Daily for a half century he has read the Bible in the original Hebrew and Greek and in recent decades also in Latin and a modern language in addition to English. And therein lie the keys to understanding Elliott and this book.

More than any other theologian I have read, Willis Elliott thinks with the Bible. If I had to label him, I'd call him a biblical humanist. Unfortunately, the word "humanist" is pejorative among fundamentalists and other defenders of biblical infallibility with whom Elliott has long had profound disagreements. What I mean is that Elliott accepts Jesus not only as the revelation of what God is like, but also as the person in whom we discover what it means to be fully human. Christian humanists, inspired in part by Christianity's classical Greek heritage, have always argued thus. But Elliott is a biblical humanist in the sense that for him, the biblical text itself establishes the categories by which we come to know what being human is all about, and the terms by which we can understand and evaluate competing humanistic philosophies and enthusiasms.

Fortunately, Elliott is by temperament inclusive. One of the great delights of his conversations is his ability to appropriate what he finds good in such things as the human potential movement, the ecology movement, and all manner of humanistic concerns. His greatest virtue as a writer is the concision with which he elucidates the wellsprings of contemporary cultural currents. He is, as I said, an exceptional listener, which means he really hears what others say or write. Turn to any of the pages that follow and you may find him inviting you into an internal conversation on "the mutual superiority of the sexes" or "stability and conflict in community" or "eyeballs for an earhole religion" or the "scrupulous godlessness" of public education and the media or "the biblical way of making sense" or how religion both messes up and straightens out the world. His range is catholic because he understands that nothing is foreign to theological inquiry.

x

We needn't always agree with Elliott to learn from his distinctions and reflections. He and I, for instance, part company on the morality of abortion, and he is rather more pious toward the environment than I am. (His home, I notice, is not only handsome and self-built, but environmentally correct.) Moreover, I am not always persuaded by his occasional diagrammatic approach to issues, perhaps because I never was much good at geometry. Where Elliott excels is in pulling words apart to show their roots and webs of meaning. Next to the Bible, in fact, his greatest love is language, which he plays with like a grandmaster at chess. Here are no deconstructionist word games. Rather, like George Steiner, he understands that the meaningfulness of human language is guaranteed by a God who speaks.

As David Tracy has also observed, the Protestant imagination tends to be dialectical, the Catholic analogical. Elliott's imagination is smoothly bicameral. To be sure, Elliott is Protestant. He is, moreover, a churchman, which is to say that he takes very seriously the need for community and public worship and recognizes the chaos that ensues when traditions are heedlessly jettisoned. But his spirit is instinctively irenic and ecumenical: he is as much at home in counseling celibate Roman Catholic nuns as he is with married couples in his own church. A respecter of traditions, he moves easily into those not his own.

Enough idle praise. With this book, the secret is out. Here is Willis Elliott for everyone's enjoyment and intellectual delight. To paraphrase Dante, abandon all hope you who enter on these pages, of remaining firmly fixed in your cherished assumptions. You're in the presence of a great conversationalist. So let the conversation begin.

Kenneth L. Woodward
Senior Writer and Religion Editor, Newsweek

Introduction

How I read a book: How do you?

Would I want to read this book if I were you? Depends on what sort of reader you are. I'll tell you the kind of reader I am. And if you're anything like that, you'll enjoy and profit from this book: I wrote it for readers like me.

First, I read the subject index. What, no subject index? Already I'm turned off. But if there's a subject index and something in it grabs me, I read those references. If there's a bibliography, I read that next: it's like exploring a fish's insides to check on the diet. (That won't work with this fish. It has digested its food, so there's no bibliography.) Even if at this point my interest has almost vanished, I usually feel kindly disposed enough toward the author, known or unknown to me, to read the table of contents. If a chapter heading holds my attention, I read that chapter. And if that trip was worth it, I make another to the contents . . . and so on.

Or instead of going to the contents, I might stare at the title, ask myself what sort of book I'd write on the subject, then sketch a table of contents, then read the author's table of contents. I prefer this approach, for it lets me get up to author-speed so my reading of the book will be *conversing, not just listening.*

There, as Kenneth Woodward has already said in the foreword, is your primary clue to reading this book: it is my end of some **conversations.** This means . . .

. . . it's for readers serious enough to sweat out their end of at least some of these half-conversations, and . . .

. . . it's *oral* literature, the opposite of Victorian children: it's to be heard more than seen. It's to be read out loud, or at least subvocalized — in either case slowly, at moron speed, to cancel that high speed you were so proud of when you took that speed-reading course.

All that is why . . .

This book needs talking with

"I learned more than they did" is a comment you've often heard from teachers. Well, now, if you talk with me, in talking with my book, you'll teach yourself more than I could teach you. God is your best teacher, you yourself are next best, and I come somewhere way down the line. But if you read me, you are in range of my convictions and opinions, which I hope will prove helpful in "stir[ring] up your pure minds" (2 Pet. 3:1 KJV) just as I'd expect to be helped if I came into your range.

What this book was

"Elliott Thinksheets," that's what. The book is a Thinksheet *sampler,* a selection from some 2,800 occasional pieces distributed by subscription, with some printing-and-distributing support from the Lilly Endowment. I took "Think-" from IBM's company motto, and "-sheet" from "broadsheet,"[1] a one-sheet (often two-page) advertisement such as that which falls out of your daily newspaper if you don't handle it right.

Unbeknownst to me, Wm. B. Eerdmans Jr. came upon some of these Thinksheets and wrote asking me to "put together a selec-

---

1. Often called a "broadside." Most of the Thinksheets are one sheet, most of them two-sided.

tion logically organized so that the reader may have, in topical arrangement, your provocative and insightful comment on the secular and religious events of our time." That states both the origin and nature of this book, almost all of whose chapters were Thinksheets. Not "thought" sheets, lecturing my readers; but "think" sheets, inviting readers' "think."

So almost all of the chapters of this book are born-again Thinksheets — some just as they were published, some slightly touched up, some completely rewritten.

"Occasion"

The **occasion** for this book is my saying yes to Mr. Eerdmans' suggestion. My Thinksheets are distributed **occasionally.** But here also lies a problem: the Thinksheets are "**occasional** literature," most of them having sprung up out of specific occasions in my life, the church's life, the world's life.

Here's the squeeze: You'd be impatient with *dated,* dead material that was, when I wrote it, vital and *timely* for me; and if I were to rub out the time references into *timelessness,* I'd destroy the whole idea and feel of my Thinksheets, turning them into essays.

My editor and I have agreed, therefore, Thinksheet by Thinksheet, on whether a time reference is so integral to the message that eliminating it would be destroying, or at least diminishing, the effect of the message. I can but appeal to your imagination, flexibility, and generosity. Where a date appears in a footnote, please try to imagine yourself in my outer and inner situation back then. You will read in this book nothing that I do not at the present time hold as conviction or opinion, but of course now I might put some things a somewhat different way.

A fourth and final meaning of *occasion* refers to the times you respond to *tolle lege.*[2] May the occasions be many and your reading

2. The children's-game words, "Take up and read," that Augustine heard and, in obeying, was converted to Christianity.

xiv

times brief. Read only until your own fires of meditation are kindled, then mark the place for next time. I make my own personal index of books I judge worth reading and saving, and leave almost no page without underlining or scribbling or both.

A further benefit to reading this book in brief snatches is that you won't be so inclined to rush through sentences and finish chapters. Read my sentences rapidly and they'll turn to mush: you need to *hear* them, with a range of pitch and volume and with full attention to punctuation.[3]

What to look for, and what not to

Since you know that each chapter was originally an independent piece, a single seashell on the beach here strung together with other seashells to make this book-necklace, you won't expect too much of the artificial organization into sections. Further, only a few can be strung on each of the sections, not enough to cover what I would say if I were doing an exposition of each section.

But what should you look for? Children sing "M-O-T-H-E-R,/Put it all together/it spells 'Mother.'" Well, when you put this book all together, your way, what will it spell? Romans 3:11 says "Nobody puts it all together so it says 'God,' so nobody seeks God."[4] Yet **God** is the one continuum you will find in my book. Am I, then, contradicting the psalmist and Paul? No; rather, supporting. For the psalmist and I are decrying the folly of leaving God out; and Paul and I are including all under the folly of sin so

---

3. Miss a comma and you're likely to mess up the sentence and miss the sense and give up in disgust, not at yourself but at me! As for boldface and italics, they are my major and minor visual and aural reading aids.

4. My paraphrase takes off from the literal meaning of the Greek word behind "understanding": συνίημι, *suniemi,* means to understand because you've left out of consideration nothing pertinent, and you've put it all together in the pattern that makes the best sense. The Vulgate here has "Nobody's intelligent [intelligens]." And the second clause in Paul's quotation from the Septuagint of Psalm 14:2 and 53:2 uses an intensive verb: "Nobody searches diligently for God, seeks him out."

that none may be excluded from the invitation to the wisdom of God's gracious forgiveness in Jesus Christ.

Some comparisons that may help

While there is some variety of genre, most of the chapters are like a **flower** whose petals point to its center but themselves are mere radii, landing strips for bees attracted to the center by the petals. A chapter's petals-sections are tightly related to its center-theme, but loosely, if at all, related to each other. You may pluck the petals and arrange them to your mind's content. It's one way for you to create your half of the conversation.

Here's a comparison from **poetry.** Of fellow poet Norman Cameron, Dylan Thomas said, "A poem by Cameron *needs* no more than one image; it moves around one idea, from one [inner-] logical point to another, making a full circle."[5]

And this one from **music.** Frederick the Great handed the great Bach a brief musical theme for improvisatory exploration.[6] What the master did with those few bars was so spectacular that the "royal theme" remains to this day a classic.

And these from the **Bible.** Look closely and you'll see some sections of the Gospels arranged around a person, an event, a type of experience, an idea.[7] Or quickly run through the letter to the Hebrews. Its structure is concatenate variations around the idea that the new age is better than the old, and the virtue most needed in the transition is persistence.

My point is this: Most of this book's chapters have a pattern you've often seen in nature and in human creations. But you've not often seen it in book chapters, which are usually linear devel-

5. From *The Collected Letters of Dylan Thomas,* ed. Paul Ferris (London: J. M. Dent & Sons Ltd., 1985), p. 281.

6. As a *ricercar,* French *recherecé,* later called *fugue.*

7. Luke 15 is three parables arranged around the experience of lostness. Scholars call a piece in such a construction a *pericope,* a transliteration from Greek meaning literally "cutting around," a cut-out.

opments within a linear-logical artifact called a "book." What you have in your hands at this moment is not a "book" in that familiar sense. On first glance it can seem episodic, fragmentary, perhaps even chaotic. Maybe it will help you see with fresh eyes if you think of yourself as the bee to my flowers. Unless you pollinate, no fruit; unless you work, no honey.

Title

The comma in this book's title signals what distinguishes us from the rest of God's invisible and visible creation: we are both flesh and spirit, part animal and part angel, living our lives "at the juncture of nature and spirit."[8]

"Flesh" primarily means our biological reality flowing through successive generations.[9] This God-made flesh is "very good" (Gen. 1:31). It's simply the you people can see[10] in contrast to the you people can't see.[11] But some friends warned me that "flesh" in the title would be a turn-off. "Sounds pornographic," said one, as in "flesh flicks." I countered that in addition to the primary meaning, I intended the secondary meaning: "The flesh is what man has made himself. . . . the total effect upon man of his own sin and of the sin of all who have gone before him. . . . The flesh is human nature as it has become through sin. . . . human nature weakened, vitiated, tainted by sin."[12]

And besides sin, evil: today, the excessive flow of human flesh is lowering the quality of the environment for ourselves and for God's other living creatures.

8. An oft-quoted phrase of Reinhold Niebuhr.

9. Qoheleth (Ecclesiastes 1:4) had the idea: "A generation goes, and a generation comes, but the earth remains." And I had the idea when almost a half century ago I took the four-hand picture that appears on the front cover of this book.

10. In Hebrew, *basar.*

11. In Hebrew, *lev,* the inner you of "heart"-spirit-mind-will-soul.

12. William Barclay, *Flesh and Spirit: An Examination of Galations 5:19-23* (London: SCM Press, 1962), p. 22.

Now, looking out over the flow of flesh in both senses is "a tiny control tower of **spirit**,"[13] a self-transcendence one flight up from that power to conceptualize and arrange ideas which we call reason. This mysterious though central part of us is like a caterpillar coming to a twig end and using most of its body to make circles in the air in hope of touching its next meal. My early life passion was natural science, to learn all I could about the twig and the caterpillar. But since my middle teens, what has most fascinated me within the whole creation is humanity, and most intensely that circling in the air, that *reach* of spirit that is more and other than the desires of the flesh — that reach for the More Than, the Other, the Beyond that is somehow also within.

If you stand on a city street and point, soon many will stop and look in the direction in which you are pointing. I am grateful to the many whose lives and words have pointed to God, leading me to pay the utmost heed to the Highest.

In Houghton, New York, where I first immersed myself in higher education, all that remains of the old church is the *hand* which for generations pointed to heaven from atop the spire. Before the railroads took over, the boats in the Erie Canal moved slowly past that church, and for more than an hour the rough boatmen could see that hand. That hand left no doubt as to what that building was for. What the church is for. What the prophets and Jesus and the apostles were for.

. . . What this book is for. To point to the Abiding from the standpoint of the ever-changing scene. To help others ponder the Eternal amid the passing as "a generation goes, and a generation comes."

---

13. A felicitous phrase of Gabriel Fackre, in *The Promise of Reinhold Niebuhr*, rev. ed. (Lanham, Md.: University Press of America, 1994), p. 15. Boldface is mine.

Subtitle

In 1941 I heard Christian philosopher Elton Trueblood say, "It's what you leave out that wrecks you." If I had not already been a **contrarian** at the time, I wouldn't have remembered it. Two-thirds of a century ago I was a member, by choice in baptism and confirmation, of a modernist church, but soon became contrarian to modernism — so much so that I wrote to the minister to tell him he was going to hell. Yes, I had experienced an evangelical conversion and had become a member of a fundamentalist church. But in a few years I became a contrarian to fundamentalism, which seemed to have its head screwed on crooked, though its heart was in the right place.

I mean that, in addition to being born contrarian, I've had practice. Besides, I'm a Protestant, an historical contrarian, practicing the "the Protestant principle" of criticizing "any absolute claim made for a relative reality."[14] And though a faithful member, I'm a contrarian within my Protestant church, the United Church of Christ.

Too extraverted to be a dropout. Furthermore, one cannot be serious about Jesus Christ without loyal fellowship in his Body the Church.

"A contrarian **Christian**," the subtitle announces. A canonical-classical Christian of evangelical-radical stamp and critical consciousness — a "libergelical."

Contrarian, yes. But a thankful, joyful, playful, hopeful, singing, as well as old, contrarian. "An aged man is but a paltry thing, / A tattered coat upon a stick, unless / Soul clap its hands and sing, and louder sing / For every tatter in its mortal dress."[15]

14. Paul Tillich, *The Protestant Era,* trans. James Luther Adams (Chicago: University of Chicago Press, 1948), p. xii.

15. William Butler Yeats, "Sailing to Byzantium," in *Selected Poems and Three Plays of William Bulter Yeats,* 3rd ed., ed. M. L. Rosenthall (New York: Macmillan, 1986).

Language

Except where otherwise noted, biblical quotations are from the New Revised Standard Version, or are my own "word for word" or "meaning for meaning" translations as appropriate to my contexts.[16] "Dynamic equivalence" is the latest way of saying "meaning for meaning."

I prefer the NRSV for its sound scholarship and its *inclusive-language* guidelines. Longtime friend Bruce Metzger and his committee came to the happy **compromise** of using gender-neutral language to replace the generic masculine when referring to humanity, but without revisioning language for deity. In speaking and writing, I never use the generic masculine — "man," "he," "his," "him[self]" — for the human being; though of course I use the masculine for the male human being.[17] But when speaking and writing of God, I follow the full biblical practice: I use both the masculine titles and the masculine pronominals ("he," "his," "him[self]").

May our words, mine and yours, give entrance to the Word to "dwell in us richly, in all wisdom" (Col. 3:16 KJV).

Willis Elliott

16. King Alfred, d. A.D. 901, said he translated "one-while word-for-word, another-while meaning for meaning."

17. Surrendering the generic masculine is, however, not all gain. For example, "all men" (generic) includes children as well as women, but "all women and men" and "all men and women" exclude children. And replacements for "man" in "God and man" and "man and nature" lack the euphony and efficiency of those dyads.

When all else seems to fail,
see the beauty!

On our regular walk to and along the ocean last night,[1] I said to my wife Loree, "As war seems more and more probable, I'm praying harder and harder against it." She said something like this: "Remember the times we were with Frank Laubach, how he encouraged prayer not against but for?" And I remembered not only that but the great and radiant beauty of Frank Laubach's being shining in his craggy old face, the face of a man whom ninety-six governments invited to teach their peoples to read. I'm in self-contradiction when I pray for peace, for I believe a) that Saddam Hussein's expansionist effort must fail in Kuwait as it failed in Iran, and b) that only the destruction of his mischief-making powers (chemical, biological, nuclear) will clip his wings. But I am clear that our need for **inner beauty,** my need for it, our country's need for it, the world's need for it, is unambiguous; and that anyone, anywhere, anytime can make a start at it, a new start; and that any human achievement in its absence will be, or become, demonic.

1. "Just wait till spring!" said a nonagenarian to me an hour ago. "It's going to be sooo beautiful! Yesterday I planted 150 bulbs!" **Beauty transcends time.** It is of the mind, of the soul. We capture it out of the past, we experience it here and now, we anticipate it in and beyond time. It participates in eternity, for it is a creature, a gift, a grace from the Eternal. That old codger's health is so iffy

---

1. 8 November 1990.

1

that he may not make it to spring, but no matter: his soul has already seen next spring's flowers — and the flowers beyond, for his faith in the eternal Benevolence is bright and beautiful.

2. The invitation to "*See* the beauty!" could summarize the contribution of the great Roman Catholic theologian Hans Urs von Balthasar, for whom — even more than truth and goodness — beauty was **the door to God.** But the words are from a nine-year-old girl, a sheaf of whose poems were given me by a counselee, her mother, in deep distress because her husband, the girl's father, spent all his free time on his yacht, away from his family. I reproduce here only the poem in which the girl is appealing to her father:[2]

GO!
Rush Rush Rush!
Can you **stop**?
God can!
YOU CAN TRY IT!
Sit down, stay a while.
He doesn't mind.
He made **peace**.
He made the green grass,
He made the sky.
Come on, stop and look.
See the beauty!

I don't know the dollar cost of purchasing and maintaining that yacht, but I do know that the invisible cost was that child, a cost no thing has any right demanding. One hopes that (as in this Thinksheet's title) all else did fail for that stupid man. If all else did fail, would it be punishment from God? Of course. Would it be a blessing from God? Of course. "Punishment" and "blessing"

---

2. In another poem: "God is my Father. /. . . My father is not my Daddy. / He is just borrowing me. . . ." And in another, of her parents: "I am whatGodgave to them to borrow."

would be the same reality from two coigns of vantage: respectively, the divine righteousness-wrath and the divine love-mercy.

3. I am eager to tell you a wondrous tale of beauty. It's about a shy twenty-one-year-old introvert who was embarrassed when handed a **peacock-feather** tickler at the 1896 Oktoberfest, the raucous annual Munich beer-chaos Loree and I experienced seventy-five years later. Far from tickling anybody (as the game was), he couldn't bear to even look at others doing it, so he just stared at the feather. Five years later, he wrote this in a letter:

The longer I carried it around with me, the more did the slenderness of its form occupy me, how it swayed on its elastic stalk, and the beauty of its head, out of which the 'peacockeye' looked at me dark and secretly. I felt as though I were seeing such a feather for the first time, and it seemed to me to contain a whole profusion of beauties which no one noticed but I. And out of this feeling the little poem came into being, which I dedicated at that time to a dear friend, a painter, of whom I knew that he too loved peacockfeathers [and whose gift and work enabled him to appreciate them more] — the harmony in the variety and the multitude of colors, all together on such a little spot. . . .

But do you know what was to me the main thing about it: that I once more saw that most people hold a thing in their hands in order to do something silly with it (as for example tickling each other with peacockfeathers), instead of looking well at each thing and instead of asking each thing about the beauty it possesses. So it comes that most people do not know at all how beautiful the world is and how much glory is manifest in the smallest things, in some flower, a stone, the bark of a tree, or a birchleaf. Grown people, who have affairs and cares and torment themselves with a lot of trifles, gradually lose entirely their eye for these riches, which children, if they are attentive and good, soon notice and love with all their heart. And yet it would be nicest if everybody would always remain in this respect like attentive and good children, simple and devout in feeling, and

3

if they would not lose the ability to rejoice as sincerely in a birchleaf or a peacock's feather or the wings of a marsh heron as in a great mountain range or a magnificent palace. The small is no more small than the big — is big. A great and eternal beauty runs through the whole world, and it is justly spread over the small things and the large; for substantially and essentially there is no injustice upon the whole earth. Thus, dear Helmuth, all hangs together a little with the poem about the peacockfeather, in which I could but badly express what I meant. I was still very young then. But now I know it better with every year and am always better able to tell people that there is a great deal of beauty in the world — almost only beauty.[3]

In almost every child's mind, I am convinced, firefly-like poetic connections stitch the darkness; but it is the poet who brings into the light the garment stitched in the darkness within, in inner beauty-truth-goodness. Romantic poets like Rilke are masters of the poetry of beauty and love. There is a cost, of course: while you're staring at beauty, you aren't seeing injustice and other uglinesses. But this Thinksheet presupposes that many of my readers lately have been staring too much at what's wrong with the world and neglecting that looking that heals, refreshes, and so energizes the soul that it glows in the sin-darkened world. And it may be that justice, as is true of happiness, can be deeply got at only indirectly, by aiming at something of which it is a byproduct, something deeper than fairness, something not of society at all but of the soul. Of that profounder something, beauty is at least a component.

3. Excerpts from this letter of the twenty-six-year-old Rainer Maria Rilke appear in M. D. Herter Norton, *Translations from the Poetry of Rainer Maria Rilke* (New York: W. W. Norton, 1962), p. 236. The peacockfeather poem, on page 27, speaks of Rilke's childhood experience of peacockfeathers and of his connecting them in his child-mind with stories "good little Grandmama / often read me of wishing-wands," and of his own dreaming that peacockfeathers are "love-tokens . . . / selves in cool night hand each other, / when children are all gone to sleep," and even of peacockfeathers' having "the crafty force of the divining rod —/ [so I] sought you in the summer grass."

Flannery O'Connor celebrated that something in the same indirect way that we must get at happiness (and justice?). A non-commercial raiser of peafowl, she often floats on a peafeather, though wryly she says "the word *beauty* never crosses my lips." But hear her in her poem, "The Peacock Roosts": "The clown-faced peacock / Dragging sixty suns / Barely looks west where / The single one / Goes down in fire."[4] She doesn't have to use the word! "Sixty suns"! Her **inner beauty**, rooted in a radiant Catholic faith, let her hard-edged mind draw hard-nosed sketches of the hard world, and do so without cynicism.

4. Some human beings become, for those near if not also far, emblems or **models** of certain *virtues,* both cardinal (prudence, temperance, fortitude, justice) and theological (faith, hope, and love), and/or certain *values* (beauty, truth, goodness). When these exemplary lives have the effect of directing their attenders to God, the biblical word for them is *"holy* ones" (French, "saints"), for they bridge like Jacob's ladder from the Holy One to the common ones.[5] When I think of that nine-year-old unofficial saint pleading with her father, the King James Version phrase "the beauty of holiness" springs to mind, as does my Shakespeare-spouting father's quote, "He hath an inner beauty that makes me ugly."

4. Sally Fitzgerald, ed., *The Habit of Being: Letters of Flannery O'Connor* (New York: Vintage, 1980), p. 56.

5. For the technical sense of "saints," see Kenneth Woodward's *Making Saints* (New York: Simon & Schuster, 1990), which he reviewed in *Newsweek,* 12 November 1990, pp. 80f: "The primary purpose of canonization is to provide contemporary examples of holiness for the edification and . . . emulation of the faithful."

All things bright and beautiful

All things bright and beautiful, all creatures great and small, all things wise and wonderful; the Lord God made them all.

1. Each little flower that opens, each little bird that sings, he made their glowing colors, he made their tiny wings.

2. The purple-headed mountain, the river running by, the sunset and the morning that brightens up the sky.

3. The cold wind in the winter, the pleasant summer sun, the ripe fruits in the garden: he made them every one.

4. He gave us eyes to seem them, and lips that we might tell how great is God Almighty, who has made all things well.[1]

I've traced this hymn through many collections and hymnal companions and — unusual for a popular sacred song — have found no variations from its first appearance in Ms. (yes, "Cecil") Alexander's *Hymns for Little Children* (1848), though two of her stanzas no longer appear. It was in the supplemental hymnal of the congregation of my long pastorate but until recently had not appeared in the formal hymnals of

---

1. From Donald P. Hustad, ed., *The Worshiping Church: A Hymnal* (Carol Stream, Ill.: Hope Publishing, 1990).

most denominations.[2] The youth movement of the 1960s put "Amazing Grace" on the map of pop songs; and British veterinarian James Herriot's four books, one for each line of the hymn's refrain, has nudged our hymn at least near the map, as has the general culture's rising eco-consciousness.

Our hymn's first word is *"All"*: **biodiversity!** It's based on the second article of the Apostles' Creed, "Maker of heaven and earth." Miss Hymphreys (her maiden name; she was Irish) was "the greatest of women hymn-writers in English."[3] "Intergenerational" is a word we would use today for her hymns for children: their simple piety embraces all of us Christians.

While our hymn proclaims divine creation, its emphasis is on **inclusivity,** the fact that *"every one"*[4] of nature's bountiful variety is a creation of God. The word "all" signals this inclusivity five times, four of the times in the refrain and the fifth at the last stanza's end. And to dispel the notion that this divine action is impersonal and en masse, the very first word of the first stanza is *"each."* In representing this inclusivity and biodiversity, an artist must suggest the whole by choosing a few of "all creatures great and small" to symbolize all. This John Lefton has done in his continuous-line bestiary I have titled "Jesus and the Beasts of Both Comings."[5]

You're smiling, aren't you? Besides being a virtuoso performance, this pen-ramble has the freedom, joy, and seriousness of a child's drawing. It's Palm Sunday, Jesus is riding on his **donkey,** and the crowd is — other animals. Wings and scales and fur and feet and horns of land, sea, and air, "creatures great and small." Other animals with which God has ordained we should share the world. Animals gathered around Jesus as birds gathered around St. Francis.

When I decided to put these drawings in this book, I marked them with meanings I saw, then asked John to critique my markings

2. The Anglicans being the exception: she was the wife of an Anglican bishop, and it began to appear in Anglican hymnals in 1916.

3. Says Eric Routley in *Hymns and Human Life* (Grand Rapids, Mich.: Wm. B. Eerdmans, 1952), p. 214.

4. The last words of the third stanza.

5. See chapter 32 for more on the artist, p. 162 for more on the drawing.

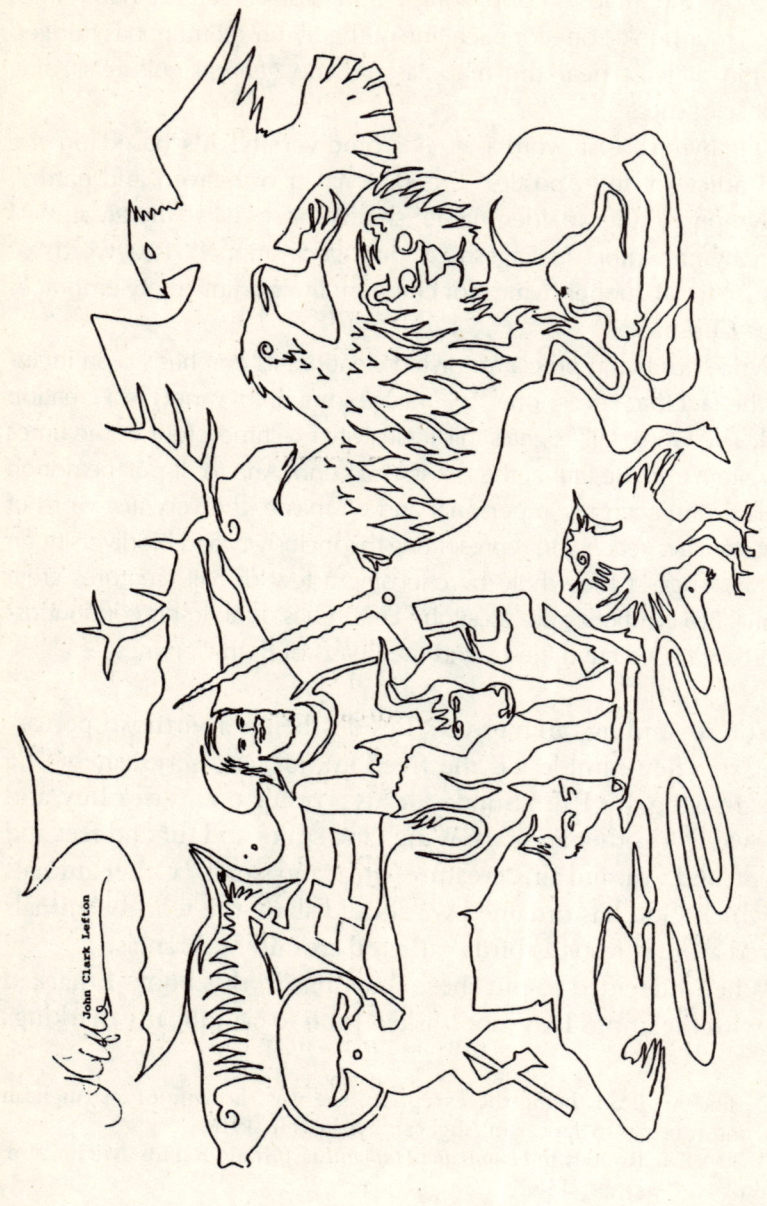

John Clark Lofton

Jesus and the Beasts of Both Comings

and to add annotations of his own. Try your hand at this, then read my notes and his combined, his in quotations marks.

Jesus on that two-Testament[6] donkey was the take-off into this natural and fantastical bunch of beasts. See Eden's **snake** (Gen. 3:14) about to bite the foot of Peter's conscience-**rooster** (Matt. 26:34, 75 and parallels), which is connected to the fabulous **unicorn,** symbol of Jesus' purity and invincible strength, in stark contrast to Peter's mendacity and weakness. The **dove,** reminding us of the Spirit at Jesus' baptism, seems to be talking into — or pecking? — his right ear. The dove reminds us also of "Noah's ark" (Gen. 8:8-12) and "the seven gifts (Isa. 11:2) of the Spirit, often illustrated in art by use of seven doves."

Contiguous-continuous with the dove is "the hind, hart, or stag, a symbol of faithful Christian longing for God (Ps. 42:1, NRSV 'deer') and of solitude and purity."

Now we come upon something surprising: the dove and deer not only flow into each other by one of the deer's horns but also are joined by the superimposition of the unicorn's horn! Carl Jung remarked that the unicorn is sometimes transmuted into a white dove. What additional meanings occur to you as you contemplate the confluence of these three creatures? To create this remarkable piece of Christian art, John would not have had to have all these meanings in mind: the spiritually sensitive often say or do more than they know, as did the prophets of Israel.

Moving clockwise, we come upon birds four and five, both of them connected to the deer. The **eagle,** "symbol of Spirit, associated with St. John the Evangelist," because "his sermons [the Gospel and the three Letters of John] soar to the heights." The final bird, bringing us through the unicorn to the first bird, Peter's rooster, is the **phoenix,** "mythical bird said to have lived 500 years, then built its own funeral pyre, lit it, fanned the flames, was consumed, and after three days emerged as a new bird"; both its fletching and the flames appear here.

6. Zech. 9:9, Matt. 21:5, and John 12:15.

9

The three-day resurrection theme appears also in the **lion** intimately merged with the phoenix. It signifies the lion totem of the tribe of Judah, but also the father lion who, finding that his three cubs had been killed, "restored them to life by breathing into them" the breath of life (Gen. 2:7, John 20:22). Again, "the lion is majestic and the symbol of vigilant protection."

Continuing clockwise and skipping the two animals already treated above, we come to the **dog**, "in Renaissance portraits a symbol of fidelity"; and emblem of the priest-pastor "who guards and guides and protects his human flock" (the sheepdog, in a bestiary, standing in for the shepherd). Suppose the artist also saw this animal as a wolf. Connected as it is to the lamb, we could then have the two of them "living together."[7]

Appropriately touching Jesus is the only animal providing a biblical name for Jesus: the **lamb**, "symbol of sacrifice used frequently in Old Testament and New Testament (Exod. 12:21 and John 1:29 and parallels)." The Christ lamb "has a halo" and as the victorious Lamb of God is carrying a cross-bearing battle flag — a mood the artist has signaled further in providing a perky tail for the lamb. The defeated-crucified is also the victorious-resurrected Lamb of God so prominent in the Bible's last book. And does that Lamb, biblically the wolf's favorite food, have its foot on the wolf's head while the wolf is observing the snake — the two animal symbols of evil?

We come finally to the Jesus **fish,** it and the cross being the earliest Christian visual self-identifications. Use your concordance to note how Jesus references fish, what connotations of "fish" we have from him. From that study you'll see how easy it was for the fish, like the Lamb, to come to mean Jesus; for as an acrostic, the letters of the most common Greek word for fish spell "Jesus Christ [is] God's Son and Our Savior."

Why does my title refer to a bestiary of "Both Comings"? Because most of the animals in the drawing blur the distinction between the Incarnation and the Return, between the historical and the eschatalogical Jesus.

7. Isa. 11:6; though here not "feeding together," v. 25.

10

This chapter started out with a hymnic celebration of biodiversity in God's pleroma, fullness, of creation. After our *song,* we went on to the *sight* of what we had sung about. I was with this artist for some years in a New York Saturday morning group called "Breakfast for the Hungry Hearted" and can testify to the profound and joyful Christian spirit behind and within this drawing: it is his soul made visible.

1995 Supplement

1. Of Ms. Alexander's many hymns, my favorite begins with a metaphor drawn from the theme that pervades "All things bright and beautiful," namely, nature: "Jesus calls us o'er the tumult / Of our life's wild, restless sea. . . . In our joys and in our sorrows, Days of toil and hours of ease, / Still he calls in cares and pleasures, / Christian, love me more than these / . . . Serve and love thee best of all!"

2. While "All things bright and beautiful" includes nature above us, all nature is **beneath** our "reach of spirit." Thus the title of the book's first section, "The World BENEATH Us: Earth." We live in nature, but our spirits reach beyond it to "The World **ABOVE** Us: God" (the title of the book's sixth section).

11

"God created . . . darkness." Why?

Something happened last night[1] in Lincoln Center before the New York Philharmonic concert, and this morning at breakfast I told fifteen beloved friends, seated in a circle, about it. As you will see, the story includes the Christmas card printed below.

Salute You!

There is nothing I can give you which you
have not; but there is much that, while I
cannot give, you can take.

No heaven can come to us unless our hearts
find rest in it today.
Take Heaven.

No peace lies in the future which is not hidden
in this present instant.
Take Peace.

1. 17 December 1993.

12

The gloom of the world is but a shadow;
behind it, yet within our reach, is joy.
Take Joy.

And so, at this *Christmas* time, I greet you,
with the prayer that for you, now and forever,
the day breaks and the shadows flee away.
— Fra Giovanni, A.D. 1513

Seating myself next to a plain-looking, late-middle-aged woman before the concert, I asked, "You are new to this seat, aren't you?"

"Yes, I am."

"My name is Willis Elliott." She gave me hers. "Where, may I ask, do you live?"

"Brooklyn."

"Ah, yes. And what, may I inquire, is your religion?"

"Strange that you should ask," she replied. "Just last night I was feeling very religious and decided to read the Bible straight through, beginning immediately. I'm Armenian Evangelical, but we don't have a church in Brooklyn so I joined the Episcopal Church. But let me tell you what happened last night. I started reading, and it said that God created darkness and light."

She paused, and I looked at her. "Why the frown?"

"Well, I can understand God's creating light, but why darkness?"

"Now, let me get this straight. Last night you started reading through the Bible and you got stuck before the third verse of the first chapter of the first book?"

"Yes."

"If you're going to bog down that easily, how many years do you figure it's going to take you?"

She appreciated the gentle humor, and laughed. "But if I don't understand what I'm reading, why bother?"

"Why indeed! The Bible is a talk-back book: you talk back to it, as you did, and it will talk back to you. Reading is one word for this process, prayer is another: God's Spirit helps us understand as

13

we reach for the light as we read. Yes, the light! You think it was not a good idea of God to make darkness?"

"Well, sometimes it seems that way."

"Yes, it does. In my pocket I have a 480-year-old Christmas card that may help. It was given to me as a greeting this afternoon by the librarian of New York Theological Seminary. The paper isn't that old, but the greeting is. It's by Fra (Brother) Giovanni, who lived joyfully for Jesus in humility and poverty." I then read it to her, pausing to look at her after each section, her smile broadening throughout.

"I think I'm ready to go on reading."

As we stood up to leave after the concert, which included Kurt Weill's "The Seven Deadly Sins," she smiled, squeezed my arm, and said, "Thank you for the Christmas card."

A few comments on this do-it-yourself, pre-commercial Christmas card:

1. Brother Giovanni gave, as a Christmas present, all that he had, the gift of challenging words closing with the gift of prayer.
2. Rest, "in this dark world of sin," is heaven: heavenly rest! And, like "eternal life" in the Gospel of John, it's available now, for the taking, with open heart and hands. So not having it is something one has deprived oneself of.
3. A hunt for mind and heart, to find the "hidden" peace here and now!
4. So much is beyond our reach, but joy is not among that much.
5. Today[2] is epiphany, day-break!

2. 6 January 1993.

14

Back to the outhouse!

We Americans have become environment-conscious enough to accept the notion that society, collectively as well as individually, is responsible for the defense of "**nature**," our bio-support system. First came the defense of the nation, 1776 and all that. Then came the defense of the citizen, the Bill of Rights and all that. Now we have the defense of the biosphere, whose health and wealth can no longer be taken for granted.

Go back about two decades, though, and consciousness-raising about our species' deleterious effects on the planet that God satisfiedly pronounced "very good"[1] was tough. If you were into it, you were thought to be some kind of nut. I was.

Back then, in the small, beautiful Westchester County, New York, village of Chappaqua, a near-Hudson bedroom town north of New York City, I started a modest campaign to convince the citizenry and thus the town board to convert sewage disposal from individual septic systems to individual **outhouses** in order to move *back to the future*. My media and mouth-to-ear effort was a counterpoise to a proposal the board was considering: the coerced installation of a public sewage system which would send the town's offal (after processing) down Hudson to New York City, paralleling our sending most of our working stiffs down rail to the same destination.

My argument was eminently commonsensical (as well as

---

1. *Tov meod,* Gen. 1:31 (resultant meaning, "very pleased").

scientific). I pictured the city as desiring to thank us twice, not just once: "We thank you for your workers, and we want to continue to thank you for managing your effluvia back home in Chappaqua." But the town's political worthies, giving only risible consideration to my proposal, removed the city's second occasion for gratitude: in went the public sewer, everywhere ripping wide gashes in mother earth's skin.

After my pitifully few supporters and I lost, I placed a piece titled "Back to the Chamber Pot: 'Improvement' Brings No Joy"[2] in northern Westchester's leading newspaper. It was a tongue-in-cheek cushion-shot, "doing theology" in relation to the basic value-rethinking we must do if we — humankind — are to survive. After the decision but before the installation, I hoped to set the sewer discussion at a new angle and at greater depth and breadth by **shifting attention** from sewer to toilet. And yet I hoped to exploit the humor inherent in the subject, to exploit it for (to use a labored phrase!) the theology of ecology: "The earth is the Lord's,"[3] not ours; we are its stewards, its trustees, and are to run it for the glory of God, who first appeared among us as a gardener (Gen 1:8). We are its renters and are to keep up the property, not just pay the rent. In this as in all else, I wanted to call attention to God, whom we forget at our peril and loss and pernicious influence.

Why this strenuous preaching from an unexpected pulpit, namely, the *potty*? It's dramatically simple and is used daily — as much so as "I am the door."[4] And it's *fons et origo,* the micro-source of humanity's direct pollution problem which increasingly demands macro-planning and more "advanced" technology. Attention to it can free us from technologism's "Big is beautiful" to E. F. Schumacher's fresh-thinking "Small is beautiful."[5]

Here are some snatches from "Values," my op-ed essay:[6]

2. Editorial page, *Patent Trader,* 16 March 1972.
3. Psalm 24:1; quoted in 1 Cor. 10:26.
4. Or "gate." John 10:7.
5. He soon moderated this radical rhetoric to "appropriate-size technology." Compare the bicycle adaptations in *The Ugly American.*
6. Somewhat revised, no change in sense.

Back to the chamber pot and the outhouse! In the cities, the chamber pot and honey wagon! . . . It sounds crazy, but it's *intelligent.* Now they're coming to tear up the beautiful gardens of our Chappaqua home to "improve" sewage disposal by pushing our problem elsewhere, NIOB ("not in our back yard"). Long-range, ecologically, that's *crazy,* not intelligent. Long-distance crazy. Like "fighting communism" in Vietnam so we won't have to in California, and then discovering consequent baleful fallout in California. Crazy, like failing to ratify certain conventions of the U.N., such as the Universal Declaration on Human Rights, because "we don't have the problem" in America. Crazy, like pushing national problems off onto the heads and shoulders of the lower classes. Crazy, like America-first resistance to the emergence of global authorities for the handling of global problems. Crazy, like refusing to think about resources and pollution in global terms.

Well, won't the processing plant eliminate effluvial disease? Even if it does, it will increase eutrophic pollution, the major problem for marine life. But wasn't pushing our problem off onto the fish "inevitable," the "progress"-minded pushers of the adopted technology arguing "Eventually, why not now?"[7] and scoffing at alternatives as unthinkable? . . . On this and many other problems of our shrinking planet, we're going to have to think again, **think anew,** if for our children's children we are to treat more gently God's green-and-blue gift of earth. This new-think will require more than the engineering mentality that gives technological reason its head and promotes ecocidal "development."

If we are to permit the "new occasion" of mega-pollution to teach "new duties," we shall have to recategorize factors under "inevitable" and "unthinkable (unreasonable)." It's not inevitable that we continue living with the same unexamined assumptions in private and public life. Growth for growth's sake is not inevitable: "zero growth" is not unthinkable: **simplifying life**

7. The decades-used slogan of Gold Medal Flour.

17

is not unreasonable but rather the reverse, the only way of bio-salvation. The American Way of Life need not continue to accelerate as a way of death.

We can begin this revolution of consciousness by redirecting our attention, literally, upstream. The *old* question was, "What happens after the flush of the toilet sends the water and effluvia out of the house?" The answers were two: a private septic system or a public sewer. But suppose we stare away the W.C. (the British euphemism, "water closet") and ask the *prior* question: "What, in the light of all factors, including the environment, are we to do with body effluvia?"

A truly progressive society, as distinguished from a merely developmental one, is not locked into old questions and answers by myopia. In its search for better ways, it's free to move both backwards and forwards.[8] In Sweden, for example, I found both a *return* to the potty + outhouse and an *advance* into what the world calls the Swedish dry toilet.[9]

In technological innovation, we Americans have been the world's model. Now we and the world are in urgent need of *pre*technological innovation, in need of liberated thinking about how we are to live in God's garden with our fellow creatures.

---

8. Long ago some of these became recycling systems. In the 1455 central European home where my paternal grandfather-in-law was born, for more than a half millenium the house-and-barn effluvia have gone into a deep sump. As it liquifies, it's pumped into the family-owned and oxen-pulled honey wagon, taken to the top of the *weinberg,* and allowed to run down between the vine rows. Voila, it is recycled into grapes, which then are liquified and run through the family. I have quaffed heartily the delicious second liquid in the cycle.

9. When we began building our home on Cape Code in 1980 and wanted to install a Swedish toilet, the government at two levels said "Fine, go ahead, but you'll have to install the water-sewer system also even if you don't use it." On balance and against that insanity, having only the dry toilet would reduce building costs, which are now so high that most young Americans cannot look forward to ever owning their own home.

Pink Lily Pond, Agassiz's facts, Darwin's fantasies

In his autobiographical film, *The Magic Lantern,* Ingmar Bergman attributes at least some of his creativity to having had, in childhood, extreme difficulty distinguishing fact from fantasy. As I write,[1] the American public is having extreme difficulty separating, in the presidential campaigns, facts from managed, spin-controlled, handled, tailored, mad-avenued fantasies fed at us in sound bites and photo-ops. This Thinksheet is a parable, a true story, a cautionary tale, for church (especially theological seminaries) and society (especially the public schools and their educationistic establishment).

1. As I write in my study, I can look through the window toward **Pink** (now called "Red") **Lily Pond,** not much more than a hundred yards away, where the world-class Harvard biologist, Louis Agassiz (who died 115 years ago) discovered, and later established the taxonomy of, the pink (water) lily. Do drop in and visit us, but don't look for that lily: it's too late to save the lily; we're fighting now to save the pond from eutrophy . . . but that's another tale.

2. Coming from Switzerland in 1846, Agassiz became a grand master of the English language, which he used with persuasive force as author and both academic and popular teacher. He founded, and was long curator of, the Agassiz Museum in Cam-

1. 8 October 1988.

19

bridge and the Marine Biological Laboratory at Woods Hole, the latter not all that far from Pink Lily Pond (and a scientific research center so important that seventy Nobel laureates in science have worked and lectured there). His byword was "Go to Nature; take the facts in your own hands; look, and **see for yourself!**"

3. One often hears or reads that Agassiz was the most effective promoter of *science education* in American history (as Edison was the greatest promoter of creative tinkering, grassroots engineering). Though I am the third generation from him, I can see and feel the glow of his cool ecstasy, his merger of passion and reason in facts-seeking: one of his students was a science teacher of my father, who never tired of passing on to us children the words of and the stories about Agassiz, one of the secular saints of my childhood.

4. I've mentioned two institutions Agassiz founded; his students, and those they influenced, founded many more in his spirit. One of these, New York Theological Seminary (founded in 1900), from its earliest days told Agassiz stories in connection with "**inductive Bible study,**" which the school came into existence to practice and promote, over against a theological educational establishment that had wandered away from the canonical biblical text. There Agassiz's byword underwent this mutation: "Go to the *Bible;* take the facts into your own head and heart; look, and *see for yourself!*" How thrilled I was, in a 1937 NYTS course I took, to find the same Agassiz spirit that I knew from my father! Even some of the same stories were told, like the one about the stinking fish that Agassiz had a student study all day, day after day, under the single directive, "Look!"

5. The Agassiz spirit was and is unsympathetic both with those who input in the interest of output (no, not computer programmers, but **eisegetes**) and those who, looking for what is not there, miss seeing what is there (yes, **ideologs**). Let's apply this . . .

a) to the **Bible.** It's a God-book, so a good place — the best literature, I believe — to look for God. "Scientific creationists" look

20

for science, historians for history, theologians for theology ("biblical theology"), sociologists for sociology, psychologists for psychology.

b) to **nature,** God's wordless book. Following his grandpa Erasmus, Charles Darwin claimed to find evolution there, an excessive extrapolation Agassiz scoffed at but "modern science" has bought (and postmodern science is questioning). On the other side of the Atlantic, Charles Darwin was as dedicated a nature-observer as Agassiz was on this side. But, said Agassiz, Darwin was insufficiently respectful of the facts he found: "natural selection" was not a respectable scientific theory but an *alien philosophical import.* . . . Darwin died nine years after Agassiz.

1995 Supplement

1. In the London home of a Darwinian atheist, I saw the first edition of every Darwin work. Eric Evans showed me that the first edition of *The Origin of Species* ends with the recognition of God as the Creator of the processes summed up, before Darwin, as "evolution." How did God get dropped from the second and all subsequent editions? I say, his atheist friends got to him; Evans said, God was slipped into the first edition by the nagging of Darwin's wife. "History" is the story we tell to confirm our vision; so is "nature."

2. Theists are eager to tell the nature story with God in-behind-above-beneath-beyond: **"creation"** is the story's title. Atheists are as eager to tell the nature story leaving God out: **"evolution"** is the story's title. Agassiz was right: there's no science in either view: "scientific creation" and "scientific evolution" are both oxymorons. To expose these two frauds as ideologies, add "ism": evolutionism (which in our public schools is taught as science) and creationism.

3. See pp. 207-9 for a religion-and-philosophy-free telling of the nature story. Because this telling is *scientific,* it's not weighted either for or against God. It is for science with its confessed limitations, and against scientism with its atheist hubris.

21

Sacred space because sanctified *place*

No, the universe-world-space-place is not holy, only God is. Yes, God has given us human beings the power-privilege of **sanctifying** (Latin, "making sacred") the space-time medium in which we have our here-and-now being. We biblical peoples, Jews and Christians, are in perennial warfare against the very essence of paganism, which is belief in the inherent holiness-sacredness of some or all of the Creator's creatures-creations. Some of us may take poetic license with the words, blurring this vital distinction. So vital is the distinction, however, that we should object to the blurring. To use the wording Martin Buber loosed on the world in 1925, the world is "it," but we've the power to "thou" it. And the need: the *eco-eco-crisis* (economics and ecology globally intermeshed) calls us to revalorize "nature" and our place in it.

1. As personal maturity demands *self*-respect + *self*-transcendence, ecological maturity demands *earth*-respect (including its sanctifiability) + *nature*-transcendence (including freedom from the pagan doctrine of sacral inherency). To be avoided are the **extremes:** pagan OVERrespect for nature and "Western" UNDERrespect. I'm distressed by the Western theologians (in particular, many preachers of "creation spirituality") who over-repent and fall into a romantic mood that unguardedly appropriates pagan expressions (in one instance, Matthew Fox, calling down Vatican condemnation of his writings).

2. *Locus is focus:* shortsight is basic to longsight; nearsight, to

farsight; land, to sky and sea. Space and place overlap: in my 3 x 5 files, the two categories are *a)* "PLACE, PLACES — See also SPACE, SPACE-TIME CONTINUUM" and *b)* "SPACE — See also SPACE-TIME CONTINUUM, PLACE." The biblical words here are plentiful and rich, and worth exploring in a Bible dictionary. I've a subcategory under **PLACE:** "HOLY place." The first card there is this, from the Gettysburg Address: "We cannot dedicate, . . . consecrate, . . . hallow this ground. The brave men. . . ." The second is from a hymn: "Jesus, Where'er thy people meet, / . . . , / . . . , And every place is hallowed ground." And here are a few behind the "**SPACE** . . . " index: *a)* "Inscape" — G. M. Hopkins and Ross Synder (on inner space); *b)* "God, when taking up all the room, enlarges, the space, my space" (from my 1977 Kirkridge lectionary); *c)* "Grief makes a unique space that God will not fill, refuses to fill" (from a 1943 letter of mine); *d)* "Locative dimensions: place, outer space, inner space." "Draw nigh unto God, and God will draw nigh unto you." "Space increases as distance decreases"; *e)* "Space is making room inside yourself for another" — Gabriel Marcel; *f*) and cards on Hebrew-Greek-Latin roots for placed-spaced experience.

3. Paradox: The prophets use the divine **transcendence** to speak to very concrete human realities: the priests use God's **immanence** in specific places to ritualize God's general presence in human life. The authentic and necessary *tension* in this double paradox is the biblical prophylaxis against the extremes, primitive numinous nature and Platonic-Neoplatonic immaterialism. In *The Prophetic Imagination,* Walter Brueggemann lucidly exposits this creative tension.

4. The two pregnant expressions I remember Sidney Mead for are a book title, *A Nation with the Soul of a Church,* and this sentence from his *Lively Experiment: The Shaping of Christianity in America:* "In America space has played the part that time has played in the older cultures of the world."[1] A recent book — Belden C.

---

1. Sidney Mead, *The Lively Experiment: The Shaping of Christianity in America* (New York: Harper & Row, 1963), p. 6.

Lane's *Landscapes of the Sacred: Geography and Narrative in American Spirituality* — could well be viewed as a commentary on Mead's sentence. A comparison occurs to me: as sociology of knowledge studies knowledge vis-à-vis its social context, so Lane's (I shall call it) **demography of spirituality** studies American numinous experience vis-à-vis its place contexts (the inner city [e.g., the Catholic Worker movement], the forests and plains [Native American spirituality], New England [the Pilgrims and Puritans], etc.). Compare, in the making of the biblical mind, Canaan, Egypt, Babylon.

 5. Scott McCarthy, author of *Creation Liturgy: An Earth-Centered Theology of Worship* — as solidly Christian as is Lane — applies the sanctification of life to our ecological need for a **second naïvete** vis-à-vis nature. "The universe is in the dynamic process of being prepared to become the Kingdom of God."[2] "Matter matters."[3]

1995 Supplement

 Place + space = **land**. Religions could be classified according to their relative closeness to / distance from / *Lebensraum,* the devotees' "living-room," place-space in which they live.
 Primitive or aboriginal peoples have so little distance from, transcendence over, where they live that when they are forced off their turf, they lose their religion — for example, Native Americans. At the other extreme is Buddhism; Gautama left home and land, and the religion stemming from him has never taken strong hold in his native India.
 The "holy land" of promise was lost to Israel in 721 B.C. and to Judah in 586 B.C., and in Babylon the Jews transferred land sacrality to book sacrality ("holy Bible").

 2. Scott McCarthy, *Creation Liturgy: An Earth-Centered Theology of Worship* (San Jose, Ca.: Resource Publications, 1987), p. 93.
 3. Ibid., p. 90.

The mutual superiority of the sexes

Not just my enemies, but also my friends agree that my wife is superior to me. Loree was under me in doing her college major in religion and philosophy, but in marrying her I married up — not upscale, but up-quality. At the altar of God I got me a good deal, a better deal than my woman got.

At all that, my wife-woman, the only full life partner I've ever had, laughs. Her heart of hearts claims she got the better deal. She can't understand why my enemies and friends — especially my friends — can be so stupid.

Me? I'm nonpartisan on this one. I think everybody's right. Which means, if you'll pardon a personal reference, that I hold myself to be *both inferior and superior to my beloved Loree.* I could bore you with the evidence for both. Or I could rush to the generalization that I've arrived at through personal and other evidence: the sexes are inherently and existentially mutually superior, the superiority or inferiority of each divinely designed for mutuality, for partnership, for the human wholeness impossible within one skin.

1. My doctrine of the sexes is not egalitarian; it is hierarchical. Friendship is egalitarian: friends are **equal,** and friendship can and should exist between sexual partners. But the notion that the sexes are equal is false and has multiform pernicious effects — and, when extended far enough by radical feminism, ridiculous, move-ment-damaging effects.

25

2. What do I mean by **hierarchical mutuality**? That the full, body-and-soul interpersonal relationship of woman and man is doubly vertical, not horizontal: each is naturally superior to, and therefore the leader of, the other. And this superiority is again double: it is both of hormones and of genes.

3. Consequently, what is to be honored is neither sex over the other but rather each person's own unique hormonal-genetic makeup. The Eleventh Commandment is "Thou shalt honor thy neighbor's hormones and genes." A man may have less control-drive than his woman, and is not less a man for it: a woman may have more control-drive than her man, and is not less a woman for it. Here lies the **righteous revolution** against traditional societies' rigid sex role assignments. It's against the human grain, and against the will of God, that boys and girls, women and men, should be forced into life tasks misfitting their individual constitutions.

4. It's a social principle that churches should take the lead in living: we are to discover and release, in each individual, the **gifts** God has given by nature and grace.

5. Since the androgens are more leading and the estrogens more nurturing, it should surprise no one that more men than women will be **initiators** and more women than men will be **carers.** This fact must not be used as a biology-is-destiny excuse for men not caring and for women not taking the initiative. But the fact should not be obscured, as it is by radical egalitarians.

6. Growing up in a household where woman presence was 5:2 over man presence, I never considered women inferior. Ashley Montagu's *The Natural Superiority of Women,* when it came out years later,[1] had nothing to teach me. Further, my father taught me an

---

1. Not long after his 1952 debate with me on "Is God Love, or Is Love God?" Macmillan's revised edition was 1968; paper, 1970.

26

awesome respect for woman as God's mysterious, same-yet-other creature. **Patriarchalism** has always been repugnant to me.

7. But not **patriarchy,** the male lead in male-and-female mutual partnership decision-making, and the male's primary responsibility to protect and support the female and offspring, the family.

Here the latter-day battle of the sexes has a **counter-hubris.** Against the hubris of patriarchy's overreaching and becoming dominance, that is, patriarchalism, radical feminism pits the hubris of attacking patriarchy as though it were always and everywhere patriarchalism. Patriarchalism is sinful; patriarchy is hormonal. Patriarchalism dogmatizes that no family should be matriarchal; patriarchy accepts the plain fact that most families will be patriarchal, and the dismal fact that most matriarchal families will be manless.

8. Radical feminist theologians read **sexual egalitarianism** into the deity, using their two darling texts: from the Old Testament, Genesis 1:27 ("God created human beings, making them like himself . . . male and female"); and from the New Testament, Galatians 3:27 ("clothed with the life of Christ . . . there is no difference . . . between men and women: you are all one in union with Christ Jesus"). To pull off this eisegesis, one must neglect both contexts. In the former, the divine Patriarch takes the initiative in producing a pair of creatures whose symbiosis expresses sexually a polar dynamic within the divine; nor should the order, "male and female," be obscured. In the latter, the same order, "men and women," is observed; and a man, "Christ," "Christ Jesus," envelopes the "no difference."

9. The radical feminist project of bowdlerizing the Bible into **inclusive language** runs up against an awkward set of facts: *a*) of the world's religions, Christianity is the most masculine, the god coming only as a man[2] and the deity being represented in the sacred

---

2. In *Divine Principle,* Sun Moon points this out as a defect in traditional Christianity. When Messiah comes, says he, they will be a male/female couple, overcoming the inherent sexism of the orthodox doctrine of the Incarnation. On

27

writings almost exclusively as masculine;[3] and *b*) in spite of all this masculine conceptuality and expression, Christianity is, among the world's great religions, the most sensitive to women and the female values and virtues.

10. While inclusive language is disingenuously used for purposes of historical theological revisionism and is doomed to fail at both, I use and promote inclusive language **today**.[4] General interpersonal relations should be treated egalitarianly, in the friendship and legal modes. And I'm happy that our newer English Bibles are removing masculinisms unsupported in the Hebrew, Aramaic, and Greek originals.[5]

11. "**Man**" is the general generic, the theological generic, the scientific generic, and the Germanic radical (root for a huge cluster of words referring to our species). I have given up the first of these four: I no longer use "man" to include wo-man (an instance of the Germanic radical, which English can't give up; other instances are hu-man-ity, hu-man-e, hu-man being).

---

the contrary, I see the masculine Incarnation not as trascendentalized politics but as immanentalized reality, in the vein of the patriarchy paradigm. It is God's initiating behavior, not just "his" titles — Father, King, Lord, God — that is masculine, so much so that "he" should be referred to by the masculine "he-his-him." Efforts to avoid this, especially in the public reading of Scripture, are awkward and amusing, entertaining congregations rather than enlightening them. The Bible's God is what he is, not Pascal's "God of the philosophers" or Tillich's "God beyond God," but the historical God of the biblical story.

3. Acquaintance with other religions highlights the masculinity of the biblical God. For example, Hinduism is not "sexist," with no goddesses; and what I call Protestant Hinduism, i.e., Buddhism, is not "sexist": in its original, pure form it has neither gods nor goddesses.

4. I'm not against desexizing hymns in nonbiblical expressions, as long as the deviation is somehow noted after the hymnist's name. For some years I rewrote, using inclusive language, the hymns sung at New York Theological Seminary commencements. But I do resist the radical changes of meaning I see in the inclusive-language hymnals.

5. The Inclusive Language Lectionary is a camel's nose in the tent toward the bowdlerized Bible. If it fails, it was a waste. If it succeeds, it will be a tragedy.

28

But "man" will continue in use theologically (our creature name in relation to God) and scientifically (our species name). It's our only plain word serving the locus-function relative to God and nature (e.g., Ps. 8). But when a culture becomes, as ours has, amnesiac about God, "man" deteriorates into "male" — as it does also when we lose our proper sense of place in nature, which we then rape and pollute. Instead of surrendering the theological and scientific use of "man" under radical feminist pressure, we'd do better to revive "God" and "nature" as its historic analogue-antonyms.

12. My doctrine of the mutual superiority of the sexes, over against the doctrine of the equality of the sexes, implies that feminists, instead of denigrating and denying male superiority, would do better to **celebrate female superiority.** Efforts to desex the Bible and the Anglo-Saxon base of English are worse than foolish, they're pathogenic: they foster alienation of this and future generations from the Bible, the great English classics, our powerful-simple-resonant ground-diction, and most religious talk and writing in our own time; they spread false idealism; and they feed a self-righteousness that rejects any who don't conform to the verbal guidelines of feminist fanaticism.

I'm not worried about the future of "the man/woman thing." A self-correcting gyroscopic homeostatic principle seems to be at work to return sexual-theoretical wanderers from their fantasies and ideologies to reality. Rather, I'm worried about the excessive human **costs** of antisex neo-Victorianism with its twin doctrines of individualism and egalitarianism. Against that I developed my doctrine of the mutual superiority of the sexes, a doctrine that honors sex, each sex, each person — and God.

An etiological dissertation on hugging

I had two phone calls the other day on hugging from a woefully underhugged human being, a man who, in the middle of his years and living alone, has become conscious that he is desperately **hug-hungry.** I want to thank him here, for he got me going toward this Thinksheet.

Reader, please keep two things in mind: (1) poetry's truth-reach is greater than that of prose, as religion has always known, and as the new physics has, along many lines, discovered; and (2) the Bible's poetic descriptions of God's being-feeling-doing give us permission to fantasize in the same vein and to do so without blaspheming. So don't suppose either that I "believe" (prosaically, unpoetically) what you are about to read or that my words blaspheme. Know that I believe, without blasphemy or even unorthodoxy, the One who is in, with, and under the sacrament of my words.

The **Adon Olam** (Eternal Lord), hungry for more communion than he could have with any creature he had made, bethought himself to make a creature more like himself, in hope that it might do the trick. Being desirous also of a garden to walk about in the cool of the day, he lit upon the idea of making the communion-creature a gardener "to cultivate" (Gen. 2:5, 15) the garden he had only in his heart.

Now, you might think that A. O. (Eternal Lord) would make the garden first and make A. K. (**Adam Kadmon,** primordial man) next. You would be wrong. First he made the communion-creature-man (Gen. 2:7), "then . . . planted a garden" (v. 8) and

30

"placed the man in the Garden of Eden to cultivate it and guard it" (v. 15). Communion first; only then the place of communion. But surely Y. E. (**Yahweh Elohim,** the Lord God) could have cultivated his own garden? Impossible! With what? No tools. Not even any hands. We all have our limits, you know. Limits are the downside and underside of powers, and God's bodilessness — as we see now and will also see later — had its limits as well as its powers. Creativity itself is both a power and a limit . . .

. . . as E. (**Elohim**) was discovering. For while the upside of making a creature like unto himself was communion, the downside was the danger that the creature would have other ideas. Things were under control as long as God was storytelling with deeds of command, but they got out of control when God tried to continue the story with words of communion, words communicating A. K.'s limits as well as powers. A. K. didn't take well to the idea of limits, and said so in a single deed. Y. E. sighed and said, "The risk of his disobedience was the price of his freedom, and his freedom was the price of communion. I just don't know what's going to happen now, except that I'm not going to give up on him."

Well, what did happen was A. K.'s *loneliness*. A. O. Y. E. hadn't figured on that possibility, and felt hurt. "How could he be lonely when in communion with me? But I have to face it: he is. I see now that 'it is not good for the man to live alone. I'll make him a suitable companion'" (Gen. 2:18). So God made "all the animals and all the birds, . . . but not one of them was a suitable companion" (vv. 19f). God frowned, not with anger but with perplexity. "If my need for companionship can be satisfied with man, who is less than I, why cannot man's be satisfied with the inferior creatures I've made for him?"

Cloning is what the Lord God hit upon: take a piece of Adam and make another Adam. But He didn't go through with this plan. "That would be mere duplication, and how could duplication enable communion, which requires difference as well as likeness?" That, children, is how we got *sex*. Not out of the earth, from which he'd made man, but out of man, the Lord God made wo-man, **Eve**. And Adam cried out (v. 23), "At last, here is one of my own kind!" Adam had to give up being A. K., but it was worth it. Yet

31

think of the new risks! Eve might do Adam as Adam had done God! And Adam and Eve, infatuated with intercommunion (v. 24, the recapitulation of A. K.), might forget all about communion with God! Especially since A. and E. could do for each other what God could do for neither of them: *hug*.

And A. O. Y. E. discovered that A. and E. didn't just want hugging, they needed it, could provide it for each other, and couldn't get it from God. When it came to hugging, God was out of the competition. What to do? Send a storyteller to convince the man and the woman that God is not limited in the power of loving except by their will not to love God; what needs he cannot supply directly he meets indirectly. Hugging. *Babies*.

Long after A. K. and also A. and E., the bodiless One embodied himself (John 1:14), but that is another story for another time.

1995 Supplement

1. "Thou shalt love the Lord thy God with all thine **imagination**" as well as with all those other good things he's given you. Being playful about Bible stories is not so much innovation as extension; the playfulness, the play of fantasy and humor, is implicit in many of the stories, though we must guard against reading our cultural consciousness into them.

2. Salvation cometh not by hugging, to which the law of diminishing returns applies. But this chapter shamelessly pushes hugging because it's far more often underdone than overdone— says this shy man, to remind himself not to fail to hug when hugging's appropriate.

3. Our thinking about God, always both necessary and insufficient, should be free to roam between the **intimate**-personal (on the model of our limitations) and the **ultimate**-suprapersonal (without limits of power [omnipotent], knowledge [omniscient], or place [omnipresent]).

All institutions are KICKING COWS but some of them give MILK

God and I are more interested in people's *piety* than in anything else about them, so I usually inquire of this when meeting strangers. (By piety, I mean *inward* soul-orientation and *outward,* including institutional, praxis.) As it's been my practice for sixty years (ever since becoming more interested in piety than in anything else) to ask, in these words or other words to this effect, "What, may I ask, is your religion?" I have stored in my synapses thousands of responses.

Responses, in order of frequency:

1. "In my childhood, I attended the _____ church (or synagogue or temple or meeting), but now I'm a member of _____."
2. "As a kid I went to the _____, but I haven't gone regularly anywhere since."
3. "I'm not religious, never have been, but I do believe in God."

NOTICE: All the responses are *institution-conscious.* The first has religious institution as part of personal identity, though further conversation is needed to discover the degree of institutional participation. The second is ex-institutional. And the third is non-institutional. Any more responses? Of course, but these are the three most frequent. And also of course, these three are nuanced in many directions.

ONE CONCLUSION: Religion as institution is in the mind of most Americans when asked, out of the blue, *What, may I ask,*

33

is your religion? Almost everybody thinks religious institutions are important, though not all live what they think important.

Important, yes, but **necessary**? I try to get my responders to speak of their inward piety, but most of them flee to religion's outwardness, many of them to reject it: "I'm a Christian, but I don't go to church. You don't have to go to church to be a Christian." When I insist that you do, since church-going is the only distinctive thing Christians do, most of these answerers, their usual defense penetrated, become irritated, defensive, sometimes even hostile. *Anti-institutionalism* is rampant in our country, and especially religious anti-institutionalism.

What did Ramakrishna mean by his analogy (in this Think-sheet's title), put various ways, when disciples asked him why they should pay any attention to religious institutions, when, they said, "All we need do is follow you"? Do your own ruminating on his response. Here is some of mine:

1. R. goes to the heart of the usual objection to institutional religion — that it's *more trouble than it's worth.* So much kicking going on! Clericalism and anticlericalism, laicism and antilaicism. Fights over coteries and group decision making, especially hiring/firing and budgets.

2. R. raises the question, What is the worth of religious institutions? *Extraneously* they may have a tranquilizing effect on the populace, but that cannot secure their worth to participants, though it may to potentates. Indeed, in R.'s own country, institutional religion often is destabilizing, as right now[1] Hindu fanatics are attacking mosques built on property where a Hindu temple formerly stood (or even occupying a refurbished temple).

3. *Participants* who want milk, the spiritual nurture that can come through religious institutions, notice that the cow kicks, but pay greater attention to the udder.

4. When Goodwife Loree was a small child, her preschool chore

1. 27 July 1991.

was to milk a nonkicking cow or two: kicking cows are for bigger girls and boys to milk. But when it comes to religious institutions, there are no nonkicking ones: that's R.'s **realism,** which includes staying away from dry kicking cows.

5. R. avoids **cynicism**, the sneer that no cows (no religious institutions) give milk, feed the soul and society's spiritual needs.

1995 Supplement

1. In the past decade, America's *individualism* has been better documented than have its two social consequences, namely, the weakening not only of **institutional** loyalty (for example, to employer or political party) but also of **community** (for example, family, neighborhood, church). While in the long run this social pathology may be self-correcting, in the short run all suffer — persons, communities, institutions.

2. R., a Hindu philosopher, might have been expected to disparage both community and institution, in the pattern of the holy man at age forty abandoning society to become an anchorite in the mountains. Instead, he invites us to be affirming of community and discriminating among institutions, warning his disciples away from (to use a Christian expression, Heb. 10:25) "neglecting to meet together, as is the habit of some." (He was neo-Hindu, making his own mix of his native religion and Christianity.)

3. **Privatism**, a secular version of the holy man off alone in the mountains, afflicts all of American life, but especially religion. "Spiritual" folk affirm the soul in meditation and perhaps devotion (as the ancient Gnostics), but deny the institutional body (as did the ancient Manicheans vis-à-vis the human "physical" body). At the other extreme, **ritualism** is "religious" in the bad sense, all body and no soul, "holding to the outward form of godliness but denying its power" (2 Tim. 3:5). But the body/soul split is evil, and in all its forms doomed as violating human nature and the will of God.

35

Mutual blasphemers, love one another!

Imagine that this Thinksheet[1] is the continuation of a conversation that I, a double goy (both parents gentile) had with a hybrid (as it was, yid mother and goy father). Further, suppose you were thinking *Christianly* but going regularly to synagogue rather than church. You would be, would you not, in transition to Christian commitment. Or suppose a reverse, which is my friend's case: thinking *Jewishly* ("Jesus is a blasphemer," and thus Christians are also), he goes regularly to church. But is he in transition to regular synagogue worship? Probably not, for he would view that as retribalization. Judaism is "tribal" (and therefore unacceptable); Christianity is "blasphemous" (and therefore unacceptable). Yet instead of being in the secular no-man's-land between the two religions — secularly neutralized — he is as God-intoxicated as was Spinoza, who was excommunicated from the synagogue for (yes) blasphemy. And his God-intoxication has deep roots and rich fruits in both Christianity and Judaism.

I hope this Thinksheet doesn't entangle its two feet and fall over. Its two purposes are *a*) to spell out the title and *b*) to present my friend as a living symbol of the problems and possibilities of relations between Jews and Christians today and tomorrow as we face a world increasingly hostile to our faith (the biblical faith, which historically has taken the form of our two religions).

1. This was, in the main, written 3 September 1988 and bore the pre-title "Jews and Christians confront one another AND unite."

36

1. Jews and Christians are theoretically committed to loving one another and existentially in the habit of not doing so. Unless we are to continue in hypocrisy, this **bad habit** must be broken — broken existentially by being together and developing affection for one another, broken intellectually by thinking together ("dialog"), broken spiritually by interfaith occasions of worship (private as well as public), and broken actionally by mutual confrontation of violations of the biblical way of seeing, and living in, the world.

2. **Honesty** is not optional if dialog is to be humanly productive. And honesty here demands mutual confronting of the fact of mutual **blasphemy.** "Blasphemy!" — the single word on a poster being carried up and down in front of a Boston theater showing *The Last Temptation of Christ* — is a gut-and-mind reaction in the presence of what is felt and thought to violate the holy, the fount and origin of all value and virtue. I have been known to shout it out in a public meeting, so I can understand both Jews who did it in Jesus' presence and Christians who have done it in the presence of Jews. (My former reference is to the Jesus of the Gospels, who makes claims which, to Jews, appear to be excessive for humanity and encroaching on the territory of divinity. This is the Jesus, Jesus Christ, of Christianity. I believe this Jesus to be continuous with "the historical Jesus": I am a Christian. Anyone who knowingly denies this Jesus is to me, to Christians, a blasphemer, as rejecting God come among us in and as Jesus, "Immanu-el.")

3. Can light (holiness as commitment to a holy, a religion) have fellowship with darkness (denial, rejection, of that holy)? In nature, light and darkness do have fellowship; they are a continuity. And our two religions commit us to mutual love in spite of the structural mutual blasphemy. Why is all of this, so obvious, usually left unspoken? Because of the **danger**: the gut side of blasphemy as gut-and-mind reaction is a deep cause of anti-Christianism and anti-Judaism. Honest and informed dialog shifts the weight from gut to mind, freeing us to **admit and accept** the mutual blasphemy as built-in, something

37

nobody from either side or from outside can do anything to eliminate. Yet the actual situation qualifies the starkness of the double-blasphemy dilemma. Uncommitted "cultural" Christians and "cultural" Jews can get along together without the blasphemy element, as neither belong to the holy: such Jews do not really believe that the Jewish people are singly, only among the peoples of the world, chosen to be "a light to the nations"; and such Christians do not really believe that Jesus is God come among us (the incarnation). God bless them at least for supporting their mutual goodwill by humanistic considerations. For the imperative of mutual goodwill, however sanctioned, is the ground common to the uncommitted and the committed. Humanism's sentimentality, blurred vision and slurred speech, however, cannot promise any depth of improved Jewish/Christian relations.

4. Judaism and Christianity are blasphemies to each other: religion and philosophy are **scandals** to each other. As religion sees it, philosophy commits the scandals of *generality* (wanting the fruits without feeding the roots) and of *rarification* (neglecting, if not also despising, concretions, and adoring, if not also reifying, abstractions). As philosophy sees it, religion commits the scandals of *particularity* (insisting on at the least the interdependence of the concrete and abstract if not claiming the dependence of the latter upon the former, as in idolatry and magic, and also sacrament); and of *provinciality* (explicitly or at least implicitly teaching the superiority of one's tradition and commitment, an insistence that makes interreligious, intertribal, international conflict unavoidable, and global unity unattainable).

5. As an infant, my friend was baptized after being ritually circumcised, a "solution" satisfying nobody and continuing to confuse him, so he's made no commitment to either religion but instead has made up his own religion as he's assiduously pored over the world's spiritual classics. He's a *gnostic* in worshiping through nouns, a *poet* in worshiping through images, and a *singer* in worshiping through psalms and hymns in a half-dozen languages. Given that pious history of idiosyncrasy, let's see what he

38

does with a sacred text — for example, **Jeremiah 10:10**, the centerpiece of our conversation.

Hebrew, by using nouns with adjectival and adverbial force, plays into the hands of our goy/yid's gnosticism. Transposing our verse's nouns into English nouns produces this monstrosity: "Lord God truth, you God life and king universe." Gnosticism reverses the first clause from "God is truth" to "Truth is god."[2] And on this model of reversibility, "God is love" becomes "Love is god." On this pattern my friend is free to deify, really only to reify, abstractions, thus *reducing religion* to ethics (i.e., values and virtues), thus blaspheming both his parental religions. He's in the gnostic sky above his parents' conflict over religion; and by blaspheming both religions instead of only one, he is rejecting neither parent. His personal tragic confusion and artificial transcendence make interfaith marriage look bad. Such a marriage neutralizes religion, the children growing up secular; or makes religion a battleground (each spouse living with a blasphemer), the children afflicted with various religious aberrations. (If one spouse surrenders religion to the other, the marriage is not interfaith.)

6. Highly pertinent is **John 8**, where the early Christians ("Jesus") argued with the Jews (here called "the Pharisees") as the child, Christianity, and the mother, Judaism, were in the process of mutual anti-shaping. Each group saw God as its father and the devil as the other group's father. This eristic expression of paternity was one way the mutual blasphemy got expressed on both sides. We would be wrong — and false also to the Gospel of John! — to read that heat literally, as an excuse for either Jews or Christians today to think-speak-act as though the devil were the other's father, and so to give 'em hell.

At issue was and is *emeth-alitheia,*[3] **truth.** Note the close parallel, in tone and content, between Jeremiah 10 (our section 5) and John

---

2. Contrast two honest, responsible translations of the verse: *a*) *Jewish*: "the Lord is truly G" (adverbial; Tanakh, 1985); and *b*) *Christian*: "You, Lord, are the true God" (adjectival; TEV, 1976).

3. The hyphen indicates that the Greek of the Fourth Gospel, as is true of the Greek of the earliest Christian Bible, the LXX Old Testament, has Hebrew close behind and within it.

8: "true" religion resisting untrue-false-unreal. Both use resistance language, from the lexicon of controversy. Use your concordance to see how often, and with what forces, this author used "truth" in his Gospel and three letters. Now note John 8:31-32: "If you obey my teaching, you are **truly** my disciples; you will know the **truth,** and the **truth** will set you free." The last two phrases are carved in a stone arch of the University of Chicago's divinity complex, and usually misread by passersby as meaning that truth frees you (the message of the school's Latin motto, which says that as knowledge increases, life exfoliates, opens up). Face to face with challenges to their community's integrity and even existence, Jeremiah and John closely associate their deity with truth, verity, reality: Κύριος *(Kyrios)* is "the LORD" YHWH God in the Christians' first "Bible" and in the New Testament usually refers to Jesus.

For Jews, this is a blasphemous identification; for us Christians, with our high Christology, it is a quite natural identification, a trinitarian-incarnational continuum. Jesus is "full of grace and **truth**" (John 1:14, 17), and can say "I am the **true** and living way" (John 14:6). Note the startling resemblance to our Jeremiah passage, the full verse 10: "You, Lord, are the **true** God, you are the **living** God and the eternal **King.**" In the Fourth Gospel, the Holy Spirit comes to confirm Jesus as **true** and to guide Christians in Jesus' **truth** (14:17, 16:13); Jesus prays "Dedicate them [my disciples] to Yourself by means of the **truth;** your Word is **truth**" (17:17); Jesus says "I was born and came into the world for this one purpose, to speak about the **truth.** Whoever belongs to the **truth** listens to me" (18:37; followed immediately by Pilate's asking "And what is **truth?**").

7. In the living context of every religion, activists, mystics, poets, and philosophers produce their **versions** of truth in the process of ingesting (whether or not personally practicing) the environing religion. That process has been the central passion of my friend's life. Paradoxically, he is both irreligious (as not practicing any particular religion) and consumingly religious (interiorly, and as exploring **religions proper,** i.e., various religious praxes). Let's do a visual on this:

Phenomenology of Religion

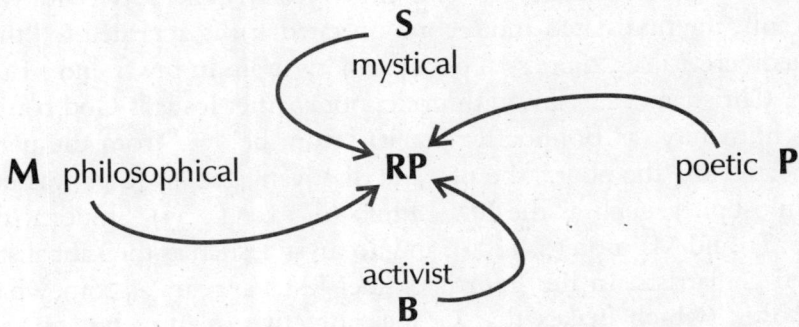

RP is religion proper, religious praxis, being observant or "active." These folk are "the continuity," without whom a religion dies, ceases to be one of "the world's living religions," becomes a dead (and soon forgotten) religion; and its parasites (nonobservant mystics, philosophers, and poets) die with it.

As for the positioning of the four versions, **S** is spirit, **M** is mind (analytic), **P** is psyche (intuitive, imaginal, fantastic), and **B** is body, here for "activist," i.e., getting involved, under the impetus of the religion proper, to make a difference in the world. My friend is into all four versions of religion-tinged activity — in my opinion, in this order of importance to him: poetic, mystical, philosophical, activist. The arrows show him as dependent on, but not contributing (by praxis) to, religion(s). Were he to make a religious commitment and become faithful to that religion's praxis, the arrows would have heads on both ends: he'd be both contributing to and dependent on that religion.

8. "I knew immediately that is my faith," said my friend, of **Maimon**(ides)'s *Guide to the Perplexed,* which he has just read for the first time. At least for the time being, he has found a spiritual companion, a fellow-shaped soul, in history; and the discovery has brought him a measure of peace and joy. Here was a bridge between

us. He was pleased to hear that the *Guide* is on my personal list of the world's 150 greatest books.[4]

9. My gnosticizing friend finds **Jesus** unattractive at two points, the first stated and second unstated: *a*) he appealed to "the mediocre." (Yes, there's an elitist, snooty strain in my friend.) But we Christians view this with pride, not shame: Jesus is God come to humanity (as Bonhoeffer put it) "from below," from the perspective of "the poor," the un- and disadvantaged. *b*) Jesus was no philosopher, such as the Jews' Philo (d. ca. A.D. 54), Spinoza (d. 1677), and Maimon (d. 1204), and no mystic, such as the kabbalists and gematrists. In the Fourth Gospel Jesus appears as somewhat gnostic (which makes that Gospel attractive to him, but not as attractive as the Gospel of Thomas, in which Jesus is, like my friend, a gnostic). At least for now, my friend's basic scriptures are Hindu and Buddhist, and he has a tough time reading Jesus in that light. Yet the three Western religions "are more **life-affirming** than the religions of India and China." Taking history seriously, as the religions of India and China do not, why wouldn't the Western religions be more life-affirming? But taking history seriously is what prophets — not philosophers, poets, mystics — do; think of Abraham, Moses, Jesus.

Said my friend, "God is the force of love and peace in the universe." The roots of this religio-ethical conviction of his are chiefly biblical (Old Testament and New Testament). For me, God is not an impersonal "force"; rather, God transcends the very real bright and dark forces, and ultimately controls them.

10. **Shoah-Holocaust** has an as yet unexplored potential for helping us mutual blasphemers, Christians and Jews, both confront and love one another.

4. Maimon's doctrine of God as noncontingent Being finds a parallel in "The Unconfinable," my Bates College Annual Religion Lecture, 1972. But the balancing truth is that the biblical God chooses *contingency* (to be the God of creation and history) and even *confinability* (most radically in the incarnation, especially the cross and tomb).

Stability and conflict in community

Fellow citizens of the Kingdom that is and is coming, as Father Avery Dulles[1] graciously sent me his cool, collected, comprehensive, and highly competent paper[2] before I wrote this, I have the joy and advantage of being able to complement his work. Joy because my mind delights in the solidity and clarity of his thought and my heart agrees with his conclusions; advantage, not in the dialectical sense — for the dynamics of this "Salvation and Community" colloquium do not demand conflict between the two papers — but in the archetectonic (system-building) sense: I can build on and alongside his work, throwing some beams across to my own and sharing a common foundation, which is Jesus Christ as Lord of the future. In process and event, however, I shall be grateful to him if he points out what he may consider illegitimate

1. Jesuit theologian Avery Dulles and I were, respectively, the Roman Catholic and the Protestant lecturers for the 1970 (June 7-11) National Council of Churches' National Faith and Order Colloquium. For use in spring-summer seminars in theological seminaries, we each prepared a study paper. His was titled "Authority and Diversity in the Christian Community." Mine bore the title of this chapter, to which were appended 66 study notes keyed into the text — "not so much to buttress arguments as to open doors and suggest journeys." This chapter includes little from those study notes.

2. The media had small interest in our two papers, but were hopeful of getting him to make some bridging remarks between what he and I were endeavoring and the family facts that his father was the chief architect of the country's current foreign policy and his uncle started the CIA. They were disappointed.

extrapolations from his building, as I shall try to be open to any among us who would in any way critique my building.

Roughly, the land-plots of our buildings are (1) his: **authority and diversity** in the church,[3] with implications about *Homo sapiens* in any society, and (2) mine: **stability,** an effect from the proper exercise of authority; and **conflict,** present everywhere because of diversity, with implications for the church as social phenomenon (though my focus is wider: the phenomenology of community in soteric perspective). A visual aid can exhibit that all four factors are necessary for the human space we call *freedom:*

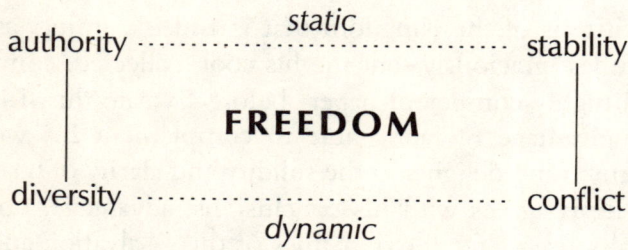

Why this theme for the National Council of Churches' 1970 Faith and Order Colloquy? In my *Tempo*[4] article on the 1969 Colloquium, I said "The Fifth Colloquium will extend the theme of salvation into the corporate dimensions of lostness and savedness: 'Salvation and Community' is to be its theme. The planning committee intends that the cumulative force of the previous colloquia be applied to issues agonizing church and society and to the human potential for salvation from 'the principalities and powers' now threatening humanity's joy, fulfillment, and even existence."

3. In the subsequent years, this has been Father Dulles's area — in scores of articles and a small shelf of books — of major contribution . . . . What his paper says about church has penumbral meanings for world as inclusive of church; mine stresses the saving/damning experiences of human beings in community in general, with adduced implications for the Christian community.

4. A National Council of Churches periodical.

To be action oriented, one must be world oriented; to be world oriented, issue oriented; to be issue oriented, power (i.e., promise-and-threat) oriented. Accordingly, I choose the "radical" stance for this paper: its fundamental reference is to the psycho-sociodynamic root of "stability and conflict in community," that is, those tangible and intangible **sanctions** (positive and negative incentives, promises and threats) that move groups and individuals. For while my mind is pessimistic about the human future, my will is hopeful for the emergence of a leadership, in church and society, appropriate and adequate to the new age that is upon us — hopeful that "all shall be well and/All manner of thing shall be well/By the purification of the motive/In the ground of our beseeching."[5] For me, that purification both is and leads toward salvation, by the power and love of God in Jesus Christ, for this corrupted and polluted planet.

The remaining development of my theme is in outline form.

I. **WHAT IS A SAVING COMMUNITY?**

A society that meets its members' needs, both delivery and deliverance.

A. What are these needs?

1. **Conscious** needs:

   a) A life-supporting environment: air, food and drink, clothing, shelter.

   b) Protection from lethalities of nature and humanity: stability and peace.

   c) Face-to-face relationships with one's fellows of both sexes and all ages.

   d) Repair of ruptures in those relationships: forgiveness, reparation.

5. T. S. Eliot in *Four Quartets.*

45

e) Physical and psychic distance from those relationships: oscillation between society and solitude.

f) Protection from other members: "law and order."

g) Damages: legal requital, "justice."

h) Rebellion: illegal demand or pressure on the ground that "the system" is incurably oppressive and unresponsive.

i) Protection from nonmembers: diplomatic, economic, and military sanctions.

2. **Preconscious** needs:

a) Arousal, external stimulation: excitement, exploration, adventure, experiment, risk.

b) Play: fantasy, physical manipulation, contest.

c) Direction (by *positive* sanctions): group-and-personal-value guided goals.

d) Discipline (by *negative* sanctions): group-and-personal correction of deviance from these goals.

e) Freedom to develop the self in positive and negative orientation to these goals.

   (1) Order/chaos as the polar context of this development.

   (2) Ecstasy: celebration, euphoria, eudemonia (happiness, joy), orgastic and mystic experience, praise, thanksgiving.

   (3) Unruliness, rebellion, "liberation" from repetition (deliverance from dailiness, from dull and dutiful routine).

f) Freedom to develop relationships.

g) Availability of other members.

h) Covenant and promise: covenantal security, shame, and guilt.

i) Will and skill to make strains on covenants creative.

j) Hope: faith and trust.

k) Love: touch, identity, sensitivity, affection, tenderness, caring, loneliness, grief.

3. **Unconscious** needs:

a) Homeostasis, both physical (biostability) and psychic (tranquility, reverie).

b) Disequilibrium: challenge, threat, yearning.

c) Creation/destruction: positive and negative use of the human energy systems (physical, psychic-imaginative, mental-rational, spiritual-decisional).

d) Depth nurture: awe, wonder, worship (religious response to the numinous), collective primordiality (the primitive within), personal primordiality (child of one's past within).

B. How does a saving community meet these needs?

1. By providing **a pro-human environment** for its members. It has adequate power for their and its surviving and thriving, i.e., for obtaining life-maintaining resources and for protecting both its members and these resources against nonhuman and human predators.

2. By structuring **order** (an instrumental value) in the interest of **freedom** (socially, the ultimate value). Here are the problems of authority and of individual vs. collective.

47

3. By **mythologizing** its existence and common values (space-transcendence).

4. By **sacralizing** its myths and thus solemnizing its common values.

5. By **defending** its sacralized value-world against pollution, erosion, and substitution (replacement).

6. By **interiorizing** its sacraments in the interest of its members' inner freedom: prayer, meditation, mysticism, religious education.

7. By extrapolating this inner freedom in the forms of **innovation and hope** (time-transcendence; eschatological community).

8. By affirming the community's **solidarity** with and potential **contribution** to humankind.

9. By purifying and renewing its vision and institutional life in the light of the community's origins and potential contribution to humankind. This is the prophetic-theological task, requiring **remythologizing**.

II. THE CHURCH AS SAVING COMMUNITY

In the light of all the above, what does our traditional-classical Christian doctrine of "salvation" look like? And what, in the light of Christian existence today, does Christian "lostness" and Christian "savedness" look like in its communal expressions?

A. Freedom from fate, hate, and fear.

B. Freedom to share in the feast of Love, to receive a divine mission, and to renew one's self-understanding as the church renews its own in changing circumstances.

III. RIVAL SALVIFIC MOVEMENTS AND INSTITUTIONS

"Salvation" in the Christian traditions is in cultic competition with movements and institutions more or less effective in their counterpromises and counterthreats.

Can we work with them toward pro-human goals — or will they not let us, or will they corrupt us, or will they take us over or quit cooperating on failure to do so?

Do they encompass the entire "world" exclusive of the church, or is it paranoid to imagine so?

Do they offer only other "salvations" and/or fraudulent substitutes, or do some of them have power to encourage and even nurture "Christian salvation"?

And what is "salvation" in the competing lifestyles of contemporary America: what is "a lost hippie" or "a lost business executive"? How can "Christian salvation" speak to the increasing Apollonian/Dionysiac polarization in our country: shall we consider heresies and schism (if, indeed, we identify such) as full-fledged "rivals"? Can we divide the rivals into religions and ideologies? Perhaps not, but let's try:

A. Religions

1. **Old** religions

Islam is the most dangerous abroad and Hinduism, in many guises, at home. Coming on fast are various versions of Buddhism.

2. **New** religions

a) Romantic-mystical

Much of so-called New Age movements; Alan Watts' version of Zen; Meher Baba's and the

49

Maharishi Mahesh Yogi's mix of Oriental religion and Western science and psychology, as well as the older Bahai.

b) Romantic-educational

All forms of educationism, salvation by education, neo-gnosticism, including Fritz Perls's liberation by self-gestalt. He had one foot in the old Freudian psychoanalysis and the other in the human potential movement, both in this subcategory of new religions.

c) Romantic-political

All the revolutionisms are rivals of the Christian revolution in spite of the fact that most of them contain Christian elements. Overlapping American religion-tinged political revolutionism is Sun Myung Moon's Unification Church, and in Japan, Soka Gakkai.

B. Ideologies

1. **Tribalism and racism**

Political energy is shifting from detribalizing to retribalizing, political atavism; from integration to multiculturalism.

2. **Nationalism**

A bad bargain, to purchase stability at the cost of security and chauvinistic pride at the cost of contiguous and global realities. And when nationalism is powered by tribalism and racism, as in Nazism, the mix is suicidal and demonic. The bright side of "civil religion" is the critical undergirding of public life; its dark side is politolatry, nation-worship, the fatal merger of faith and nation.

3. **Secularism**

a) Philosophical-ethical

As the romantic-educational movement deserves to be called a new religion, this deserves to be called a new ideology. Focus is on human behavior, ethics, morality — for example, naturalistic ethics with an evolutionist base.

b) Philosophical-political

Most rampant of these in the U. S. is dialectical materialism, i.e., Marxism, which blurs the distinction between religion and ideology.[6]

IV. **SALVATION AND CONFLICT**

Because "shalom" is wrongly narrowed down to "peace" meaning the absence of conflict, conflict gets bad press among Christians despite the fact that Jesus and Paul were men of conflict. Our Faith and Order planning committee asked, "Can fragmented churches be healing communities?" My answer has two parts: (1) Jesus and Paul were healers while in conflict; and (2) an unfragmented church, given human nature redeemed but not completely transformed, would be a wounding community. This chapter's title is "Stability and Conflict in Community." Stability and conflict are circular: each leads toward the other. What conflict calls values, stability calls norms. As Father Avery Dulles put it in his lecture, "It is scarcely possible to speak of stability without discussing authority, or of diversity without referring to conflict." Authority provides stability, conflict assures diversity.

---

6. Now, a quarter-century later, I must add "4. **Radical feminism**."

A. <u>Ethology and human conflict</u>

Naïve ethologists (e.g., Lorenz, Ardrey, Morris) jump the gap too easily between human beings and the other animals. They overextrapolate from Delgado's electroded bull's brains and Calhoun's altruized mice. This moves us more toward Huxley's *Brave New World* and Orwell's *1984* than toward a truly human society.

B. <u>Roots of conflict</u>

U. S. turbulence in the second half of the 1960s stirred up studies in conflict and its causes, and experiments toward higher tolerance for frustration, anxiety, and strife. The human-potential marathon was one salutary form of this development.

1. Unresolved **interpersonal** tension

From deficient childhood socialization, poor handling of conflict in schools, little or no discipline of the spirit, low or no conflict-management skills in institutions of work, worship, and leisure. Oversold on psychology, our society tends to therapeutize, i.e., to define the situation in terms of sickness/healing, and the church too easily falls into this analysis and its language.

2. **Racism**

The victim defense for underachievement is overworked, to everybody's detriment. But racism is real, and perhaps, under the conditions of history, ineradicable, though its baleful effects are reducible.

3. **Poverty and hunger**

The shifting definition of "the poor" is problematic, but hunger is more manageable, except in the Third World.

4. **Oppression**

An elastic word, here meant to address mainly gender and class.

5. **Dissent**

The more repressive a society becomes, the more it needs healthy dissent and its supports.

6. **Coercion**

Polarities tell the story: coercion/persuasion, order/freedom, authority/chaos, coercion/justice, law/violence. A society not legally restrained in the interest of all will be brutally coerced in the interest of a few; a society resistant to change and legally restrained in the interest of a few (oligarchy) or even of a majority (majoritarianism) will be politically unstable.

C. Revolution

While revolutionaries suffer the same or similar illusions as those in power, revolutions eventuating in democracy (as the American) rather than tyranny (as the French) produce a net good, an incremental advance toward a more humane society. Stasis, the motionless social wheel, is doomed; a quarter turn of the wheel is reform; a half turn is revolution (its literal meaning being the "revolving" of a wheel: Jesus' "the first shall be last" and his disciples "overturning the world"). The gospel will call for active resistance more often than for violent revolution.

V. **SALVATION AND STABILITY**

In church and society, conflict is normal and stability depends on the normative. Excessive conflict results in no community; excessive stability results in no liberty. In IV and V, "salvation" is the common term.

53

A. Creation and stewardship

I thought of Psalm 24:1 when I heard a sci-fi flick end with "it [cosmic order] all depends on the will of the Landlord." The One under whom we are stewards, trustees, is not only the Landlord but also the land-Creator. Both these doctrines are stabilizing factors, in church and society, to the extent to which they are believed and lived.

B. Christian unity

Scripture connects salvation-unity-mission; but the latter two are somewhat at odds: unity is a gathering, mission a scattering. I have little regard for structural unity, high regard for the functional unity of being on local and larger mission together.

C. Global unity

War has now shifted from being mainly centralizing to being mainly decentralizing, by the principle of the agitation of opposites: even a minor intranational political upheaval can produce a global tidal wave. But the means of protecting nations against such waves are increasing, so chaos is being quarantined, while at the same time national borders are becoming osmotic.

D. Peace

Those in power claim to want peace, but they're happy to settle for quiet, the price for peace being justice, which challenges their power. Our historic spiritual resources for panhuman dreaming and action have been overwhelmed by our love affair with technology and its products, the powers of wealth and the blandishments of leisure. Temporary quiet perhaps, but shalom eludes those who fail to attend to "the things that make for peace" (Luke 19:42).

VI. THE FUTURE

A few questions, with only one answer (among many possible) each:

A. What makes human survival improbable?

Uncontrolled population-growth and therefore uncontrollable detritus-pollution.

B. What gives humanity a fighting chance?

The new youth.

C. Will conflict increase?

Yes, if only as an inevitable concomitant of rising pluralism.

D. Is there some rising stabilizing force that may offset the rising conflict by solving the problems of survival and justice?

Yes, the new planning.

E. Will there emerge, at all levels, political structures appropriate and adequate to instrumenting humanity's surviving and thriving?

Humanity's historic adaptability says yes; time pressure says no, but religion can help speed up the adaptation.

F. Will Christians and ecclesial institutions survive and thrive? And serve the world's surviving and thriving?

We'll share (and help shape?) the world's destiny, and have a destiny of our own.

The two rosaries of reasoning on abortion

It's Martin Luther King Day,[1] and after participating in yesterday's anticipatory celebration, I have freedom-liberation on the brain and in the heart: **God's** freedom from the evil forces in the universe, including in humanity, and the **biosphere's** freedom from its only intraterrestrial threat, namely, humanity. **Humanity's** freedom from what the old baptismal formulas call "sin, death, and the devil." The freedom of both **minorities** and **majorities** from each other's ever-looming tyranny, both instances of the freedom of the **weak** ("unempowered") from the **strong** ("advantaged") and vice versa.

All this came together with Goodwife Loree's taking a rosary to a dying Methodist (as a Hospice chaplain, she thought he might find spiritual comfort through the touch of a sacramental he'd known and used before his conversion to Methodism), and with the upcoming Craigville VI Theological Colloquy theme, *"Human Beginnings*: Deciding about Life in the Presence of God," to produce this Thinksheet's title.

1. President Bush wanted a "kinder, gentler America," and the abortion controversy promises to make us a meaner, bitterer America. As the gutsiest of our social issues, it's the hardest internal test of our democracy to arrive at an amicable settlement of an issue or to live with its unsettlement. Pray hard, think hard, try to speak

1. 16 January 1989.

softly. I speak softly in interpersonal situations, but must not do so in public.

2. In my Thinksheets, the context is the **content,** the order is the **intent.** This Thinksheet's introduction thus reveals both my content and my intent. You can see, for example, that I care relatively little about the future of humanity — relative, that is, to the biosphere's; and relatively little about the future of the biosphere, which may turn out to be a failed divine experiment — relative, that is, to God's future. You can imagine, then, how far down the line of my priorities is that class of human beings whom I cannot know personally: zygotes-embryos-fetuses!

3. **Every zygote is a *unique* human being,** and few zygotes become *individual* human beings (most fail — by miscarriage, by embryonic or fetal natural death, or by abortion — to become neonates). Yes, every individual is unique, but only those unique human beings who are jostled about outside the womb among other unique human beings get to be individuals: "individual" is the antonym of "social": God makes individuals not in mother's womb but in society's womb (including "Mother Russia" and "Mother Church").

4. What do I mean by a *rosary of reasoning*? A rosary is *a) sacred,* thus appealing to the transrational (that of the real that's unavailable to reason), and *b) circular,* a closed string of beads, emblematic of an enclosed paradigmatic world with its own internal logic irrefutable from beyond the charmed circle. Rosaries are wise devisings combining the tactile, the attentional, and the intentional. But when Khomeini used one with the fifty names of Allah (the first one being "The Compassionate"!) and then committed mayhem on the minds and bodies of his own people, something was missing. Like everything else, rosaries have their downside. The downside of my **pro-choice** rosary is that it's easily abused to present abortion as just one among many equally acceptable conception-and-birth prevention procedures (as in Japan, where 53% of embryos

and fetuses are aborted); and also to lessen the social sanctions against promiscuity.

5. The downside of the **pro-birth** (with rhetorical insult, "pro-life") rosary is manifold. For a starter, consider this bogus logic, which I've extended to reveal its flaws: *a*) The fetus is a *"unique individual"* (misunderstood as an intensive tautology). *b*) Each "unique individual" is a God-made *"person"* called to eternal fellowship with God (a claim equally applicable to the hundreds of billions of dead human zygotes).[2] *c*) The unrepeatable is inherently *sacred*. *d*) The sacred is *inviolable*. *e*) The willful death of a human being is *murder. f*) Abortion (and war? and capital punishment?), being the willful death of a unique, individual, unrepeatable, sacred human being of infinite meaning and ultimate value, is murder. *f*) Aborters, or at least abortionists, should be judged under the criminal code as *murderers*.

6. Just think of the much more raped and polluted condition of the earth were God not (to cop a phrase from the antiabortionists' lexicon) "in the abortion business"! As early as sixteen years ago, the (Rockefeller) Federal Commission on Critical Choices put the **environment** at the top of the list. That they were right in giving the threats to the biosphere priority over all other human problems has become steadily clearer through the intervening years.[3] To take a single but horrific instance, Brazil's rainforests have been suffering a blight so serious that it's easily visible even by the higher satellites; their blight is us, the flow of human flesh, which Brazil with its 2000% inflation seems powerless to stop even though the world's atmosphere is being degraded and 90% of the world's species of flora and fauna are facing extinction. In view of ecological nightmares such as this, **every abortionist is a worker**

2. Medieval debating as to when "soul" enters "body" was, and remains, speculatively lame.

3. The United Nations Conference on Population, Cairo, 1994, detailed the shocking worsening of such threats since the Rockefeller Commission's report — and rightly focused on women's needs.

58

together with God. Every abortion is a victory for the biosphere against its number-one enemy. Yes, there are other perspectives for viewing abortion. I'm saying this is one. Holistically, globally, it is the most important. It is also the one that causes the greatest revulsion, repentance, and humility: our flesh is the world's worst cancer.

7. Except for members of the International Flat-World Society, humanity has made the Copernican shift from geocentricity to heliocentricity: facts undermined the Ptolemaic paradigm, and it collapsed. Now we face an even more consequential paradigm shift (call it **Copernicus II**): from anthropocentricity to biocentricity, from the *narcissism* of centering in our species to the *realism* of centering in the biosphere. Will the facts erode our narcissism fast enough so that it collapses before irreparable, irreversible damage is done to our planetary mother and home? I fear not. Humanity's psychospiritual inertia is too great. The technology for population control improves every year, but so does the resistance: even many Christians are committing the sin of fetolatry (fetus-worship). Furthermore, to primitive taboos against intervention in the pro-creative process, Christianity as a conversional religion adds the burden of overemphasis on the *individual,* who is the goal and subject of conversion. Our Christian religion, in most ways the best among the world's religions, is here a net negative, a liability, a hindrance to our moving into God's future. See how dismal the prospect is: Christians must be asked to *repent of their religion in order to be faithful to their faith.* Not many of us, I fear, will respond to the Spirit's call to come up higher into the new paradigm — let's call it **ecotheology**.

8. How shall we answer the charge that those of us who **promote** abortion instead of only permitting or proscribing it are hard, insensitive, maybe even misanthropic? My answer is this: Our enemies on this issue, those willfully blind to the truth that "new occasions teach new duties," are *less* kind to humanity. For their failure to promote abortion and their fight against even per-

mitting it weigh on the scale to increase the tonnage of human flesh and accordingly add to human misery by *a*) an exponentially degraded bio-support-system, *b*) starvation on a scale previously unimaginable, and *c*) triage eco-wars of the shrinking advantaged defending themselves against the expanding unadvantaged.[4] If humanity does not act swiftly to shut down the baby-faucet by all means, including abortion, we'll soon face Hobson's choice of *all* sinking into degradation (if the advantaged compassionately "identify" with the unadvantaged, which the old version of Christianity recommends) or *some* enjoying privileges earth can't extend to many, certainly not to all. Bioethicist Willard Gaylin weeps over the "terrible irony" that already we can't afford life: life-saving has become too expensive except for a very few. Then we'll be faced with *triage*: shall we draw lots to see who lives, as the disciples did (Acts 1) to replace Judas? How do we allocate shrinking resources among expanding humanity? How do we face constrictions when we've been taught to hate and deny limits? How do we dispose of our offal when we're "running out of out" (as in "throw the garbage out")? Can the liberal church demythologize "the sacredness of the individual" so as to theologize a humanity-in-biosphere sustainable system? Can we free ourselves, in time, from thralldom under Enlightenment "rights" into the freedom of biblical "responsibilities"?

4. E.g., South Africa's black-to-white proportion increasing, in only one generation, from 5:1 to 17:1.

Sex: saved (safe), dangerous, and less dangerous

Condoms and Antonyms

Last evening,[1] our Cape Cod town of Falmouth's school board decided to distribute condoms to seventh-graders without counseling. Against the public and the schools' faculties, they found persuasive the argument that "this is a *health matter, not a moral or religious matter.*" This insanely myopic thinking has, as you see, overwhelmed my weak reluctance to speak of things genital.

1. Today is the fiftieth anniversary of an event indicating my long opposition to chopping life into compartments like health, morals, and religion. The following quoted material is from my diary entry of fifty years ago. To the Plebian Forum of Chicago, "composed of economic, political, and religious malcontents . . . Henry George-ites, atheists, and radicals of every color," including communists and Bundists (American Nazis), I gave a one-hour "speech-sermon on the *interrelatedness* of the economic, the political, and the religious problem." After I closed with prayer, "they questioned me for about three hours and seemed surprised that a religionist could answer questions. (They apparently thought before that only economists could!). . . . I told them that God and Christ could not be identified with *any* human structure, and that they therefore could become Christians without accepting the American majority's equation of the status quo with the will of God." Fol-

1. 12 November 1991.

61

lowing the meeting I talked for two hours in the apartment of the leader, a Bundist, who became so angry that he kicked his dog hard enough for the poor critter to land against a wall. Next day he was seized by the FBI, and I never again heard anything of Mr. Gaul.

Think of the "alien" sickness that has come upon the world from the *fragmentation* of mind into economic, political, and religious ("alienist" being an early term for a shrink, who was supposed to help folks who'd fallen apart to get themselves together again). Without this general social sickness, and the philosophical materialism underlying it, that school board could not have narrowed its view of students down to rutting skinbags in danger of self-destruction (in the name of "health").

2. "The message of Magic Johnson" has been a Rorschach since he announced himself as HIV positive. His own meaning of "practice safe sex" is "use condoms." But even if a condom is properly used, it may permit the passage of spermata, resulting in pregnancy. And the AIDS virus, being only $\frac{1}{150}$ the size of a sperm, has 149 more chances of getting through the latex (which is somewhat more protection than animal skin)! So why has he not been more generally attacked for deception and fraud? Because, as millions are saying, "Condoms are all we've got, so don't knock 'em."

3. There's a better way, an honest way free of deception. It's to say that condom intercourse (vaginal, anal, oral) is *less dangerous* than noncondom intercourse, which is *dangerous.* What's wrong with that? It's negative, stating a degree of danger. The Falmouth school board would be in the actionable position of furthering a dangerous student activity: the use of condoms. (Any good lawyer could reduce "less" almost to invisibility.)

4. Biologically, the only form of *safe* sex is *saved* sex (sexus reservatus), abstinence till virginal marriage or at least virginal engagement to marry. Is there an honest argument against telling the children so? I can think of none. And if to biology the teller adds psychology, morality, and religion, the argument will for many children be per-

suasive. (Under "psychology" here I include all intra- and interpersonal considerations, supremely the fact that in all societies, cruising-wandering genitals are the most disruptive and impoverishing social force.)

5. On the side of creativity, crisis is *opportunity*. AIDS now provides opportunity for society to train itself in more responsible genital activity. We are in some danger that a magic bullet against AIDS will be discovered before this social improvement occurs. The social control of sex requires a complex of fears, and in our permissive society that complex has disintegrated, but is now being gradually restored by the AIDS horror (the only salutary effect of AIDS). We are, then, in necessary self-contradiction. We want AIDS to succeed as a fear and fail as a disease.

6. Where is **God** in the AIDS thing? Most Americans believe *a*) in God and *b*) that that's a nonquestion: religion is irrelevant to social conditions and moral decisions, being entirely a "private" matter of the "heart." Those of us with the burden and joy of finding God in everything are called "arrogant asses" if we suggest *a*) that the loving God punishes, *b*) that suffering should alert our minds to the possibility that punishing is going on, and therefore *c*) that AIDS cannot automatically be exempted from the punishment category. The most frequent rejoinder I've heard is, "Is God punishing an AIDS baby?" Using the analogy of the Gulf War, I say that no AIDS baby is being punished by a divine smart bomb, but God also uses dumb bombs, sometimes producing "collateral damage." Or if the thought of a divine dumb bomb whiffs for you of blasphemy, consider that even a smart bomb gets some "innocent civilians" who are too close to target.

From another angle, I ask, "Where do you see God punishing if not in AIDS?" Every time I've asked this question, the answer has been, "I don't see God as a punishing God, but as a loving God." A nonsense answer, as that God as a loving God is not in question. Thus is revealed the fact that "AIDS is not a punishment from God" is only a fragment of the complete idea of my opponent, which is that "God does not punish, so AIDS cannot be a punishment from God."

63

7. In light of all the above, how much clearer is the Falmouth school board's *nonsense* in separating "health," morality, and religion! Of course AIDS is a health problem. But it is also a socio-moral and a religious and theological opportunity. We'd better be about these opportunities before medical research makes AIDS go poof.

8. It's an uphill fight against a culture of *promiscuity*. Basketball player Wilt Chamberlin's autobiography says he's had twenty thousand lays (that's laid women, not basketballs in hoops), and Magic Johnson in *Sports Illustrated* admits "I did my best to accommodate as many women as I could" (*L.A. Times* says "thousands"), "most . . . through unprotected sex." A government pamphlet on condoms says they "reduce the risk" (which, seen from the other end, means a risk of a disease that's 100% fatal!). And *Reader's Digest*[2] says the infected "lie their heads off" to sex partners.

1995 Supplement

1. By my persuasion and with support from fellow-member Gabriel Fackre, our congregation — First Congregational Church (United Church of Christ), Centerville — became the first Cape Cod church to witness against the Falmouth school board decision. Subsequently, abstinence promotion has become secularly respectable in much of the United States, and the problem of how to restigmatize teen pregnancy is out in the open.

2. Guilt and shame, which for several generations have worked against virginity, are now beginning to work for it. Where in our society the fear of the Lord failed, the fear of AIDS and of the plague of child mothers, and the public's abhorrence of mass abortions (though more than canceled by the public's libertarian belief in choice), are pushing the loose/tight pendulum of public morality in the tight, neo-Puritan direction.

2. August 1991.

64

On not taking Mother Nature as seriously as Father God

The sexual ethics of the clergy today

No, this is not one more Thinksheet on gender language for God, though I admit to having that topic much on my mind as I'm about to complete a close study of the best backlash-book on feminine referencing of God (*Speaking the Christian God: The Holy Trinity and the Challenge of Feminism,* ed. by Alvin F. Kimel, Jr.[1]). It's about *clergy sex,* which runs this range: (1) none (i.e., clergy virgins), (2) virginal marriage + marital faithfulness, (3) virginal marriage + long-past adultery, (4) virginal marriage + recent adultery, (5) virginal marriage + present adultery, (6) nonvirginal marriage + faithfulness, (7) nonvirginal marriage + long-past adultery, (8) nonvirginal marriage + recent adultery, (9) nonvirginal marriage + present adultery, (10) promiscuity, (11) homosexuality, and (12) pedophilia.

This Thinksheet's immediate occasion is a United Church of Christ conference on the subject, for those who have *disciplinary responsibility* for our clergy.

1. Jesus says angels don't have the problem of **genital control:** no sex, because nonsexual (Mark 12:25). Without the weight of genitals, they aren't tempted to take themselves too seriously, heavily. That is why, according to that old reifier of metaphors G. K. Chesterton, they can fly: they take themselves lightly. So there's our first clue as to why some clergy drift into genital violation of

1. Grand Rapids, Mich.: Eerdmans, 1992.

65

vows ecclesial or marital: *they put too much weight on their sexual feelings.*

2. The public (the media) makes cynical grunts over news of clergy *venality* (greed), but gives fascinated attention to clergy *venery* (lust). Since the exposé of the sexual exploits of certain televangelists, that fascination has somewhat abated: news run into the ground is no news. The trial of Henry Ward Beecher (d. 1887) for alleged philandering with a counselee was big news because of his prominence and the rarity of the case, but now this aberration goes unnoticed except in the local press — except, again, in the case of prominent clergy.

3. Same-sex lust *(homosexuality)* and adult lust for children *(pedophilia,* including pederasty) are not unknown in clergy permitted to marry, but they're more common in churches forbidding clerical marriage and in monasteries, which are less attractive to heterosexuals, who must give up more.

Why do I use the pejorative **"lust"** for homosexuals and pedophiles but not for straights? Because the classical Christian position is that of the three, the only acceptable sexual desire is straight. Pedophilia remains unacceptable, indeed has become even more unacceptable since the Roman Catholic Church (facing tens of millions of dollars of claims) has tightened discipline. Sexually inactive out-of-the-closet homosexuals are increasingly acceptable in some churches, but sexually active out-of-the-closets are acceptable in few churches. The extent, if any, to which "Mother Nature" is responsible for homosexuality and pedophilia remains in dispute. All churches agree on the principle that *human beings are responsible for their sexual in/activity no matter which of the three orientations.* And almost all churches refuse the claim of some homosexuals to equal sexual status with heterosexuals. (Emphasis on "sexual": this affects no other equality-claims.)

The other answer to the question opening the paragraph immediately above is that I do use "lust" also for straights: for any nonmarital or nonconsensual genital activity except masturbation.

4. Jesus enjoins the most radical defense against wrong genital

activity, the earliest possible intervention against it: *custodia oc-culorum,* i.e., *inattention* (Matt. 5:28, looking "with lust"). What doesn't get your attention can't get you. Was he preaching against marriage? No, but he was preaching against taking Mother Nature (who's all for the lustful eye) too seriously, in violation of Father God. It's a counsel of **prudence**. To call it a counsel of perfection, as have most interpreters through the centuries, is to dismiss it "for all practical purposes," on the illogical leap that since it's extremely difficult it must be impossible.

In a permissive time like ours, such dismissal gets extended. Children "can hardly be expected" not to fornicate (the original "F-word," now replaced by the positive phrase "practice abstinence").

Now, the clergy should live at a higher sexual level, closer to Jesus' logion, than the laity. (I didn't say "should be expected to": they shouldn't be.) When they fall into low sex, the devil wins more than when that happens in the laity. So the ecclesial discipline should be *severe*. But consider what militates against such severity:

a) "unconditional **love**," which easily takes the form of low-conditional or no-conditional forgiveness. The classical Christian position is plainly expressed in an old classic, *The Principles of Christian Ethics* by Albert C. Knudson: "Moral love is necessarily conditioned love. If it were not, it would not be moral."[2] God's love is "not unconditional," for "the severity of the divine judgment awaits" for those who refuse to "yield themselves to the divine *agape* to be transformed by it." A fundamentalist ethic? No. An evangelical ethic? No. Knudson was a personalistic modernist. Postmodernism has jettisoned the divine judgment and, with it, conditional love. The sexual sinner need not depend on cheap grace. Like judgment, grace is unnecessary.

b) unconditional **forgiveness**. Marsha G. Witten, studying recent sermons on the Prodigal Son, found little weight given to the repentance side of the repentance/forgiveness transaction. The story is hyperbolic to show (as an old gospel song puts it) "grace that is greater than all our sin": it's not to be read as though the father had

2. Albert C. Knudson, *The Principles of Christian Ethics* (Nashville: Abing-don-Cokesbury, 1943), p. 125.

written "Come home, all is forgiven." Yes, all was forgiven when the son went home: the going home was repentance in action. But "unconditional forgiveness" perverts the story by claiming God's forgiveness *before* the return. Clipping off the first phrase, Ms. Witten titles her book *All is Forgiven: The Secular Message of American Protestantism*. A more-tolerant-than-thou spirit pervades pulpit and pew, making repugnant the thought of disciplining either.

5. To this *permissivism,* which now pervades and pollutes "Christian love," **suppressing Mother Nature** (despite Jesus' bold injunction to do so) is oppressive. According to the Freudians, including sadomasochist Michel Foucault, nature is oppressed by humanity's internalization of societal norms, which have behind and within them (not divine revelation) only custom, tradition-conditioned behavior. Society has reasons for proscribing certain sexual behaviors, such as pedophilia; but don't claim Mother Nature as support for such prohibitions. Father God may be, but Mother Nature is not against doing what (for any individual) comes naturally. Pedophilia, homosexuality, marital rape are not "sick" in themselves but sick only because society denies them the status of healthful behavior. Mother Nature, the Goddess, has a womb, and whatever comes forth from it is natural and in-itself good. And remember, folks: "You can't fight Mother Nature."

6. What a contrast to biblical ethics, which is *affirmative* of nature as God made it ("very good," Gen. 1:31) and *suspicious* of what humanity makes of it! We Christians are baptized, if the old formula is used on us, against "the world, the flesh, and the devil." We are called to a moral-spiritual discipline which is (in a definition I devised a half century ago and still hold to) *the systematic **violation** of our feelings in the interest of a higher order.*

7. Think of the *social context* of present clergy sexual misconduct: for almost two generations, Americans have been taught that *a)* we're individually on our own in moral decision-making and *b)* we should be, of our feelings, "a little more careful than anything" (to paraphrase e. e. cummings on love). Contrast God's treatment

of Jonah: the systematic **violation** of Jonah's feelings in the interest of God's higher order, concern for the city of Ninevah. As you read each of the four chapters, imagine how Jonah is feeling. Then, please, laugh. Laugh to be free!

1995 Supplement

1. Radical feminists, on insufficient grounds, object to the traditional **Mother** Nature / **Father** God polarity, so they'd be disinclined to give this chapter a fair hearing. But both thought and life need the polarity however the poles are named and described. In the mold of this chapter, we have our urges, our vital bio-energies, from the Earth Mother and the Ten Commandments from the Sky Father, and all things from the One God.

You may suspect that this polarity exists in a different guise as the title of this book. The correlation is real, but only rough.

2. This chapter's title does not say you shouldn't take Mother Nature seriously. But it does imply that what de-fines humanity, sets us off from other creatures, is "reach of spirit" (here symbolized by "Father God"): "flow of flesh" (here symbolized by "Mother Nature") we have in common with all other embodied sentients.

3. The libertine **myth** that "You can't fool Mother Nature" (i.e., defeat your need of sex) is a pleasant fraud. All the wandering-genital clergy I have counseled have believed it in spite of having known healthy, happy persons living without sexual intercourse.

Nothing's more basic to ethical thinking than the distinction between needs and wants. Immoral persons do not make the distinction. A moral, mature person says often "I want this, but I don't need it." The consumerist industry (production, propaganda [i.e., advertising, promotion], distribution, sales) aims to de-moralize the public, i.e., convince suckers they need whatever the industry seduces them into wanting. The motto "Sex sells" fits both the myth and the industry.

Living with and in a ruin

If a man lives long enough with a woman, I am told, sooner or later he is living with a *ruin*. ("I am told," I say, for I wouldn't want to claim an experience I haven't had.) At that stage of the relationship, the ruin will be to him either repulsive or dear, depending on how he's treated the relationship (i.e., her) in his heart and life.

Thus said I recently to my dear Loree, who is not yet a ruin, though she is living with one, one who is to her a dear ruin, as she will some day be to him. I was speaking of Bessie Dyke, who in 1811 married **Tom Moore**, who lived with her gratefully-joyfully-faithfully-devotedly decade after decade through the births and deaths of five children till finally she became to him a *dear ruin*.

When I wasn't a third of my present age, I heard an old ruin of a preacher say, "If you manage to live till age fifty, you'll be living in a ruin. And before then, you will have decided whether to let that fact depress you — you will have decided how important to your soul is the condition of your body." That joyful, humorous old codger delivered me, by the grace of God, from the fear of aging, which may be the theme of this Thinksheet, though I think it's about grateful-joyful-faithful-devoted love.

You should understand that Tom was helped by the fact that he was Irish. Besides leaning toward laughter, the Irish love **green**, *verdancy*. They'd better: Eire is not called the Emerald Isle idly. If you swim east by north off our Cape Cod beach, first thing you come to will be this huge green mass sticking up out of the Atlantic.

70

Or even more impressive, you look down from your plane and suddenly the solid blue turns to solid green!

What about all those old ruins scattered over St. Paddy's island, you say? The green crawls up and around and over them. Their gray gradually loses to a hundred kinds of vine.

In those vines' determination to cover the gray, Tom saw the power of his love to green over the graying of aging Bessie: "around the dear ruin each wish of my heart / Would entwine itself verdantly still." Not abolish the gray: the power of resurrection is in the hands of God alone. Rather, his was a **realistic romanticism**, not aging-and-death-denying but life-affirming in the power of timeless love, the only timelessness available to us on this earth.

Nor was Tom a self-victim of his contemporary romantics' bathetic-Byronic melancholy — his good friend Byron being so typical of it as to provide posthumously and unknowingly a personal adjective to describe it. (Byron gave Moore his autobiography to be published, then at thirty-six committed suicide by jumping ship in mid-ocean. Byron's life was so seamy-steamy that his family persuaded Moore to burn the book. Byron tried to bury his melancholy underneath what the KJV calls, in the case of the Prodigal Son, "riotous living," which began with — if not before — his failed marriage.)

A melancholy fact: sooner or later, gravity gets everything presumptuous and powerful enough to stand up. If it doesn't suddenly drop dead young, everything sags before it collapses. *Gray* romantics wallow in that fact. *Green* romantics accept it as fact and with *song* defy its power, with *beauty* defy its ugliness, with *love* defy its loneliness, and so with *truth* defy its lie.

Tom's evergreen, melancholy-overwhelming love was for **God** as well as for Bessie. Facing aging, sorrows, and death, he invites us — in a hymn[1] still in many hymnals — to "come to the feast of love":

Come, ye disconsolate, where'er ye languish:
　　Come to the mercy-seat, fervently kneel;

1. Written in 1816 at age thirty-seven.

71

Here bring your wounded hearts, here tell your anguish;
　　Earth hath no sorrow that heaven cannot heal.

Joy of the comfortless, light of the straying,
　　Hope of the penitent, fadeless and pure;
Here speaks the Comforter, tenderly saying —
　　Earth hath no sorrow that heaven cannot cure.

Here see the Bread of Life; see waters flowing
　　Forth from the throne of God, pure from above;
Come to the feast of love: come ever knowing
　　Earth hath no sorrow but heaven can remove.

And for **Bessie,** Ireland's foremost poet-lyricist wrote the lovesong we have been musing on:

Believe me, if all those endearing young charms
Which I gaze on so fondly today,
Were to change by tomorrow and fleet in my arms
Like fairy gifts fading away,

Thou would'st still be ador'd, as this moment thou art,
Let thy loveliness fade as it will;
And around the dear ruin each wish of my heart
Would entwine itself verdantly still.[2]

2. From *Heart Songs* (chosen by 25,000 Americans), no. 148 (Boston: Chapple, 1909). My copy is from my parents' collection of "home music," "family music." My audio-memory can hear my parents singing "Believe me . . ." before the days of radio.

Evil creeps before it pounces. When it pounces, it's too late. While it's still creeping, it's not too late.

1. When Adam asked, "Who am I? I want to know who I *really* am," he committed the first sin (which, note, was by a man, not a woman). Since the universe is theocentric, and not even the earth is anthropocentric, Adam's first question to God should have been, "Who are YOU?" I'm not just spoofing the current "middleclass" narcissism. I'm introducing God's reply to the first human question: "You are mud *(adamah)*, and your name is Mud *(adam)*." Our name has been Mud-Soil-Earth ever since. So *soil* begins this Thinksheet, with Toles' help (see next page). Soil loss correlates with **population** gain. The population of the planet has doubled since I began teaching in seminary and will, barring effective intervention, double again within the lifetime of most people now living. (Doubt that? The average age in some countries is only fifteen.)

It was while meditating on the cartoon following that this Thinksheet title's metaphor occurred to me. I watch a nature film and want to warn that beautiful gazelle approaching a clump of savannah grass in which a lion is creeping, but I cannot intervene. The lion pounces, the gazelle is dead. I did, but the gazelle didn't, see the creeping.

Pouncing evil is public, easy to film, like war in Somalia with its starving children. But the *creeping* evil of Somalia's soil erosion, depletion, impoverishment — will CNN sponsors pay for filming that? Even less will the media highlight the fundamental cause of biodegradation — just too many people. It's not "PC" for "West-

73

TOLES © 1992 The Buffalo News. Reprinted with permission of UNIVERSAL PRESS SYNDICATE. All rights reserved.

ern"/"Northern" media to call attention to the fact that they, those other people, are having too many babies. Supersensitive "minority" defenders even call that genocide! And even to suggest that "they" ought to control their populations steps on the toes of those who for religious reasons oppose contraception and/or abortion. Most Christians, and the billion Muslims, are two examples.

2. No use squabbling over statistical details. Even the lowest projections scream, "Horrors ahead!" How many children will have been added to earth's tonnage of human flesh between your breakfast this morning and your next breakfast? The Population Institute's figure is 396,000. More deforestation, more consequent

flooding, more grazing, more planting — and five hundred years to replace the **topsoil** (that's without people on the land)!

3. An evil argument is diverting attention from the creeping evil of topsoil loss. Well-intentioned, but in effect evil. It goes like this. The higher the *development* (material wealth), the lower the birth-rate. So let's encourage development, as many U. N. agencies have been doing ever since the U. N.'s founding. It sounds compassionate, just, fair. But what would happen to ecology if, for example, the thirty million people in Greater Mexico City got "developed"? That fragile environment is dependent on keeping underdeveloped those now undeveloped! As the soil sees the world, the humane project is to prevent "development." That the developed are enjoying their advantages is understandable, as the undeveloped would enjoy development if they got it. But the present development inequality is an irrational and perverse argument for development. "Rights" argumentation, however, favors this perversity and irrationality — contending, for example, that your having something I haven't gives me the right to have it, too. The reverse would be rational but unworkable: the fact that I don't have it means you don't have a right to it (though voluntary divestment is workable: "I will not have what my brother cannot have" — Eugene V. Debs).

4. The bumper sticker is **good news for the soil:** "I will live simply, so my neighbor can simply live." At least the protasis is good news for the soil, which will be less stressed if I consume less; the apodosis is murky (how specifically can my consuming less reduce the dying among my world neighbors, and for how long?). The agonizing, Gordian fact is that the more I help keep my neighbor alive (including reducing infant mortality), the more I'm guilty of increasing the stress on soil (by erosion, but also by pollution), subsoil (mineral and fossil resources), sea (pollution, and depletion of seafood), sky (pollution), and suprasky (ozone depletion).

What can I do? Every place I've lived with access to soil, the soil's been better when I left (from soil-enriching plantings, composting, rotation, refuse and rock removal). But I mustn't kid myself. The biosphere would have been better off had I never been born. I haven't been paying the rent. My bio-living has never been a pouncing evil, but it's been and is a creeping evil. Yours, too. You and I need the **grace** of God to forgive us and the **wisdom** of God to guide us . . .

5. . . . into specific, costly **actions**, such as *a*) purchasing for permanence, include repairability; *b*) speaking out publicly and privately against easily and not-so-easily avoidable waste and pollution; *c*) supporting intelligent pro-environment public decisions; and *d*) helping create an up-to-date theology of ecology.

1995 Supplement

1. Among the flora, phragmites is an **endangering** species, threatening hundreds of others; among the fauna, by far the most endangering species is *homo sapiens:* we are the enemy we continue to refuse to meet. Look upstream of the **endangered** species and there, always, you will find us — too "developed" us and too many of us.

2. This chapter, because the Thinksheet's impetus was the Toles cartoon, prays for the environment from the **perspective** of arable soil. Facing any problem, especially any global problem, we should be multi-perspectival, considering every angle. Water is the perspective of chapter four, the book's only other chapter on ecology: humanity is now suffering even more from water pollution than from soil erosion.

3. Twelve jurors, twelve perspectives. In the jury box pronouncing us "Guilty!" are flora (green things), the other fauna (two-legged, four-legged, winged, and gilled), soil, water, air, the ozone, the subsoil irreplaceables (minerals, coal, petroleum), and "the Creator of heaven and earth."

4. Ecological evils have been creeping, but they are beginning to pounce.

Sin is anything extended far enough in a straight line and anything that holds up the party

Should I apologize for this long chapter title? You will see why I shouldn't. It's because the two things I want to say about sin are said in the title exactly as I want to say them, and exactly as I've said them many times in recent years because the words "work."

Let's take them in order:

1. **Sin is anything extended far enough in a straight line.**

So is stupidity, but you can be sinful without being stupid, and vice versa. If you do something stupid, you're violating wisdom. But sinning is doing something that violates God; it is a breach of covenant, a betrayal of communion, by exceeding some limit God has set for you, crossing some boundary into territory you've no right to be in. It's being on your own trajectory as a God-unguided missile. It's coming to the margin and paying no attention to it. It's keeping on doing your thing *without thought* of God and of what God wants for you and of you in his world and in yours.[1]

Adam and Eve were eating up a storm in Eden, and the snake

---

1. It can also be with negative thought of God, as in deliberate rebellion and betrayal (e.g., Gen. 3). *Hubris,* the Greek word for presumptive overreaching and the damage it does, often in the LXX (Greek Old Testament) renders various Hebrew expressions, such as "with a [stiff]neck." The literal Greek of Job 15:26 is "runs against God presumptively." For the colorful images of the Hebrew and Greek words, see "Sin" in Bible dictionaries, theological dictionaries, and ency-

convinced them that there was no good reason to exclude the fruit of a certain tree that God had told them was out of bounds for them. They were eating in a straight line and came to that tree and its fruit looked as good as any they'd eaten, and the snake said it was even better because it would be educational in addition to being luscious (and God was lying when he said it would be fatal). Well, both the snake and God were right: Adam and Eve became both wise and dead.[2] Since it was stupid to eat fatal fruit, what sort of wisdom could have come of it? Or *can* you be sinful without being stupid?[3]

clopedias; and in general reference works, "Sins, the seven deadly" (with their remedial virtues).

Indeed, the "without thought of God" can be amnesia as well as ignorance: God the void, God the enemy, God the void again (instead of Whitehead's God the void, God the enemy, God the friend).

2. Gen. 3:1-21. They are to "become soil again" (v. 19), between soils to cultivate the soil outside the garden (vv. 22-24: access to the "tree of life," to immortality, was forbidden; the expulsion was necessary because Adam and Eve proved themselves untrustable).

3. The story's surface is simple, its depth is witty and profound, and its

If you need proof that Eve and Adam ate the same apple,[4] here you have it, the actual core. But couldn't this core have been eaten by one person? Impossible. In gestalt reversal, you can see the man on the left and the woman on the right.[5] By using the attentional insight that ground and figure, separately attended to, deliver different messages, but together deliver a single message, the artist humorously and profoundly displays the story's themes of *ambiguity* and *social sin* (sinning together presumably being more fun than sinning separately).[6]

---

reach is into the culture clashes of its origin time and ours. It hints at all forms of gnosticism as addiction, and reminds me of my three-dimensional approach to the alcoholic: you're *sick* (the medical diagnosis), your *sinful* (the spiritual diagnosis), and you're *stupid* (the sapiential diagnosis) — each to be used, separately and in combination, as appropriate to the person-in-situation.

4. Apricot, many scholars say.

5. The man is John Locke, a professor of art at Bard College, whose work is treated also in chapter 31, and the woman is his wife Joan. When he asked to study the Bible with me at New York Theological Seminary, I said "God has given you *eyes* and *hands*. Read through the Bible, as you go making a list of all the distinct visual impressions you have. Then try to capture the Bible's message in a series of paintings." The impressions came to some 3,000; the paintings, to 30, of which the applecore is the third.

As for his "Genesis 3," it's a red-and-orange silkscreen which (here) he redid as a black-ink sketch for my use. The colors of the original represent sin, suffering, blood, salvation, in all of which John and Joan have experience. Foster parents to many older children whom New York City courts have considered incorrigible and poor prospects for foster homes, this deeply Christian, joyful couple do not present themselves to their problem foster children as nonproblem, sinless adults: everybody bites into the wrong apple and acquires original sin atop original righteousness. Martin Buber says the best way into the Bible is to feel and know yourself a traitor to life, to the world, to yourself, to God. The Bible story is the story of "The Way out of Betrayal": the One we betray does not betray us, but saves us. Peter's denial results not in being denied but in being asked, "Do you love me?"

As for the gestalt-reversal technique, how appropriate it is for representing (1) the surprise of revelation, in history and the person, (2) our involvement in sin and salvation, and (3) the Bible's kind of consciousness, the theocentric-holistic way of seeing, and living in, the world.

6. At a much later time, Mr. Locke used his image for a *secondary*, positive message. Above it he inscribed "The goal of friendship" (and below) "is not to think alike, but to think together."

After hearing my straight-line sin metaphor, a Boston minister preached a series of sermons exploring the idea, "in the course of which," he told me, "I taught myself more about sin than I'd ever known before. My people have picked it up, and in teaching and counseling I'm hearing it back."

Have at it yourself, dear reader. And please tell me if you know of somebody who said it before me: almost all my original ideas derive from the simple fact that I have a bad memory:[7] "what hast thou that thou didst not receive?" (1 Cor. 4:7, KJV).

Now notice the ironic twist in the definition. "Far enough" is from the standpoint of somebody wanting to sin who is being told that it is necessary to go "far *enough*." The righteous will want to change it to "Sin is anything extended *too* far in a straight line." That the Ten Commandments are negative is positive: prohibition frees, positive command binds. Our first parents weren't told to eat a particular fruit, but only what fruit not to eat: their dietary **freedom** was almost total.

Imagine yourself standing in the center of a circle and having the freedom to wander anywhere within the circle instead of being told which radii you must or may traverse. Think of the Decalog as ten arcs, or segments, marked on the periphery, "*No* God but Me," "*No* idol," "*No* desecration of My name," "*No* work on Shabbat," " *No* disrespect for your parents,"[8] "*No* murder," "*No* adultery," "*No* theft," "*No* false accusation against your neighbor," "*No* feeding of any desire you may have for what belongs to somebody else." From the circle's center, start out on any radius, or straight line, you want to — but know when you have come to the sharp-line limit of a Commandment.[9]

---

7. In recent years my daily devotional praxis has included the prayerful recollection of the day at a half-century remove. Reading the diary entry, I relive that day now fifty years gone. It's bracing to see how *accurate* my memory has been at most points, humbling to see how *distorted* it's been at some points, and humiliating to realize that a few things I remember happening *didn't*.

8. Only this commandment is without a limit-setting negative.

9. Not the Ten Suggestions of *blurred*-line limits, but freedom within *sharp*-line limits (God's good-parenting of us children). A personal memory

Then recall how you learned to say the Lord's Prayer: was it "debts" (a monetary figure for going too far in a straight line) or "trespasses" (a physical figure for going too far in a straight line)? Many Christians, and churches, now render out the metaphors, making it simply "And forgive us our *sins*. . . ."

But why all this talk of sin? Is God the God of limits, and not of freedom? God is the God of such limits as are necessary to our freedom, and forgiveness frees us from the demonic limits that forbid our freedom — for the past, unrepented of, imprisons us.[10]

Now for that second definition of sin:

2. **Sin is anything that holds up the party**.

Jesus' opponents accused him of overdoing partygoing,[11] so it's improbable that he underdid it. Some scholars think he didn't go so far in that direction as to turn water into wine,[12] but — given the glimpses the Gospels give us into that side of his character — you couldn't put it past him.

Take those three parties in Luke 15, for instance. Three freedoms had resulted in three binds. A man is *free* to own sheep, and one wanders off. A woman is *free* to handle money, and loses some. A young man is *free* to do with his life whatever he wants to, and messes up. The coin had no freedom, the sheep had little freedom, the young man had astonishing freedom — and all three exceeded their limits. But not to worry: in heaven the angels want a rejoicing party over human recovery (vv. 7, 10), and there will be three parties on earth (vv. 5f, 9, 22-32).

Three lost-and-founds. Three sorrows and joys. Hollow joys before repentance, return, confession of guilt and shame, and faith.

---

springs to mind: before World War II, having the free run of Hitler's cruise ship *Breman* except the areas clearly marked "Verboten." (Then, converted to a super-battleship, the *Breman* had free run till the British sank it.)

10. When I tried to lay original sin on a Greenwich Village poet, he said, "You can't make me believe in original sin. But I'd like to get this *ego* of mine under control."

11. Matt. 11:19, Luke 7:34.

12. John 2, 4:46.

But the Bible's moral seriousness is always unto improving the quality of partying, so sin is anything that holds up the party.[13]

On, then, to the messianic banquet, the marriage supper of the Lamb!

1995 Supplement

1. Two threads run through the two sections of this chapter:

. . . **freedom**. Though we cannot frustrate the ultimate will of God, we are free to diminish and damage ourselves and others and even to destroy ourselves.

. . . **humiliation**, what is done to us when we fail to do humility to ourselves. It's humiliating to go so far in a straight line that it becomes apparent, to others if not also to yourself, that you are achieving a reverse of what you'd intended. And it's shameful to suffer unnecessary losses.

2. The biblical call to **humble** ourselves (e.g., 2 Chron. 7:14; Jas. 4:10, 1 Pet. 5:6) — to get down to the elevation appropriate to us as creatures, as human beings, as Christians — is a call to the freedom available to us only at the level proper to us, the level at which we are reverent toward God and respectful of our neighbors and responsible toward society and the good earth.

3. Some feminist hermeneuts call our attention to the fact that both humility and humiliation are cures for arrogance: the already humiliated have a different disease, viz. too-low self-respect, and need a different medicine, viz. a self-affirmation that will free them to their full humanity in relation to God, neighbors, society, and the good earth. The Bible speaks as persuasively to the too low as to the too high. True enough. True also that the too low are tempted to the arrogance of trading on their alleged victimhood.

13. Of course sin is also anything *not* extended far enough in a straight line, and it's trying to crash a party you've *not* been invited to. Take those, please, as further thoughts for your rumination.

Will the Beast control you through your Social Security number?

Homeless, unemployed in spite of perpetual seeking and because of low skills, and without any welfare income in spite of having four small children, the Bergers were rich in the kind of human dignity that derives from steadily seeking the divine glory. They lived the Lord's Prayer, in all things seeking to hallow God's name, including their access to daily bread.

But "the system" was against them. In fact, two systems were against them. Representing the *social* system in the southern Manhattan federal court were a stackup of lawyers — federal, state, and city — determined to force Social Security numbers on the Berger children, without which they would not be allowed welfare benefits. A young welfare-rights lawyer, and I as a biblical scholar, were sweating it out with the Bergers against "the welfare system," whose legal letter was denying its compassionate spirit.

But the other system, the dark powers unsubjected to God, threatened much worse than the denial of temporary bread. This *demonic* system (Rev. 13) will soon send the Antichrist Beast to Washington to seize the Social Security computer and through it control all who are in its memory, the digital recording making unnecessary the visible identity "mark" (v. 16). Against that, the Bergers were concerned about the registry in heaven (v. 8), that their children have the freedom and dignity of the divine commonwealth rather than grovel out their lives as slaves of the state and, later, of hell.

Yes, they were in a fundamentalist church, a humanly warm place they'd found in the cold world and a spiritually warm place in the cosmos. Having interviewed the pastor and them, I could and did testify to the sincerity of these good folk whose hearts were full of love and glory and whose minds were, according to me, full of literalistic-fantastic garbage.[1]

And that's what the great Jewish judge Jack B. Weinstein wanted to know. In refusing Social Security numbers for their children, was this couple trying to do a number on all three levels of government? Or could they be as innocent, as naïve, as their dignified demeanor suggested? What was he, who openly confessed he knew nothing of the book of Revelation, to make of their way of making sense of heaven-earth-hell things? So he said, "Dr. Elliott has testified as to the defendants' sincerity, but I cannot be convinced without understanding their thinking. And that cannot be until I have sufficient knowledge of the book of Revelation. As that knowledge begins with near zero, this is going to take some time. Until I am satisfied, I will recognize nothing said by anyone else."

For almost an hour I expounded the Bible's last book, the judge delighting me with his eager and close questioning and the government lawyers ineffectually objecting whenever I bridged from the Book to the Bergers. What it all settled out to I can represent by a vertical ellipse, thus: If our core human task is to glorify God (the upper focus, "Divine Glory"), to hallow his name as the Lord's Prayer proclaims and practices, that task, accepted as path and goal, is the core of our dignity as human beings (the lower focus, "Human Dignity"). Our *essential* freedom is so to accept and live. And our *existential* freedom cannot escape resistance, often costly resistance, to whatever demonic and human forces, structures, processes frustrate that freedom.

So understood, biblically understood, the divine glory *dignifies* humanity, and reciprocally, humanity with the glory of the dignity within *glorifies* deity.

Did the Beast get lost in all this? Well, in the Book, the Beast

1. But I am as literal as they about 1 Cor. 10:31.

does indeed finally get lost, to the glory of God. But in Judge Weinstein's court, the Beast got used, used in the service of justice, which has priority over the laws — why else have judges?

Satisfied, and against all three government lawyers objecting at once, the judge ruled for the family's welfare benefits without Social Security numbers.

Am I putting you on? As Casey Stengel would say, "You could look it up." *Stevens v. Berger.*

In *Berger,* everything fell into place for an act of **compassionate intelligence,** the moral heart of the truly human society. But what if we change some factors? Consider the following examples:

1. What if the judge were a Christian? No difference. Our two religions are rooted in one faith, faith in the holy God of justice and mercy. What if the judge were a woman? Again, no difference. Nonwhite? Still no difference. The magnificent jurist Constance Baker Motley, in the same federal district as Weinstein and different from him in those three ways, is at least his equal, as our family can testify.[2]

2. What if the judge, instead of letting reason and compassion temper each other, were either a sentimentalist or a rationalist? Without keen intelligence and high respect for reason, a judge would dishonor the *letter* of the law and thus fail to function as the structural officer of public order. And without a "heart of flesh," she or he would violate the *spirit* of the law, the humane spirit that is prior and superior to all institutionalizations thereof, including the legal co-

2. Another case of refusal to register, this time for the military draft, was brought to Motley's court. In *United States v. Mark Elliott,* she ruled that the government was persecuting an individual who, desiring to make a personal protest against his country's action in Vietnam, appeared before his draft board, but refused to sign. The defendant's counsel Marvin Karpatkin proved the government had all the information it needed to draft Mark, but his number was so high that he never would have been called. The judge rebuked the draft board for arrogating to itself the power to force a signature "to make an example of" the accused. Whatever the specific words, the court thus served both "the glory of God" and "human dignity." As I am Mark's father, his case moved me even more deeply than the Berger case.

85

dices. Sentimentality leads to anarchy; rationalism, to tyranny: to both the French Revolution, in contrast to ours, testifies.

3. And what if our society were not founded on the conviction that the Really Real, from whom and to whom are "all things" (Greek for "the universe"), is the Holy One of love and justice?[3] There would be no government help for the Bergers: no welfare-rights lawyer and no biblical scholar contributing their time to an otherwise socially invisible family.

So much is wrong with every social system, including ours. But think on this: every workday, in some cases in some court-rooms, God is honored in human victories of the bright powers;[4] the motives and motifs of divine glory and human dignity converge; the ellipse becomes a circle.

4. Finally, what if the ellipse were to collapse into a circle without the bipolar center, one of the aims being lost? Lose attention to *human dignity,* and religion rationalizes crimes against humanity. Lose attention to *the glory of God,* as is the situation in our secular-pluralistic society, and humanity puts on divine airs, public-school children being taught to leave God out of their thinking and learn to center on such humanistic "values" as "the infinite worth of the individual" and "self-esteem." We should not be surprised at their deepening estrangement from the roots and reach of Western civilization.[5]

3. Of course the tension between love and justice appears in all civilizations, but in ours it dominates ethics, moral reasoning, and law. Early Egyptian Christians used Osiris as a Christ figure: the old religion preached that justice (Osiris's whip) and love (Osiris's shepherd's crook) would converge in the afterlife, where Osiris is god; but the Lord Jesus, dying and rising in this world, offers that unity here and now.

4. Dietrich Bonhoeffer's antonym for "the dark powers."

5. This estrangement was sadly true of the federal lawyer in the Berger case. Petulantly, after she lost she said to me, "Why do *you* care about *them?*" "Well, to begin with," said I, "I'd be scared not to, remembering Jesus' opinion of clergy who 'pass by on the other side.'" Contrast that to the defendants' lawyer, who wrote to me that it had been "the most rewarding experience of my legal career" and had led to his return to Christian faith and observance. And the judge, whose thirty-five-page decision showed keen perception of what was at stake and solid learnings from the materials I had provided him, including photocopies from twenty-one books.

In the court of fate, none are guilty

*Are there metaphysical underpinnings
for moral responsibility?*

"If it isn't local it isn't real," I remember hearing the World Council of Churches' Visser t'Hooft saying. On the street, on the phone, in meetings of all kinds, and in the local media (especially the newspapers, still), the **soul-and-society-shaping** conversations occur day by day. On Cape Code, a tragic local accident has crowded out the wider news these past few days. The president of the Barnstable High senior class, a paragon, died in a 6 A.M. car crash after the junior prom, to which the seventeen-year-old driver had invited him. Up all night, the girl fell asleep at the wheel. A stream of visitors said to her, "It's not your fault; it could have happened to anybody." When an eminent journalist chimed in on the same note, it was — as you can see by my *Cape Cod Times* letter here — just too much for me. It was like saying that the Holocaust was just one of those terrible things you can't explain. Only it was worse than that: Paul Gauvin could and did explain it: "fate" was the "culprit." Gauvin's godless column, prominent on the OpEd page, undoubtedly satisfied many if not most of his readers — hungry for a secular reading, suspicious of religious readings.

Belief in fate cuts moral responsibility

In ancient Rome, Jews and Christians were persecuted for believing in God. Their pagan neighbors, and the government, believed in fate.

If he'd lived then and there, Paul Gauvin would not have been persecuted. His May 22 column, "the pain and blessing of fate,"

87

is a confession of belief in fate. Horrors happen, and he concludes that "fate is the real culprit."

First, that belief makes nonsense of the heart of the Jewish and Christian religions, which refuse to deny that God is the Lord of nature and history, the Sovereign over all that happens. Oddly and backhandedly, Gauvin expresses this faith in asking, "Why did sleepless providence (lower-case 'p') choose to take from us" this boy? But tragedies are "preordained" by fate, says Gauvin.

Second, belief in fate cuts the nerve of moral responsibility. The girl, so the press reported, was under a midnight parental curfew. Six hours in violation, she's to blame for the boy's death. But Gauvin blames fate.

The Bible teaches us the courage and wisdom to search for meaning in life's downs as well as ups and to believe that the center of the search is Providence (upper-case "P," as in Roger Williams' naming of the capital of Rhode Island), God as Lover-Creator-Redeemer. Gauvin bespeaks the diametrical of that faith when he agonizes "the inequitability of fate's enigmatic process of random selection."

We should not be surprised at America's rising faith in fate. The public schools do not teach faith in God, so what else is there?[1]

1. If "the public square" does not hear godly interpretations of local and wider horrors, what happens to the biblical-pastoral claim that God is not only relevant, but *central*, "when," as the hymn says, "we are in deep distress"? God becomes an optional, then an alternative, finally an embarrassing source of insight and wisdom and guidance. We may go to church, but we leave God inside when we leave. The price? If God is not struggled with and for outside the church, the meaning will leak out of him inside the church.

2. Things happen by (take your pick) chance or fate or Providence. Especially since Darwin, **chance,** the random concatenation of atoms-molecules-cells-environment, has been the minimal,

1. *Cape Cod Times,* 3 June 1993.

88

least painful hypothesis for explaining good/bad "luck." Add the notion of predetermination, and chance yields to **fate.** Put the two together and you get Gauvin's "random selection" (an oxymoron, as is its parent, Darwin's "natural selection"). The mood this throws you into is not resolution but resignation, because whatever's going to happen will happen *(que sera, sera).* Most of the extant ancient Greek dramas are "tragedies" in that the doom denouement is unavoidable: not so much tough luck as destructive destiny, a goddess (Diké, "Justice") having been offended and another goddess (Moira, "Fate") administering the punishment.

The Bible offers the third way: **Providence.** In explaining untowardnesses, begin your sentence with "God . . ." even when you don't know how you're going to manage to get to the period. This explicative paradigm would be smooth going if God hadn't granted the angels and human beings *freedom.* There would have been no righteousness (from accepting the *responsibility* implicit in freedom), only rightness in a clockwork-smooth cosmos without chaos. Job and Ecclesiastes counter the simple deuteronomistic faith that observably, the righteous are rewarded and the guilty punished. But the prophets used that faith in refined forms, teaching the people to say, for example when they were dragged to Babylon, "We must have been doing something wrong." That assumption makes for a profounder and more productive reading of history than do views that see only negativity in *guilt* and *shame,* those inner-life pains signaling that we've used our freedom irresponsibly. By contrast, as this Thinksheet's title states, "in the court of fate, none are guilty." As for the subtitle, the biblical "metaphysical underpinnings for moral responsibility" are the nature and will of the biblical God. This will is Torah-taught (revelation) and conscience-reinforced (Kant's "moral law within").

3. "What do we understand by the *providence* of God?" asks the Heidelberg Catechism. Answer: ". . . the almighty and ever-present power of God whereby he still upholds . . . heaven and earth . . . and rules in such a way that leaves and grass, rain and drought, fruitful and unfruitful years, food and drink, health and sickness, riches and poverty, and everything else, come to us not by chance but by his

fatherly hand." The answer assumes a society whose sanctions derive from Torah-and-conscience and whose institutions, family and wider, act on the sanctions to reward and to punish. (To this year's Harvard Law School graduates, Attorney General Janet Reno said that **rewards/punishments** should be so clear and instant that every child understands them by age three. I agree, but it's a tough sell in a society that believes more in fate than in providence and disbelieves in pedagogical punishment. But here is hope: a recent RNS release says American "teens overwhelmingly believe that God loves them, watches them and will reward and punish their actions.")

Providential rewards/punishments do occur in this world, but not so neatly as to be under the control of our calculation of the future or interpretation of the past. The emphasis here is on "control": we are free, but not free to manipulate God, who works out his purposes beyond as well as within our powers of knowing and predicting. As for the *afterlife* as the ultimate sphere for the resolution of justice and therefore for our present calculation of consequences, it has some force in Judaism, more in Christianity, and most in Islam (the Qur'an being heavily laden with vivid pictures of afterlife luxuries for the rewarded and horrors for the punished).

4. Christian ethics combines chance, fate, and Providence thus: God *provides* us with all we need to "do everything for the glory of God" (1 Cor. 10:31), with everything we're given (*fate*) and everything that comes at us (*chance*). In that sentence, "fate" and "chance" are transformed, domesticated, baptized (as ancient rival deities were demoted to angels under YHWH). We have many maxims for this, such as *a*) Do the best you can with the hand you're dealt. *b*) You're not responsible for what comes at you, but you are responsible for naming it. *c*) God will ask not what happened to you but how you took it.

I must stress the captivity of fate and chance to providence, if "fate" and "chance" are to be used at all by Christians. The Bible realistically deals with the fact of the variety of "fortunes" in human life and the inevitability of death, but it does not come out where Calvin does:

No Greek *moira* or Muslim *kismet,* no fatalism, but God **rules** the world personally and directly, determining all destinies (Isa. 45:1-8, Amos 3:6, Matt. 10:29-30, Luke 12:24-28), yet making space for our freedom-responsibility-accountability and granting us grace (Heb. 4:14-16). Norman Gottwald ended his Society of Biblical Literature presidential address thus: "What begins as fate becomes ultimately a gift."[2]

2. *Journal of Biblical Literature,* spring 1993, p. 22.

Who are "the poor"?

Who are "the poor"? "Persons of low income," said a 1973 federal directive forbidding the use of the terms "the poor" and "poverty" in official documents.[1] Low income because trapped in the culture-cycle of poverty? Because oppressed? Because undermotivated? Because highly motivated? Yes to those and many more questions. "The poor" is a complex category even when confined to economics. And there are many forms of poverty other than "low ($) income"!

1. Take Jesus, a *double* case of *voluntary poverty.* Rich in heaven, he "gave up all he had."[2] "Rich as our Lord Jesus Christ was, he made himself poor . . . to make you rich by his poverty."[3] And rich

---

1. This instance of federal doublespeak is to be faulted not just for its lame euphemistic effort to avoid the shame and disgrace that "the poor" and "poverty" connote but also because the substitute, "persons of low income," oversimplifies the problem with the implied suggestion, time and again proven flawed, that the solution is to throw money at "the poor" to improve their "income."

2. Phil. 2:6-8, the *kenosis* (self-emptying) of the Incarnation.

3. 2 Cor. 8:9. Paul loves the dialectic of diametricals, a familiar of the Greco-Roman diatribe (public address), of which he was a master. For Jesus' descent from riches to (comparative) rags, note two parallels in this Corinthians statement. Paul uses the same trope with regard to himself in 2 Cor. 6:8-10, ending with "we seem poor, but we make many rich; we seem to have nothing, though we possess everything." Paul only "seems" poor. A cultivated trilingual citizen of Tarsus and a Roman citizen, in his pre-Christian days in Jerusalem he was certainly — given his fine education, his high connections, and his skilled craft (tent-making) — not poor. But he "seemed" poor, as a peripatetic Christian preacher, both because he couldn't

on earth, he gave up being a builder[4] to become a peripatetic preacher-teacher, dependent on handouts.[5]

2. Our *identity* as Christians includes our being rich in God, and we are called to *identification* with "the poor" — some of us with those of unchosen economic poverty; others with those of other types of poverty — spiritual, intellectual, cultural, interpersonal.

---

give much time to his craft, which he pursued only when afraid of being accused of doing religion for money, and because, as all other peripatetics of his time, including Jesus his Master, he "lived off the land."

4. "Carpenter" was too restricted a translation. It was used partly because "builders" (the generic meaning of the Greek word in Mark 6:3, where Jesus is "the builder," and Matt. 13:55, where he is the son of "the builder") who worked in heavily wooded lands built mainly of wood: builders in sparsely wooded lands would be mainly "masons." Recent research inclines to "builder" as Jesus' trade or profession. See "Building, Constructing," in J. P. Louw and E. A. Nida, *Greek-English Lexicon of the New Testament Based on Semantic Domains* (New York: United Bible Societies, 1988), sec. 9, p. 520. A *tekton* is "one who used various materials (wood, stone, metal) in building." The term implies multiple skills, which paid well in the building-boom "Galilee of the Gentiles" of Jesus' day. Since his father preceded him as a builder, it's touching but untrue to think of Jesus as "born poor."

5. The Evangelists (authors-redactors of the Gospels) observe that Jesus accepted handouts, but they balance this with his miraculous power to supply food (feeding of the 4,000 and 5,000, miraculous draft of fishes; parallel with his unused power to defend himself with "legions of angels").

As I was writing this on 7 August 1989, a peripatetic witness to "justice and peace" appeared for supper and overnight. Alan Anderson, who describes himself as "independently impoverished" by choice after a half century of affluence, is walking from church to church 4,000 miles in two years, so far having witnessed to ad hoc congregations in 150 churches stretched out along 1,800 miles. A layman seeped in scripture, he says, "I read the Bible until a void appears and God steps into it." With his fifty-pound backpack he's homeless nowhere but often treated as though homeless. He's finding witness along the way as exciting and nourishing as witness in the churches. Everywhere, people are interested in his motivation, which leads to conversations about spirituality even more than about justice and peace. Evangelical and ecumenical, he conforms to no party but is a faithful member of the United Church of Christ. He understood, agreed, and laughed heartily when I said, "If you were wandering around like this in the first-century Mediterranean world, you'd be normal; in our society, you're crazy. Wonderfully, creatively, joyfully crazy."

93

3. I must complain against the romantic-materialist **distortions** of liberation theologians for whom "the poor" are a lumpen proletariat to whom "God must come first in the form of bread." Yes, there has been and is much economic exploitation on this sad, suffering planet. Yes, not all missionaries distanced themselves from the economic and military-political advantages of their culture. Yes, racism survived the death of slavery and classism the birth of democracy. Yes, these are the bitter roots of liberation theology, an intellectual adjunct of the struggle of the economically poor for a place in the sun. But none of this excuses these thinkers for their historical revisionisms and their arrogance toward Christians at work in other vineyards.

4. Take *Jesus* again. A midsummer 1989 document confected by theologians in seven Third World countries, "The Road to Damascus: Kairos and Conversion,"[6] wrongly says "Jesus was born in poverty," becoming incarnate "as one of the poor and oppressed."[7] This historical untruth fits neatly into the document's use of the divine sanction: We can "see the face of God in the poor. . . . God is on the side of the poor, the oppressed, the persecuted."

6. Available from Sojourners, Box 29272, Washington, DC 20017.
7. On the contrary, see note 4. As for Jesus' being "oppressed," in comparison with what? For thousands of years, life in the Near or Middle East has been an oscillation between chaos (severely hard on the people) and empire (usually somewhat less hard on the people), with short bursts of successful self-government for some ethnic populations in between (e.g., the Jews in the Maccabean period), and even some small empires between big ones when the big ones were weak (e.g., the Israelite empire, Damascus to Egypt, under David and Solomon). As for the Roman Empire, it used only enough force, "oppression," to quell uprisings and secure its borders. Under the Roman "oppression" of Palestine in Jesus' day there was law, order, and prosperity. Rebelling, the Jews briefly (A.D. 66-70) became "free," at the cost of miseries and destruction unknown when they were "oppressed." The terms "oppressed" and "free," so casually bandied about by liberationists secular and religious, are so highly political as to have almost no objective content. Sometimes the denotata are even reversed: Beirut, when "oppressed" under the French heel, was prosperous and cosmopolitan, the city open, the citizens without fear: now it is "free" and terrified and virtually uninhabitable. The anti-imperial dogma of "freedom for all peoples" is a utopian dream that time and again, when morning comes, proves to be a cruel hoax.

5. As for the **arrogance** of this theology, the document dismisses opponents as motivated by "selfish purposes." It denounces "all forms of right-wing Christianity as heretical," as "rejecting or ignoring parts of God's revelation and selecting or distorting other parts in order to support the ideology of the national security state." Irritated by the successes of the competition, the liberation party complains that "they" are not like "us." *They* consciousness-raise about personal sin rather than about "blatant injustices." *They* "blaspheme" by saying occasional kind words about "imperialism." Rather than trying to politicize the church, *they* accommodate to the status quo in society.

6. Given the Bible's concern for the whole range of poverty — of body and soul, of society and the individual — **poverty partisans** on the right and on the left cannot succeed in co-opting Scripture to their causes. That does not stop them from trying, however, nor from claiming that they've succeeded and that their opponents have failed. Fortunately, the advance of biblical scholarship today is weakening both partisanships and strengthening those who refuse all narrow definitions of "the poor," those who preach, teach, and live that "salvation" and "justice and peace" are a continuum.[8]

7. A poverty analysis of **the Lord's Prayer** will help us feel the depth and breadth of the biblical teaching. Taking the poor as the "**have-nots**," note that *a*) we're all poor in that the Kingdom of God has not yet come on earth "as it is in heaven"; *b*) some are

8. While I gladly give the credit to those who have influenced me from right and left and middle, for more than half a century this continuum has been for me a given. I've been both a traveling evangelist and a social radical, both under the impetus of the one gospel, the one faith, the one Lord. Because of my observation and conviction that it's what you leave out that wrecks you, I have been an evangelical among liberals and a liberal among evangelicals: I cry out what is being left out, as in my 1966 National Council of Churches Triennium debate with Billy Graham, who at that time had not yet added the social note to his evangelistic appeal. A humorous note: after the debate, *The Christian Century* editor said, "Willis, I'd like to print the debate, but evangelicalism is a dead horse, no future: our readers wouldn't be interested."

"bread" poor; *c*) all are in the position of beggars for forgiveness from God and our neighbors; and *d*) all are in need, time and again, of deliverance from evil.[9] We may acknowledge or deny any of these visible and invisible poverties. We may be poor in physical, psychic, or spiritual energy; in hope against despair; in joy against depression; in faith against fear; in love against self-concern; in freedom of body or soul; or in environmental conditions — social, economic, political, or ecological.

8. In answering the question, "Who are 'the poor'?" a window may help distribute the entities:

	acknowledged	unacknowledged
material-visible	A	B
spiritual-invisible	C	D

Basic poverty in the *Bible* is **C** when we confess it and **D** when we deny it: we are shutouts from the Garden of God, who calls us to "turn"[10] from our poverty back to the riches of communion with God. Dialectical materialism, as in *Marx,* sees basic poverty as **AB.** Caution: the Bible is concerned also with **AB,** and Marx is concerned also with **CD.** It's a matter of emphasis, as it is between the two parties in "The Road to Damascus: Kairos and Conversion."

9. Not having is one dimension of poverty; **alienation,** being and feeling distant from and strange to something, is another. Feuerbach's virulent atheism rooted all poverties in our projecting our

9. Or, almost certainly better, "the Evil One." Jesus saw the dark powers as cosmic, not just historic, structural, interpersonal, and intrapersonal.
10. In Hebrew, the physical base of the metaphor for "repentance."

human dignity onto God, before whom we stand poor in self-inflicted groveling. What Marx did with Feuerbach's projection theory outside the skin, Freud did inside the skin: Feuerbach's general alienation became socio-alienation in Marx and psycho-alienation in Freud. The atheist cure? To restore human dignity by reclaiming what is rightfully yours, that is, self-and-species-*esteem* (humanism) untrammeled by religious illusion/delusion; to deliver yourself from poverty and restore your wealth by reclaiming the means of production (Marx) and the means of self-determination (Freud).

10. To *define* is to *con*fine and *re*fine: definitions are active and intentional. "Secular humanism" in philosophy (Feuerbach), sociology (Marx), and psychology (Freud) defines fundamental poverty as *theism* (losing your dignity into God), fundamental riches as *humanism* (reclaiming your dignity), and the process of salvation from poverty to riches as *atheism* (getting rid of God). At every point this is the **rebellious** diametric of Scripture, which teaches that we are rich when our dignity is in God, poor when in self-pride we claim dignity for ourselves (currently, "self-esteem"), and lost when out of communion with God.

11. Why is the opposition so radical? Because it is rooted in a profound **hatred** of the biblical God. This right-wing Christians know, or at least sense; but left-wing Christians, wittingly or not, tend to obscure it, at the cost of failing to sense how complicitous they are with "the principalities and powers" of the *mind,* ironically while attacking right-wing Christians for accommodation to "the principalities and powers" in the *world,* meaning ecopolitical power.

12. While we Christians are developing a middle cohort that, to use older terms, promotes both individual and social salvation, the *gap* between the two mentalities is widening in both church and society. The Christian left is tempted to abandon Christian language ("God-talk") both to communicate with the God-ignorant and because the increasing God-absence in public education and the media makes

97

God-amnesia normal:[11] the public mind has become so godless that God-referencing seems an embarrassing violation of the law of parsimony.[12] In America, God-witnessing Christians are becoming an underclass minority, a church of the cultural catacombs; we have lost out in the struggle for respectability, and the cultural quality of our witness has been steadily declining.

13. As mainline Christianity continues to lose respectability, **hope** increases that Christians on the right and the left will become sisters and brothers in cultural humiliation and that this new church of the "meek" will somehow "inherit the earth," or at least learn to pray the Lord's Prayer — the prayer of the poor, the humiliated, the humble — with our whole being and yearning.

14. This **humility** is normal in our religion. Before we talk of "identifying with the poor" in any sense, we should face the reality that we ourselves are poor in the profoundest sense, daily dependent on handouts of bread and grace from God, timelessly dependent on God for the gift of the Kingdom.[13] Set against this mindset are two forms of *Constantinianism: a)* Christians *using* the state, or secular forces, to work their purposes, to achieve their ends. In the West we had about sixteen centuries of that, for bane and blessing. For our self-understanding as Christians and Christian institutions, it was more bane than blessing; *b)* Christians *trusting* the state, or secular institutions, to work their purposes, to achieve their ends. Because America is "a nation with the soul of a church," though we have "separation of church and state"

---

11. To the theme of forgetting God as the baseline betrayal — a prophetic note — the Bible adds the wisdom theme that fools have no thought of God in their hearts, no recognition of God in their lives.

12. The logic law of minimum hypothesis: if one can "think" — analyze-criticize-synthesize — without God, how can adding God do anything other than subtract from clarity if not also honesty? But if God is the center, then all other things have the character of additions and come under the critique of the law of parsimony.

13. "Stop being afraid, little flock! Giving you the Kingdom gives the Father pleasure" (Luke 12:32).

we have, far less than the West's other nations, less separation of the two visions of the good society. But here a distinction is crucial: We Christians, individually and corporately, should try to *persuade* the state, or secular forces, to act in the interests of humanity as we understand those interests. And in the give and take of public life we should refine our own understanding of those interests and of the skills and processes toward addressing them.[14]

But we should not delude ourselves into imagining that government at any level can be the savior of "the poor" or even the primary resource and actor toward that salvation, or that governmental social achievements will be either free from corruption or of assured permanence. Our *trust* is to be in God, not in "horses."[15] And our aim is to help "the poor" to dependence on God, which gives dignity and freedom, not on government — a dependence that rots soul and body.

15. Like everybody else, we Christians are forever in danger of becoming infatuated with one or another **ideology** as though it has salvific potency. Christians on the right have been gullible about consumer capitalism in spite of its downdrag into materialism. And Christians on the left continue to hope for good results through the application of Marxian class analysis (as in "liberation theology"), despite its rootage in materialism. Moving from economic to political ideology, Christians across the spectrum are tempted by promises of "freedom": negatively, freedom from "oppression," "imperialism," and "colonialism"; positively, freedom for "self-determination" and "national sovereignty."

16. How does **Jesus** answer the question "Who are the 'poor'?" Cautioning ourselves against reading our modern concep-

14. During the decade of the 1960s, about half of our work on the United Church Board for Homeland Ministries was concentrated in various aspects of the civil rights movement. My part of it proved too radical even for that liberal establishment to stomach.

15. Ps. 20:7.

tions into him,[16] we can make a few assertions: *a*) All the needy, whatever their needs, are *demonstrations* of humanity's overarching need for divine Rule, in contrast to the world's chaos and misrule. Jesus had the courage to look at the needs, to point to them, in God's name and power to meet some of them, and to pray and teach "Your Kingdom come." *b*) Being thus the focal demonstration of the need for the Kingdom, the needy are the (anticipatory? mystical?) *locus* of the inbreaking Kingdom and of its Messenger.[17] *c*) The fact that the Kingdom is now in the process of coming relativizes all institutional processes for meeting human needs and highlights the *individual*'s direct compassionate action.[18] *d*) In the Beatitudes, his version of the traditional Benedictions, Jesus puts the needy *first* and closely associates them with the Kingdom, saying it's "theirs," "yours."[19] *e*) While Jesus was classless in his appeal, the more one was "invested" in the present "age," the less was one apt to be pleased by the announcement of wealth redistribution,

16. The classic caveat on this is Henry J. Cadbury, *The Peril of Modernizing Jesus* (New York: Macmillan, 1937). Millar Burrows, in *An Outline of Biblical Theology* (Philadelphia: Westminster Press, 1946), p. 300, may unwittingly instance this modernizing in saying that Jesus' "dominant concern [was] for spiritual values" (Luke 4:3-4): rather, his dominant concern was directing penitent-expectant attention to God and only thus indirectly to "spiritual" values. But Burrows is right along with Cadbury: in light of "his eschatological expectations," Jesus "made no effort to improve economic conditions." We may be following Jesus if we make secondary efforts to improve economic, social, and political conditions: in my opinion, we're not following him if we fail to make such efforts. But we are not following him if we make such efforts our primary aim.

17. Matt. 25:40 is one of a number of Gospel sayings on visualizing the Lord in the poor — which Mother Teresa says is her steady, daily practice. Abraham entertains needy strangers, who turn out to be divine messengers. And Christians exercising hospitality may be ministering to "angels unawares" (Heb. 13:2).

18. The fact that people responded to Jesus as individuals must not be generalized into religious individualism. His converts formed a community centering in his presence before, and in the Spirit after, his death and resurrection. Institution preserves and promotes memory and community; it is concerned about *faithfulness*. Spirit critiques and reforms institution; it is concerned about *freedom*.

19. In Matt. 5:3, those poor by choice; in Luke 6:20, those poor by circumstance.

not to mention reversal: his "indicated" audience, his natural "market," was those for whom there was no way to go but up, those who were conscious of being "down," needy, poor in the power to meet their needs and wants. Consequently, "the poor" came to be a *technical term* for the positive responders to Jesus (a use anticipated in some of Israel's later prophets).[20] His call was universal, but he found himself working mainly with the unadvantaged. *f)* Jesus was *theocentric* here as everywhere: he illumined people's multiple needs and pains and their causes with the character and will, and the promises and threats, of God. *g)* By the nature of his prophetic-peripatetic role, his call to discipleship was a call to poverty by *choice,* a discipleship that was to be lived chiefly among those whose poverty was by circumstance. *h)* Jesus inherited and *intensified* the duties of prayer and almsgiving (charity) and the conviction that God directs society's attention to the disastrous lower-class effect of Torah-condemned middle-class and upper-class behavior. *i)* Jesus cannot be cited in support of any single-cause theory of poverty, such as deuteronomism[21] or classism or racism or sexism or etatism-imperialism. Within the limits of his culture, which was complex in comparison with cultures before it but simple in comparison with ours, he can be cited as witness to the *multivalence and mystery* of what we call evil, including poverty. Thus some poverty is punishment; the devout can be blessed despite poverty; and one can be blessed — indeed, bless oneself — through poverty embraced in order to honor-glorify God by serving the poor.

17. As the biosphere becomes impoverished of irreplaceable flora, fauna, and mineral and fossil wealth, of clean water, land, and

---

20. Perhaps even a proper name for the early Christians; see Rom. 15:26.

21. The moral theory, severely attacked in Job, that a straight line can be drawn backward from trouble to sin, trouble thus being punishment. The theory had the virtues of simplicity, of uniting cosmos and history, and of honoring God as center and source of life and circumstance. Its unfortunate defect was that it was a mismatch for reality, which is more complex, murky, mysterious, calling us more to kindness than to judgment (Matt. 7:1-5).

air, and of topsoil, trees, and groundwater (the desertification process), the whole human race and many of our fellow living creatures are sliding into **eco-poverty.** Pogo's "We have met the enemy, and it's us" needs an addendum: "We have met the poor, and we're it." Taken seriously, this massive evil will force a new look at traditional answers to many ethical questions, including abortion, euthanasia, and even suicide. "The sacredness of life" will need expanding beyond the human individual, even beyond our species. Only God is holy; only the biosphere itself deserves first-level respect as sacred. And the words we use for turning from our sins against God — "repentance," "conversion" — we will need to extend to our sins against the biosphere, God's good earth.

A libertarian argument for
capital punishment

How can the death penalty be justified in any decent society? I'll tell you if you'll listen. Trouble is, chances are that if I put the question that way — with the loaded "decent" — you won't listen.

Recently here on Cape Cod a man was caught with five million street-worth dollars of cocaine. How can any decent society justify allowing continuing life to anyone who, with the sale of this stash, would have been responsible for, guilty of, massive human misery in individual and societal disintegration? Chances are that if you were to try to tell me, I wouldn't listen — seeing that I used the loaded "decent."

Death issues — abortion, euthanasia, capital punishment — are hot, totally involving, tempting to the inflammatory rhetoric of self-righteousness. Can I keep my cool long enough to make this Thinksheet's point?

Today[1] a druglord, extradited from Colombia on the charge of laundering $1.2 billion "earned" in the United States, arrived here. Both countries need courage: the Medellin drug cartel threatens to murder, for each extraditee, ten Colombian judges and five American judges. The cartel, the *de facto* government of Colombia, regularly murders judges who dare to sit a case against them — 110 in recent months.

Two reasons no judge is sentencing any druglord to death are a) no judge is sitting, the courts aren't functioning (with a few, highly

1. 7 September 1989. The numbered sections were written 24 October 1988 (as Thinksheet #2268), just prior to the presidential election.

103

guarded exceptions); and *b)* Colombia doesn't have capital punishment. The country's judges are free to die but not free to kill. Colombia is ruled not by law with the power of death, but by bribery and terror with the power of death. The official government is fastidiously against the death penalty; the underground government has no compunction against its use.

Yet so great is the *de jure* government's compunction against capital punishment that there may be no more extraditions. President Bush says the extraditees deserve death: the official Colombian government asks, How can we send any of our citizens to a country where the law may treat them more severely than would our law?

The case displays the irony of straight-line reversal: respect for human life is elevated by law so high as to help produce a situation of extreme disregard for human life. Here liberalism has gone not just to seed, but to rot: doing evil by doing an excess of good.

It's about 87% clear in the public mind, say the polls, that the bottom-line meaning of "coddling criminals" is that the behavior of none of them is considered serious enough to merit execution: the people's killing of criminals is more heinous than anything the criminals have done against the people.[2]

Besides being *humanly* serious, the death-penalty debate is *politically* serious, serious for politicking and for the functioning of people-power in the shaping of society.

1. The minority opinion, ACPT (the anti-capital-punishment taboo), is most dramatically displayed in Michael Dukakis's second-debate abject **failure** to make a convincing response to the opening theoretical question about the rape and murder of his wife: would he

2. Murderers agree with the liberals in a high view of human dignity. Two witnesses to it are quoted on a single page of *Newsweek* (11 September 1989, p. 15): (1) "Moments before being executed," a rapist-murderer (who'd stabbed his victim 42 times) said "'What is about to take place is a murder.'" He kept his dignity, his sense of self-worth, of self-esteem, and his skill at blaming the victim (society) to the very end — unfortunately. (2) Charles Manson says if he gets out he'll "kill a whole bunch of people . . . to get even. It would be an honorable thing."

come down all that hard, CP-hard, on the rapist-murderer? No, he wouldn't. After that, it was all downhill for the Duke. "We the People," as George Will put it, don't want a president with no guts and "no nerve ends." Worse, the people just didn't believe that the Duke would behave the way he said he would; the people have been wondering whether he's real, and now they "know" (i.e., conclude) that he isn't; and the people are worried about a candidate who doesn't know how he'd behave in an emergency.

2. How did liberals get so solidly **boxed in**to the ACPT? Its force, now, is as mindless in the liberal social world as is that of the AAT (anti-abortion taboo) in the ad hoc, single-issue alliance of the old-Catholic and right-wing Protestant social worlds, and for the same numinous reason: "the sanctity of human life." (The ACP-AA-AW seamless-garment antiviolence coalition is so small as to be politically invisible: it's against capital punishment, abortion, and war. *Ahimsa*[3] all the way.)

3. It's serious. There's about as much chance of putting an anti-capital-punishmentist in the Oval Room as there is an anti-abortionist — no, less. Another question is, Why do liberals so often behave unpolitically, self-destructively? For the same reason the radical right (e.g., Pat Robertson) does: **blind ideological arrogance.** In 1980, instead of standing solidly behind Carter's bid for a second term, the liberals, rather than hunting Reagan, shot themselves[4] in the foot.

4. 'Twas not always so. The ACP taboo is a **late development** in the history of libertarian-liberal thought. Until World War II it was only a minor plank in the platform. What made it major and now *de rigueur?* Among other factors, Shoah (the Holocaust), Gandhi's nonviolent success in convincing the British Raj to quit India, and our civil rights movement's rhetoric and victory.

3. Sanskrit for "noninjury" or "nonviolence."
4. On most issues I'd say "ourselves," since I tilt at least 60% liberal.

5. The *old* libertarianism focused myopically on the individual as autonomous and corrigible, a focus the American Civil Liberties Union continues. Opposition to the death penalty arose from this myopia. The *new* libertarianism considers "liberty and justice **for all**" to be a value transcending the individual's right to life.

6. This Thinksheet will state but not develop a new-libertarian argument for capital punishment. I want to present an extended example of the antilibertarian effects of the ACPT. My **proposition** is this: the dignity of the person-in-society demands taking full responsibility for one's behavior. If the social consequences of one's behavior are not life-and-death but only life, then one is not fully responsible and so does not have full-range dignity vis-à-vis society. Society and nature are nonparallel. Vis-à-vis *nature,* one does have full-range dignity: some behaviors, like jumping off a high cliff, result in death. But in a *society* in which the ACP taboo prevails, one is denied full-range dignity; one can do anything one pleases without fear of law-administered death.

Furthermore, the people are less free in an ACPT society: the victims of Willie Horton, a murderer furloughed in spite of the Massachusetts court's sentencing him to life imprisonment "without parole," were not living, as they thought they were, in a society guaranteeing them "life, liberty, and the pursuit of happiness," that is, in a liberal-liberation society. Only capital punishment perfectly protects the public against the loss of freedom and even of life. Yes, some innocents are executed; but very few in comparison with those who are murdered by murderers given sentences other than capital punishment and then released. Bush's argument here is compelling: "Who[m] are we supposed to be protecting, the murderers or the public?"

7. The story I'm about to tell, a true story printed in the 30 September 1988 *Wall Street Journal,*[5] counters the argument that

---

5. The article is well titled (with an unspoken play on "slum lords"): "Lords of the Slums."

capital punishment brutalizes society. Society, the story and I say, is more brutalized by the absence of capital punishment — a counterargument paralleling the one just stated, that more innocents die from the absence of capital punishment than by its practice. I've added some personal reminiscences and reflections in my retelling of this story.

Robert L. Dordies "served 11 years in prison for the murder of a 66-year-old man, from whom he stole $17. Now 32, he is a ranking member of the Black Gangster Disciples," a criminal network terrorizing and controlling much of Chicago's public housing, including the Robert Taylor Homes, the largest complex. An avid learner, Dordies has profited grandly from his basic, mid-level, and advanced training in America's school of crime, our prison system, where he mastered the skills of survival, manipulation, and domination. If society were masochistic, governed by the death wish, it could hardly have done better than to provide this murderer with those opportunities to train his mind and hone his skills for the continuance of his life of crime.

"Mr. Dordie exercises iron-fisted control over his territory," a territory I knew well before, during, and after World War II. When I was pastoring there, no public housing had yet been erected, and there were no gangs. Then, when south Chicago experienced a flood of rural folk utterly unprepared for urban life, the old neighborhood life yielded to **anarchy,** and gangs sprang up — at first unarmed — to provide some order. (Not law and order, which the police, as unprepared for the influx as the newcomers were unprepared for urban living, were unable to provide.) The first of these gangs to gain public notice was the Blackstone Rangers, whose leaders I met with in connection with certain churches' encouragement and cultivation of them — including providing them places to meet. As police efforts to create and maintain tranquility continued to be inadequate, gangs' interrivalry got bloody. I was there to witness the transition of the BRs from unarmed to knives but had left by the time of transition to guns, without which the gang could not have survived. Ironically, the BRs unwittingly modeled benevolence for the criminal gangs. Alex

Kotlowitz in *The Wall Street Journal* says the gangs are working to "ingratiate themselves with the neighbors. They have learned from the El Rukins gang, previously known as the Blackstone Rangers, who in the late 1960s and early 1970s were a political force, conducting federally financed job-training classes and organizing social events. They even sponsored their own singing group."

In the absence of a competent city government, the gangs constituted the secular **infrastructure** of the ghettos, including "the projects." The sacred infrastructure, the churches, were comparatively ineffectual in the chaos, and tended to privatism in spite of Saul Alinsky's Industrial Areas Foundation's effort to rouse them to sociopolitical action. "Says Irving Spergel, a University of Chicago professor of social-service administration, 'the gangs are an institution, and we're just beginning to recognize that.'" As with the breakdown of civil government in the Roman Empire, when the churches took up the slack, the bishops becoming the mayors,[6] so in the projects the gangs, in the absence of effective civil-city governing, rule by rough approximations of executive, legislative, and judicial structures, including capital punishment of deviants and resisters. The spy system is so well developed that even though there are many viewers of crimes, there are no witnesses: whenever the police arrive, a gang member is present to note who said what to the police and/or who spent secret time, out of gang view, with the police. Cold Black, Dordies' streetname, "controls a small army of teenagers and men in their 20s. . . . The 'soldiers' in Cold Black's army often commandeer apartments in the high rises, where they sell drugs and store guns." "Protection money" is the form of taxation. The social pathology is so deep that resistance from within the territory is virtually nonexistent. As a terrified resident put it, "'You fail to make normal reactions to abnormal situations.'" The Chicago Housing Authority estimates that 60,000 are living illegally in the facilities.

No capital punishment?

6. A situation that continued well into the eighteenth century in some places, such as Salzburg, Austria.

108

Jesus and the isms

It isn't given to human eyes, outer and inner together, to "see life steadily and see it whole."[1] But — and this reveals that I am a Christian — Jesus came closer than anyone else. For reality compasses the heart of God and all that has sprung forth from the mind of God, and Jesus' vision of the whole[2] is mine, too.

A religion is a way of seeing the world: a *vision,* a world-picture, a world-view, a world-story, a paradigm. So is a philosophy. But a religion is more. It is a way of living in the world: a manner

1. But Matthew Arnold, lover of the Hellenic world (against the Hebraic, which he saw as controlling his Victorian age), in "To a Friend," made this claim for "the Attic stage," specifically Sophocles, "Who saw life steadily, and saw it whole." Many times my mentors, from my childhood days onward, quoted this line to me as a proper exhortation to curiosity, courage, and honesty in facing life. All wisdom traditions have ways of saying that few people can stand much reality, and all people make considerable efforts to avoid it. Emily Dickinson puts it gently: "The truth must dazzle gradually / or every man be blind." Jesus' parables are gradual implosions of a new consciousness.

2. Paradoxically, modern Gospel scholarship is rendering the Gospels' details more problematic but the mind of Jesus less so, more clear, more accessible to both the believer and the doubter. The old games are gone: he can neither be *separated* from Judaism (as though he were an historical *de novo* revelation) nor (by finding similarities in Jewish literature) *absorbed* into Judaism. Fragmentary as the Gospels are from the historian's angle, the stamp of his person on the mass of the materials is less and less mistakable. Though we cannot know him as a fleshed-out historical figure, we can know his stamp, his impact, his spirit, and in this sense his person. And we Christians claim to know him "in the Spirit," we in him and he in us.

109

of life, a lifestyle, an ethic, a *life*. From Jesus' vision and his living it and dying for it and rising with it there are implications[3] as to how I am to see, and live in, the world, my world.

If I'm to follow Jesus as "the true and living way,"[4] some things are ruled out: *solipsism*, creating a fantasy world of my own and living in it;[5] *prejudice*, feeding the false comforts and unfair advantages of one's class, race, tribe (nation, state, occupation), or sex;[6] and *ideology:* it's ludicrous, and blasphemous, to try to use Jesus as a mascot for a prejudiced "us" against an unadvantaged "them." Or to try to baptize him into some ideology so as to recruit him against rival ideologies. Instead:

In Jesus,
God has come to us

3. Implications, not spelled-out directions. The First Gospel sees him as the second Moses (Matthew's five speeches paralleling the Pentateuch), but the Gospels' materials do not permit our constructing a Christian Law. The Fourth Gospel is doubly at the other extreme: it's the last canonical Gospel, and Jesus' message through it is not "Do this . . ." but "I am. . . ." To paraphrase the end of Albert Schweitzer's *Quest for the Historical Jesus,* he comes to us almost without name or claim; but whoever will walk with him will find out who he is and what he asks. Through our daily practice of his presence, he magnetizes our lives *to point toward God,* whom he calls "Abba" (the first word in the simpler version of the Lord's Prayer, Luke 11:2). Our hearts and minds facing in that direction, we are free to receive "directions" in the Spirit as to how to live (or, to put it hebraically, what to do with our feet). The cost of that freedom is Christian pluralism, a wide and clashing variety of Christian opinion. This freedom's cost is not excessive.

4. John 14:6.

5. Creating fantasy worlds, as J. R. R. Tolkien's Middle Earth, is a proper and can be a productive exercise of a God-given power, the imagination. I'm speaking here against choosing to *live* in a world of your own. We can learn here from those who, without willing it, live in worlds of their own: autistics and schizophrenics. And we can learn from the computer's heightening of our imaginal power — through computer-simulated, artificial, virtual reality — but again, with the danger, to which some great works of fiction witness, of canceling the real world.

6. In "ism" terms, the prejudicial isms are *classism, racism, etatism (nationalism), and sexism.* At New York Theological Seminary I taught courses in how to use the Bible in confronting them, including confronting them where they appear in the Bible.

110

and proved he's for us and wants us to be for him.
As man among us modeling humanity face to face with God,
Jesus lives a **trust** that will not quit and
    a **love** that will not waver.
I am his disciple because he calls me to this trust and this love.
I am his disciple because for me the Truth within and
    beyond the facts
  is what I find in him:
    a **trust** that will not quit and
    a **love** that will not waver.
I continue as his disciple in spite of my trust's
    sometimes quitting
    and my love's sometimes wavering
because he knows my heart knows itself to be at its best
when it prizes, more than anything else,
    his trust that does not quit
    and his love that does not waver.
What temptations did he have to surrender such trust
    and such love?
  "He was reviled, . . .and we esteemed him not."[7]
What securities did he have to sustain him in such
    trust and such love?
Not family.
Not position in society.[8]
Not office in state.
Not wealth.
Not friends who'd stick with him through thick and thin.
Nothing.

---

7. Isa. 53:3.

8. Nurtured by institutions as well as the Spirit, Jesus was not an institutional man. A friend of mine asked me to critique his latest book manuscript, *The Sayings of Non-Institutional Jesus* (in fantasy, what Jesus has to say after walking around today's Manhattan for a week). But Jesus was not anti-institutional; and without institutions we would never have heard of him. Further, his ministry is *irreducible* to any category of leadership — rabbi, apocalyptic preacher, wisdom teacher, revolutionary, mystic; nor can he be identified with any party or school. He is, says Eduard Schweitzer, "the man who disrupts all patterns."

Not the cozy support of prejudice.
Not the false security of any ideology —
    pacifism[9]
    zealotism [10]
    Marxism[11]
    or any other ism.

Therefore, I say, *In him was life, and that life is our light.*[12]

1995 Supplement

1. In this chapter, as whenever I'm talking about Jesus, I avoid both uncritical **maximalism** and hypercritical **minimalism** — both the literalistic underuse of analytic intelligence and the reductionistic insistence on "just the facts, please." But I try to honor the truths distorted by these fundamentalisms on the right and left:

2. The truth in maximalism is that the Christian worshiper holds that everything in canon, the Old and New Testaments, is grist for the mill of the heart. Minimalism's truth is that scholars should strive to arrive at what can be said in the public domain, without benefit of, or privileged appeal to, faith.

9. Because he was noninstitutional and anticoercive, Jesus is easy to make a pacifist of; it's the easiest way to modernize him falsely. Two authors who do this attack me for pointing to the evidence that this inflammatory man, who was executed as a radical disturber of the peace, cannot honorably be recruited for the cause of pacifism: John Howard Yoder, in *The Politics of Jesus* (Grand Rapids, Mich.: Eerdmans, 1972), and George R. Edwards, in *Jesus and the Politics of Violence* (New York: Harper & Row, 1972).

10. Brandon and Schonfield are among the scholars modernizing Jesus into the role of deliberate revolutionary.

11. Almost all liberation theologians Marxize Jesus.

12. John 1:4. Jesus' life and light are not party-available; no ancient roles or titles were a good fit on him, nor are any modern prejudices or schools or ideologies. Be he was, and calls us to be, steadily *available to God.* I remember a Christian of humble social station putting it this way: "The main ability God wants in his servants is availability."

Inscape: Thinksheets as inner conversations

The front page of a Cape Cod newspaper says a school here is concerned about the "emotional health" of schoolchildren whose two fellow students died in a house fire.

Why isn't the school interested in the children's *total* inner health, not just their "emotional" health? Well, as you know, the school thinks that when you say "emotional," nothing is left out: the human organism has bio- and psycho-processes, as is true of the other animals, from whom we differ only in that at least our psycho-processes (signaled, under positivism, by the word "emotional") are more complex. In contrast, the word "**inner**" a) is not biased toward materialism, b) is not religiously loaded (as is, for example, "spiritual"), and c) alone among its rivals, is *inclusive* (covering feelings, emotions, ideas, fantasies, memories, prayers). The exteriority-orientedness of our techno-consumer culture leaves the public ignorant, awkward, and embarrassed about interiority. The inner world is parched with the hot winds of passion and pock-marked with robbers' caves where obsessions, idols, lie in wait to snatch the unwary . . . about as far as possible from what Gerard Manley Hopkins meant by "inscape."

Now, this Thinksheet is about **inscape**, *interiority*, primarily what goes on inside the reader, and only secondarily what went on inside me when doing the writing. I don't care about me when you're reading, because then what's going on inside *you* is what's important to me: I'm not primarily concerned about you when I'm writing, because then what's important to me is what's going on inside *me*. The Thinksheet

113

you are now looking at is a product of these two carings of mine — which are also two prayings meeting.

Once you get the hang of these erstwhile Thinksheets, you'll know that they typically dribble off, after making their point, to fill up the rest of the space with mutterings which you read, if you do, in hope that one or more of the mutterings may speak to you even more than does the point, the burden, of the Thinksheet. So now it's time for the mutterings:

1. Your "**soul**," by which here I mean your interiority, is compounded of *all the conversations* you've ever had — with other human beings, with God, and with yourself. That's only one angle from which to describe your soul, but it's a vital one, theoretically developed by social-psychologist George Herbert Mead (as the social origin of consciousness), and clinically tested and developed by a man I studied with, Hugh Missildine (as "the child of the past within"). Mead died before I could get to him, but he got to me through his writings. Both men have been important in the shaping of my understanding of interiority and thus in my devising the Thinksheet genre.

2. Right now, our society is *health crazy:* it has made itself sick by overconcern about health. On the plus side is this: you get attention when you come at whatever you want to from the health angle. So here I go: you're **crazy** if you're low on *inner* conversations (as you go crazy if your REM sleep is continuously disturbed so that you can never finish a dream, which itself is an inner conversation).[1] You are crazy also in the sense of being *unwise,* since there are many ways you might go to enrich your inner conversations. You're crazy in both senses if you do not take time for significant *outer* conversations, within and beyond the family. Your soul can maintain health and growth with nothing to feed on but

---

1. A recent NIH study indicates that street people who talk out loud to themselves are not as crazy as they would be if they didn't. As Thinksheets are for me muttering to myself out loud, I am not as crazy as I would be if I didn't write them.

memories of conversations past no more than your body can be nourished by yesterday's food.

3. But our culture is groaning with **conversation substitutes,** with the tube at the top. Conversational skills are so underdeveloped that *a*) the general public has only low hopes of inner payoff from conversation, and *b*) people face the double fear that if they reach out for a significant conversation, they will be exposed as inwardly empty and will, discovering inner emptiness in the other, be stuck, with no exit. When thus stuck, it's awkward to switch to the Super Bowl, especially if it's a bad year. And the weather is even worse as an escape. All in all, most folks feel efforts at depth conversation are just too dangerous.

A reader of my Thinksheets, anticipating speaking at his fiftieth high school reunion, asked me what I thought he should say. I said, "Speak what is deepest within you; it's your only shot at them." Strange how much easier that is to do in a public speech than in a private conversation! Some old maps mark *mare incognitum* (unknown sea) with "Here goeth sea monsters." As far as I know, Nessie is the world's only remaining putative sea monster, and the Scots use her only to improve tourism. But soul-nurturing conversation on the map of modernity is an expanding *terra incognita*, its monsters ever more frightening. One concern I have about this is evangelism: since one-to-one conversation accounts for some 85% of church-joining, who is to do the converting? TV evangelists? Door-to-door fundamentalists? The cults?

4. When I awake, I find myself already into inner conversation. Almost every morning, Loree and I have some soul-nourishing conversation before we split for the workday. I usually then give the rest of the morning to the full range of **inner conversings**, sometimes including the crafting of a Thinksheet. I pray the Bible, the newspapers and classics[2] — this morning, including stanza 95 of Tenny-

---

2. As we Christians are to "pray without ceasing" (1 Thess. 5:17, cf. Rom. 1:9), I teach my students to commune consciously, verbally, with God whichever

son's *In Memoriam,*[3] an all-night soliloquy on conversations he had half his lifetime ago with a now long-dead friend. Through the "silent-spoken words" of memory he explores — as had their conversations — life, love, and the limits of language to express life and love. "Matter-moulded forms of speech" proved "keen thro' wordy snares to track / Suggestion to her inmost cell. // So word by word, and line by line, / The deadman touched me from the past, / And all at once it seemed at last / The living soul was flash'd on mine, // . . . And came on that which is, and caught / The deep pulsations of the world. // . . . To broaden into boundless day."

5. Yes, there's the danger that by excessive recollection, one will get lost in the past. Engaging in that form of inner conversation while in prison, Boethius (d. A.D. 524) warns himself against all hypertrophies of *interiority*, but balances that with warnings against all hypertrophies of *exteriority*.[4] His **balance**, centering in the goodness of God, deeply influenced Dante and translators, including King Alfred, Chaucer, and Queen Elizabeth I.

Ideally, **aging**, which physically is like imprisonment in an ever-smaller cell, as "I can't do all the things I used to do," is release from the prison of world-business, of activism, the soul becoming more active as the body becomes *less*. It is another kind of balance: life-stage development. The traditional intergenerational wisdom here is society balancing itself through conversations between the old and the young. To these three healthful balances add that which can emerge only from mutually respectful fe/male conversation.

So what conversing and muttering do *you* do to keep from going crazy, and to enrich life for yourself and others?

---

of the three they are reading. An early exercise in this discipline is to write prayers all over a newspaper's first page, then read what is written aloud in a group whose members also have written prayers on their own copies of the same newspaper.

3. *The Poetic and Dramatic Works of Alfred Lord Tennyson* (New York: Houghton Mifflin, 1898), pp. 186f.

4. In *The Consolations of Philosophy*.

Day by day, O Lord

An old pop-prayer popped up in *Godspell* and became popular: "Day by day, O Lord, for these three things I pray: to see thee more clearly, love thee more dearly, and follow thee more nearly — day by day." Join that with the "One step enough for me" line from "Lead, kindly Light" and you have the following succession of daily **thoughts, one per day,** to "put all in mind of eternity."[1]

Suppose you agreed to write a few fifty-five second ("not more!") meditations and then read them for one-a-day use on early-morning commuter traffic radio. What would you write? Try writing one before reading this batch of mine.[2] Imagine yourself trying to catch and hold the attention of hurried-harried fellow citizens who have on their early-morning minds anything but eternity, the Eternal. And caution yourself with Frederick Buechner's words that "If it's not in their language, don't kid yourself that they're listening." Well, Fred, the best I can do is compromise between their language and mine.

My editor suggests that you read just one of these thoughts each day. After you've meditated on one, check it off so you'll know where to read and meditate the next day.

1. Charles Wesley's motive for asking a family he was visiting to sing a hymn. An insight also into why he wrote four thousand hymns.
2. My taped reading of these thoughts was aired for southern New England at 6:15 A.M. on successive weekdays. My sign-off signal was "In Jesus' name, amen."

117

1. The Bible leaves no doubt as to what life should be about. Jews call it the sanctification of the Name of God, and so do Christians in our Lord's Prayer: "Hallowed be Thy Name." Life should be lived from the Center, from God, the Center and Source of the universe. *Worship* is the word for living that way, and it requires daily attention and courage, the courage to apply what we applaud. Here as elsewhere Jesus is the model for us Christians. He was "the Word become flesh": because he **did** what he **said,** ordinary people were able to see God.

2. Do you have a friend who's so good a friend you feel free to say anything without coming out with one friend less? The 150 psalms in the Bible are things said freely to God, the psalmists' central **Friend** — including some things you might think they should have been embarrassed to say, but weren't. Sometime today, read a psalm. Do you agree with everything in it? Possibly not. But do you feel the psalmist's *freedom* to pour out his whole heart to God, the full range of his feelings and ideas? I hope so. And I hope you too today will do the same; for God can be trusted with the whole range of the reality that is you.

3. God cares, hears, and is here. There's a wondrous single word that says all that. It's **grace.** Grace, God's caring presence, supervenes over and interpenetrates your every day. It's the food within all food, the comfort and strength within all assurance, the song that sings itself within all moods. To know this is light, to live it is life eternal. The Love that will not let you go will not let you down. Depend on it, then; and may God find **you** dependable.

4. We are the **size** of the questions we're living and the answers we're testing. This day, today, God invites us to live the largest questions and test the greatest answers. What are those questions and those answers? You can sort them out by weight, by the effort it takes for you to lift them. How worthwhile the effort proves to be! It's called reflection or **meditation**, and it frees you from feeling trapped and pushed around. It undergirds your days

with excitement and vital adventure. It's a spiritual journey that lets the Light shine on, into, and through you.

5. With God and our fellow creatures we are participants in the splendor and suffering of our endangered planet. Our **roots** are in the Love that rules sea, sky, land, and soul, and all the storms therein. Our **reach** is for the wisdom and courage to match our task, that we may please the One Spirit before, within, and beyond heaven and earth.

6. **Truths,** like forgiveness, commitment, guidance, and deliverance from temptation, are **values** only when we own them, claim them as our own, and live them. In themselves, without the touch of God's grace and our personal investment in them, truths are only facts; and mere facts never saved, or even helped anybody. The *mind* grasps facts; only the *spirit* gives them importance, shape, direction. Lord, in your mercy, direct us!

7. If in prayer we ask more for the sense of the Presence of God than we do for anything else, whatever else we get will be more than enough even when it seems nothing. Through the practice of this kind of prayer, the God-*longer* becomes more and more the God-*lover* ; and all the lesser loves, however delectable, become *dispensable*. The saints make this truth undeniable; and the demons make it, with the cooperation of most human beings, unavailable. Go with God this day, praying for the Presence.

8. The Bible teaches **soul-realism.** Repenting is even harder than forgiving, which is hard enough. Wanting what we *need* is tough when we're wanting something else. Stopping what we're doing when we're liking what we're doing is almost as difficult as doing what we don't want to. Good religion pleases God, but it's not always pleasant for us. Yet the old truths abide: The joy of the Lord is your strength, and underneath are the everlasting arms.

9. Ours is not to choose whether we endure or perish. Ours in only to choose, while perishing, whether to live for *long* dreams

or *short* ones, for petty aims or great visions, for our little sovereignties or God's kingdom. As we choose, "the grace of our Lord Jesus Christ," who perished for us and wants to live in us, stands ready to surprise us with eternal life today and every tomorrow and even beyond tomorrows.

10. I hope you are not one of those under the illusion that one can be a Christian without *going to church*. Of course not everybody who goes to church is a Christian, but all Christians go to church. In fact, it's the only distinctively Christian thing we do. And we do it to praise and thank God in the community of our fellow believers in our Lord Jesus Christ, in the Spirit. Go next Sunday, and don't let yourself be distracted by what's wrong with you or others or, in your opinion, with the service.

11. Every trouble is a darkness, yes. But the balancing truth is this: Every trouble can be a **lens** concentrating, intensifying, the light of God. You will never be without troubles, troubles of your own or burdens you help others bear because you care; but also you need never be without the light of God's presence shining more brightly in the darkness of trouble. "Yea, though I walk through a valley of deep shadow, even the shadow of death, Thou art with me. . . . And I shall dwell in the house of the Lord forever."

12. The universe with one less prayer, your prayer, is not the same universe. How is it poorer? One less investment of good will. One shimmer less of love intended, sent. One less surge of power for the New Creation. One less dream of peace and resolve of justice. One less act of yielding to the **Holy Purpose** within and beyond the world.

13. People fight over what's **important** to them. When religion is important to them, they fight over it: if they didn't, that would prove that religion is unimportant, at least to them. So it's an honor to religion when people fight over it. Of course it's a greater honor to religion when, not from indifference but from

love, some people cease fighting over religion, because it has become for them *more than* worth fighting over. More, not less. Be fair to religion when you see-hear-read the news.

14. What do I know about my neighbors near and far? That they hurt as I *hurt,* and bleed the same color. That they *hunger,* and need the same nutrients I need. That they *hope,* and — like me — perish when vision fades. That they *are loved* by the same Love I am loved by, and betray that same Love, and by that same Love are offered upon repentance the same forgiveness and **newness of life** I'm offered. So look around you today: you won't find any strangers.

15. Nobody knows enough to know whether the world's getting better or worse, but everybody can see it's *changing*. Right now, it seems to be changing faster than usual, yet not fast enough to protect our God-given planetary home and prevent mass social catastrophes. There is much that we can do, but without God we cannot do enough. For the Love which seeks to prepare for us a new world, and to place us in it as new creatures, is predisposed to "**make all things new.**" What is *my* predisposition?

16. It is possible to abide in the eternal without keeping up with the temporal, but it is not Christian. A Christian has the good news, the Bible, in one hand and the news in the other. A Christian doesn't just see-hear-read the news; a Christian *prays* the news, offering to God, bit by bit, the whole wonderful wild mess of it. Try praying the news today; at least you'll find it less depressing, and the energy of your prayer will be added toward the coming of the Kingdom of Love, and God will be pleased with you.

17. Our two basic American religions — the basic religions of the Bible, Christianity and Judaism — teach us to love not just our family and friends but also our neighbors. Jesus heightens the commandment: love even your enemies, he says. Jews and Christians can't agree on everything, but we can agree to love one another, to treat each other with **active good will.** It's what God

wants; and on the side it benefits us with better feelings about one another, about ourselves, about the world, about God.

18. What do you do when "things just don't make sense anymore"? You could give up trying to make sense, but that would land you in the misery of cynicism. You could try to satisfy your soul with separate bits of sense. You could try to see patterns of meaning: scientists have begun to say that even chaos has its patterns. Or you could read **the Bible** daily and discover that whatever sense you do or don't make of this or that is not as important as the sense of God's Presence and what sense God's Presence makes of you and yours and life and the world.

19. Religion isn't something to believe in, it's something to believe *through*. When you believe **in** it, you help it mess up the world. When you believe **through** it, you become a "worker together with God" in straightening out messes, including the messes religion makes. We are no more trapped in our differences than Jesus was in the tomb: the long reach and stride of God's resurrecting grace can make us good news to each other and to the whole earth.

20. If listened to aright, every sound is **music** and all music is praise to God. If seen aright, every sight is *art,* do-it-yourself art, and all art is praise to God. Our senses this day can be, are meant to be, sacraments. God is holy, but the world — our life — is only as holy as we make it. "Our Father, hallowed be Thy Name. Thy Kingdom come, on earth. . . ."

21. None of us, not even the atheist, is godless, without God. God chose the Jews to witness to his love for all people. Christians add that this love shines forth in God's coming to us in **Jesus**, who lived and died and rose again for us all. All this being so, let's live this day in conscious joyful gratitude to God. Let's live today not unaware, as though godless, but prayerfully, knowing that God cares, hears, and is eager to help us in ways we can and in ways we can't foresee.

22. The Kingdom of God is both the goal toward which we strive and the reality in which God allows us to participate here and now, this day. The allowing is *grace,* the striving is *works,* and the King is with us as we battle the inner temptations and outer realities of lust, greed, malice, disappointment, disillusion, despair. If they promised us life would be easy, they shouldn't have. Today is ours for facing life's difficulties, in and toward the Kingdom, the Rule, the Sovereignty, the Reign of God.

23. What gets your attention gets *you,* and what holds your attention is *your god.* If you are driven to distraction by the world's attractions and distractions, you did it to yourself. If you are small and lonely, it's because you've worshiped some small god who isolated you. Instead, today be the lord or lady of your attending. Pay attention to the one true God of heaven and earth!

1995 Supplement

1. Many of these brief meditations, at least in substance, appeared once each during the eight years I wrote the "Kirkridge Readings and Intentions," the devotional publication of the Kirkridge Community, Bangor, Pennsylvania.

2. It's been a long time since I licked out an all-day sucker, but it's a life-long habit of mine to lick away for hours, sometimes a whole day, on some "word fitly spoken" (Prov. 25:11), powerfully though not always sweetly put. Quite possibly the habit started with "memory verses" in Sunday school: you'd get a pin if you programmed in enough of them; something like now getting (I'm told) a ribbon if you lose a certain number of pounds in Weight Watchers.

3. For CBS Television's "Wake Up and Live," I did some experimenting with professionally read quotations, including some of the above.

Babes in prayerland

"Out of the mouths of babes," I have often heard said when a child says something startlingly wise. In a KJV culture, the listener silently completes Psalm 8:2 with "hast thou ordained strength." In Matthew 21:16 Jesus quotes it (though Matthew takes it from Greek, LXX). And on his own, Jesus thanks God for revealing to "babes" a spiritual wisdom which God has hidden for the worldly wise and the learned (Matt. 11:25, Luke 10:21).

This Thinksheet's title is a takeoff on Victor Herbert's operetta *Babes in Toyland*. More often, the Bible uses "babes" with the opposite meaning, as less knowing. American slang uses "babes" as a disparaging reference to attractive young women. And "babes in the woods" means gullible, easily dupable poor souls. So we must abandon the King James Version's "babes" for "young children" — as in *Children's Letters to God: The New Collection*.[1]

While children are often theotropic on their own, we can assume — can't we? — that the children who wrote these letters to God were asked to do so. Obviously, however, the asker was not laying a pious trip on these little ones. The prayers are too bold, even brash, and too familiar, for that.

"Dear God, I think about you sometimes even when I am not praying. Elliott." A pure, disinterested theotropism that touches me twice (especially since he spells his name right). By

---

1. *Children's Letters to God: The New Collection*, compiled by Stuart Hample, et al. (New York: Workman Publishing Co., 1991).

124

Elliott's distinction, almost none of my praying is praying; and the proportion of praying in my praying has declined with the years. The upside way to put this is that the amount of my inner thinking about God, a communing without specific adoration, thanksgiving, petition, or intercession, has increased through the years. Warning: habitual praying without praying leads to the dead-end of not praying at all. Neither private nor public prayer is optional for the Christian. Part of the power of Islam lies in the Qur'an's repeated command to "perform the [five-times-daily] prayers." What does not repeatedly get your attention soon ceases to get your attention at all — which is the unforgivable "sin against the Holy Ghost" ("which," I said in a church discussion group today,[2] "you haven't committed if you worry you may have").

"Dear God, I don't ever feel alone since I found out about you." The years have deepened my conviction that precisely that was, for me as a child, the central feeling about experiential religion, the feeling of companionable Presence repeatedly confirmed and, at sixteen, decisively affirmed in conversion and, soon after, in call. It follows that, from the fact that this communion is not in spacetime (i.e., has "eternal" quality, is with [Moffatt's translation of Elohim] "the Eternal"), it is for me untouchable by bodily death, which is spacetime-bound.

This one is on *chesed,* leal (loyal)-love of God, faithful devotion no matter what, and thus long-suffering. **"God: [Noah got laughed at,] but he was smart, he stuck with you. That's what I would do."** Last night our six-year-old granddaughter said "Bruce is going to hell because he says bad words, but I'm going to heaven with Grandma and Grandpa." Grandma and Grandpa don't figure on going to heaven soon, and we like even less the thought that Em(ma) might go with us at her age. Then of course she's in danger of moralism, legalism, censoriousness, works-righteousness, pride, and whatnot. But she's got a good fix on *a)*

2. 6 March 1992.

125

the fact that deeds have unending ripple-effects; *b*) wisdom calculates consequences at hand and remote; *c*) reflection on consequences is a wall against temptation; *d*) we are responsible for choosing our optional associates, knowing that (as the KJV puts it) "evil communications corrupt good manners" (1 Cor. 15:33; TEV is better: "Bad companions ruin good character"); *e*) God knows and cares about what we do ("He sees all we do, he hears what we say, my Lord's awatchin' all the time"). (Bruce, by the by, is a public-school classmate of Em's.)

"Dear God, how did you know you were God?" In me, that releases a hopperful of Hebrew, Greek, and Latin words I'll not let fall on you.

"Dear God, who draws the lines around the countries?" Yeh, yo, who! From the Balfour Declaration of 1917 through U. N. 242, the Jews were promised not a state but a "homeland." Can there be a homeland without boundaries — say, for the Kurds, "Kurdistan" overlapping the boundaries of four nation-states? The white-white Canadian-U. S. boundary is no problem, but what about the brown-white Mexican-U. S. boundary? And the currently embattled boundaries of eastern Europe, of Africa, and of Asia? It's good, now, that children can see not only the political globe but also boundaryless earth from space.

And who draws the lines around cultures, religions, families, management/labor, races, the sexes? And do "good fences make good neighbors," as Robert Frost's neighbor insisted because his father believed it?

"Dear God, do animals use you, or is there somebody else for them?"

"Dear God, is Rev. Coe a friend of yours, or do you just know him through business?"

"Dear God, I am Amearican [*sic*]. What are you?"

126

"Dear God, are there any patriarchs around today?"

Unintentionally ironic!

"Dear God, what does it mean you are a jealous God? I thought you had everything." God has everything except what belongs to "idols," i.e., God's competitors for adoration and obedience. Well, what do the idols have that God hasn't? The God-resisting, both angels and people. Here's the humor of displacement: God is jealous of non-*relationships;* the child is thinking of non-*possessions,* in the child-world experience of visible things "mine," "yours," "his/hers/theirs."

"Dear God, my grandfather says you were around when he was a little boy. How far back do you go?" A short hop from grandpa to infinite regress — the mystery of time-depth, of the beyond. And to the child, yesterday is more real than is tomorrow.

"Dear God, I know all about where babies come from. . . . But where are they before that? . . . Please answer all my questions. I always think of you." Dear child, the fact that you "always think of" God is the answer to "all" your "questions." Biology? No problem. But the metaphysics of the "soul"? Big problem! Was Augustine right that the soul enters the fetus on the sixtieth day? And think of Arius's trouble with Athanasius for Arius's saying "There was a time when he [the Son of God] was not"!

"Dear God, thank you for the baby brother but what I prayed for was a puppy." Please, please, always thank God when you get something other than what you prayed for. Why? Because since life is what happens to you when you had other plans, you'd never get around to thanking God if you waited for things to turn out "right." Furthermore, who wouldn't prefer a noncompetitive, always affectionate puppy to a neonate sibling? Then again, once in a while you are surprised by getting what you prayed for and what you planned. Then you can be super-grateful. The life-tone is the thing, as the tonic in music. The habitually grateful never become the grumbling ingrates everybody wants to steer clear of.

"Dear God, please send Dennis Clark to a different camp this year." What was the name of that bratty kid you just couldn't stand when you were a cute, lovable, positive-thinking kid? Now, today, anybody you just can't tolerate? Punish yourself by prayers of goodwill toward that person, and so bless yourself.

"Dear God, I bet it is very hard for you to love . . . everybody in the whole world. There are only 4 in my family and I can never do it." Honesty and theology have kissed each other!

"We read Thomas Edison made light. But in Sunday School they said you did it. So I bet he stoled your idea." Do you remember how public school and Sunday school mixed it up in your young heart? But what of the millions with no religious education? Do they think that God (i.e., religion) "stoled" his ideas from scientists and inventors?

Try reading these prayers in your family or other group. After each one, ask for comments, then read mine. Part of the fun and profit will be in fresh additions to the list.
"Out of the mouths of babes. . . ."

If a hymn lifts you like a wind, your wings were spread

Today[1] a single, solitary, New Year dejected, aggressively antireligious, fiftyish gentleman wandered into a New Jersey church and, at the appropriate time in the worship, sang #376 in *The Presbyterian Hymnal*, the 1747 Charles Wesley hymn "Love Divine, All Loves Excelling," and not long thereafter phoned to discuss with me what happened to him in the singing. I am following up that phone call with this open letter to him.

Dear _____,

1. I humbly thank God that you shared with me today a precious experience of your soul. Since you have long been antireligious, I was a bit taken aback when you said, describing your strange experience in singing that hymn, "God plays tricks on us" — and vigorously agreed with you! But consider this: God cannot lift us on the winds of his Spirit if our wings are not spread, if we are not ready — consciously or not — to be lifted. You were lifted; ergo, in spite of your confessed depression, perhaps even because of it, **your wings were spread**. Not only that, but:

2. Sometimes — surprise! — we are lifted when our wings are unconsciously spread yet consciously beating. Every day I see the

1. 2 January 1993.

129

waterfowl on our Craigville ponds, but not one of them can rise simply by the spreading of wings. There must also be the beating thereof. You were **beating the wings** of your spirit when you showed up at the worship hour in that church this morning. If you wanted to avoid a spiritual lift-off, you were in the wrong place at the wrong time. You are, if you will understand I'm saying this gently, a reverse hypocrite. Hypocrites talk a better line than they live. In appearing in a church at the time of public worship, you were living a better line than you talk.

3. What happened, you said, was that well before the end of the hymn, you were singing in your thirteen-year-old barmitzvah voice, and that loud enough to attract considerable attention. Unembarrassed, you were overjoyed; and you wanted my help to *understand your joy.* You told me the joy was not from reverberations of human love: you have known no great human love, of parent or contemporary or child. Yet **the great Love** was calling you, and you were responding out of the experience of longing, not out of the experience of love. **Logically**, you rail against the idea that God loves his creation, and against it point — as did Darwin — to the cold evidence of "nature red in tooth and claw"; but **spiritually** you find, in the existence and persistence of the good, as in Steven Spielberg's *Schindler's List,* that the mystery of creative and redemptive love weighs more heavily on the scale of meaning than the mystery of evil.

For more than sixty years I've heard and read the nutty notion, derivative from British and American empiricism, that human beings can't understand anything that's not been written, by personal experience, on the original *tabula rasa* of their brains — in computerese: nothing in, nothing out. One of the pillars of feminist theology has been that since nobody had a perfect father, and many have had horrendous fathers, calling God **"Father"** is an impediment to true spirituality. The argument errs twice, neglecting two laws of the mind: *a*) the law of imagination, that by imagination we fill in the blanks of experience; and *b*) the law of compensation, that by longing we correct the defects in our experiencing. Both the person who has no personal experience of father and the person whose father-experience

130

has been negative can give full-hearted allegiance and love to the
"Father" whom we Christians address in the Lord's Prayer. As for
those of us who had good, albeit imperfect fathers, as I had, the
allegiance and love of the heaven-Father is easier to come to.

These thoughts ran through my head yesterday at Harvard,
where Loree and I heard the Boston Baroque Sander's Memorial
Hall First Day All-Bach Concert, which closed with Cantata 51,
"Jauchzet Gott in allen Landen!" (Acclaim God in all lands!). That
sophisticated audience got in the German-English libretto a full
dose of patriarchal (!) classical Christian theology, Trinity and all.
God's goodness "shines anew each morning," an event we anticipate and pray for, trusting in "that *Fatherly* constancy" *(die Vater-
treu'),* in response to which "a grateful heart may show through
godly living that we are Thy children." The concluding aria, "Alleluia!," crescendoed the baroque permutations into a burst of **joy**,
and audience acclamation at least of Bach and the musicians if not
also of God! And in between the "Fatherly constancy" and that
glorious Alleluia we heard "Glory, praise and honor to God the
Father, Son and Holy Ghost, who would increase in us that which
He promised out of Grace . . . therefore sing: Amen! We will attain
this if we believe from the bottom [Grund] of our hearts."

What am I saying? Your unexpected joy this morning, while
partly from the breaking out of your age-thirteen beautiful singing
voice, was also from the presence of the *Father,* the "Love divine,
all loves excelling." Am I trying to rope you into Christianity?
Certainly not. Roping is done on small cattle, to immobilize them
for branding. The Love divine does not rope, does not rape. Do I
think the wind that lifted you was the Holy Spirit, whom Jesus
sent to continue his work in and witness toward the Kingdom of
God (John 16:7)? Of course I do: I am a Christian.

4. We are still in the Twelve Days of Christmas, so the hymn
you sang was appropriate to the season, in which Christians honor
the **"Joy of heaven to earth come down."** You said you were
moved by the first five words of the hymn, but had to reject the
rest of the first stanza, which is on the incarnation and the in-

dwelling ("Enter every trembling heart"). But the rest of the hymn you could sing with full heart, including the hymn's ecstatic climax, **"*Lost* in wonder, love, and praise."** The paradox that we cannot be found until we are lost! First, we confess we are lost *without* the operation of God's blessing (the Hebrew way to put it, as to "say the blessing" at meals), God's grace (the Greek way to put it, as to "say grace" at meals), God's forgiveness of our sin of severance from God and our sins of falling short of God's holy will and ways. Then lost *within* our experience of "wonder, love, and praise," of which we have anticipatory experiences such as yours this morning.

5. Brothers John and Charles Wesley had, just a few days apart, such an experience in early manhood. John expressed it as being *strangely warmed,* as by an internal Fire, in an evening service in that unheated Aldersgate Street (London) Anglican church. You can feel, can you not, that warmth in Charles's hymn? The brothers Wesley asked what that strange warmth was, as now you are asking what that strange movement of your spirit this morning meant. They worked out the meaning over a number of months. I hope you don't quickly foreclose on the meaning of your experience. As long as you are sweating the question, your wings are still spread. And without **wingspread**, you're not going anywhere in this world or the next.

6. Please see the film *Shadowlands,* the love story of a man who didn't meet "her" till he was sixty-five. He was C. S. Lewis (played by Anthony Hopkins), prominent British atheist and, after conversion, author of numerous Christian works of fiction and argumentation. She was Joy (Debra Winger), dying of cancer when he met her, whose death resulted in his writing an instant classic on bereavement, *A Grief Observed.* That book, and his autobiography *Surprised by Joy,* remark that the two factors leading him from atheism to Christianity were **reason** and, more important, his frequent prior experiences of inexplicable sudden bursts, upwellings, of **joy**. The figure is mine but the idea, his: the experiences were like dots a child is asked to connect sequentially, to get the surge of happiness upon recognition of the otherwise hidden face or animal or plant or building. Using his vast

132

learning and remarkable rational skill, he connected the dots of those joy-bursts and saw "the light of the gospel of the glory of Christ, who is the image of God" (2 Cor. 4:4 NRSV, my reference; "the grace of God dawned" on him, Tit. 2:11). The upwellings of joy were instant, punctiliar, iterative; the conversion was gradual, linear (which, too, describes my own case).

7. You explained to me that what you are yearning for, longing for, is some way to get to what human beings need, in themselves and in unselfishness toward others, without going through the particular religions, which by their very diversity, and even more by their mutual coldnesses and even animosities, frustrate the very human unity that fulfilling the goal of humanization demands. Your experience this morning seems to have landed you in a *via media* between walled-in particularities and utopian generality: can one celebrate the **universal *through* the particular**? I say YES! It is what I do. . . . Grace and peace to you!

1995 Supplement

Yesterday I told our pastor to relax: if his sermon doesn't lift Loree and me, the hymns will; they always do. Earlier in the day I heard a pastor tell James Galway that his best lift when down is Galway recordings. There are three possibilities for aural blessing: words without music, words with music, and music without words. A fourth often lifts me: poetry, which is words without music but with musical qualities.

Part of the great flautist's response, which included his gratitude to God for his Belfast Protestant rearing, was this: "When I take on a new student, I can always tell immediately whether he or she had the blessing of a religious rearing: those who didn't, lack reverence." For those of childhood religious nurture, all their lives it's a shorter distance to the mood of being "lost in wonder, love, and praise," and almost no distance at all for those who daily practice the Presence.

Dignity derives from. . . .

One handle for grasping America's current cultural crisis is marked "dignity." We're in a crisis of dignity. Most of us have a pretty good feel for what it is. Certainly it includes *self-respect, self-regard,* in all relations and situations a sense of *self-worth* ("dignity" deriving from the Latin word for worth, "worth" in Old High German meaning the dignity of being worthy and thus valuable).[1] It's something the United States Department of Education is finding everywhere in high-achieving public schools among the so-called disadvantaged — so it's something that transcends turf, though turf may predispose for or against dignity.

That seems to be a good place to begin a list of completions of the generic stem "Dignity derives from . . ."

1. **Achievement,** as in the case of the children mentioned above. One essential for the healthy society is that the citizenry have adequate opportunity to achieve and thus to reap the harvest

---

1. I avoid "self-esteem," the current code word of humanists for the dignity of the individual viewed as autonomous. Rather, children should be taught to *respect* themselves and one another, and *esteem* their betters, who are "superior" to them. *The Random House Dictionary,* 2nd ed., uses the now-no-no word "betters" to define the plural of "better." When I was growing up, I understood "betters" — meaning my parents, teachers, and other authorities and worthies over me — as a put-down on any false dignity I happened to be claiming when the word was put down on me. I needed to acknowledge betters in order to have the *dignity* of right judgments as to my place, and the *security* of being put in my place when I got out of it.

thereof in dignity, the dignity of *self-satisfaction*. A society is sick to the extent to which such opportunity does not exist.

2. **Freedom,** decisional power over one's life — one's time and potential. Without social regulation ("socialism" of some kind), this freedom — and attendant dignity — will exist only for those of high gifts, high energy, and high drive (ambition). Society will be sick, for few will have freedom-dignity and achievement-dignity. But the flipside is that society will be sick if the state co-opts everybody's decisional power: the state will have *coercive* dignity, the citizenry will live without freedom-dignity, in subjection, in fear, in virtual or actual slavery. Under any ideology, a prison is, by this definition, a sick society, which in doublespeak is called a "correctional institution." One argument for capital punishment is that, on this angle, it has more dignity than imprisonment: the criminal may die with dignity instead of being forced to live in indignity. The counterargument that life under any conditions is better than death demeans humanity; it's mere vitalism, as appears also in the techno-medical sustaining of life in the brain-dead.

3. **Divine Origin.** Life has dignity, according to our Declaration of Independence, because we are "endowed by our Creator with life. . . ." It's an anomaly that the Supreme Court is hearing public-school cases in which "creation scientists" are claiming that it's okay to teach creation science because it's to be done without reference to, or even the implication of, the dignity motif in the Declaration of Independence! At the bedrock of the founding fathers' moral vision was this sanction of divine origin, and it is silly and insane that government schools — pledged to continue and promote the American heritage — are forbidden to engender this motivation. Secularistic efforts to marginalize this sanction in our founding documents, as though it were as peripheral as the embroidery on the founding fathers' shirtcuffs, are disingenuous, pernicious, and at the moral level of the former Soviet historical revisionism.

4. **Loyalty.** Maybe there's not always happiness in lying in the bed you made, but there's dignity in it. Dignity in "my word

is as good as my bond." Dignity in keeping covenant, fulfilling contract, being faithful in relationship, not making promises with convenient mental reservations. No, loyalty isn't everything. My point is that dignity derives from (among other things) loyalty, which is hanging in there by will-power when self-aggrandizement seems to lie in becoming disloyal. In the Bible (and so in Judaism and Christianity), loyalty is the heart of religious and sexual commitments: cult-code-creed and marriage (not "love" or "intimacy," which are to be bound by and nurtured within marriage).

5. **Discipline,** the prophylactic, pedagogic, and punitive removal of freedom. If *dignity* is the end, then freedom (as in section 2) is merely *a means to dignity* and (as here in section 5) should be denied when the interests of dignity supervene. But if freedom is the end, as in *permissivism,* then discipline is an attack on dignity — the main argument used by libertarian forces (such as the American Civil Liberties Union) in battles against the public-school use of fear and physical pain (seen thus as forms of "child abuse" — overlooking the fact that the underdisciplined classroom is a time-delay form of child-and-society abuse).

Outside the sphere of this Thinksheet is the means/end criterion applied to dignity itself. In biblical religion, dignity is instrumental to *devotion,* "holy living" and "holy dying" (as Jeremy Taylor, scholar-saint, put it), which is instrumental to *the glory of God.* But all this is way beyond the allowed sanctional range in American public schools. It's a severe problem, though, that to stop with dignity, and not go on to devotion and "the glory of God," is to overweight Renaissance-Enlightenment values over against biblical values; far from teaching the Bible in the public schools, it is teaching anti-Bible in the public schools. The myth that our public schools are neutral on religion is promoted by those whose religion, humanism, is being taught, without competition, in our public schools.

6. **Integrity,** active respect for truth and honesty in word and deed in one's living and relating. You feel good about yourself, or have dignity, if you pay up when you're tempted to cheat on truth,

honesty, relations, or possessions. Integrity-dignity demands that you treat with *dis*respect what you see, in others' feelings and ideas and actions, as lacking dignity. This is *a*) the only form of disrespect that dignity permits, and *b*) a disrespect that dignity requires.[2] I have found that obeying the dictate of this integrity-required disrespect reduces the number of one's friends to the point where they do not overimpose on one's time and energy; friendship becomes a manageable factor in day-to-day living.

7. **Divine suffering** and **human self-offering for redemptive suffering.** A specifically biblical root of dignity, this. It is found in Judaism, but heightened in Christianity as *a*) "Christ died for me" and *b*) "Take up your cross and follow me." Mother Teresa knows about this dignity, but it's undervalued in "mainline" religion in the United States.

8. **Participation in the Holy Spirit.** For Christians, this is a *community* dignity. Immanu-el, God is with us in the Jesus community of caring-with-God for "the saints" and "the world." Only this can deliver the local church from being merely a religious club.

9. **Heritage.** In addition to horsethieves, everybody's family tree has saints and near-saints in it. And also — why not? — tribal and racial and ethnic pride, contributing to dignity if tamed by continuous awareness of the pan-human context of all claiming and celebrating. Theologizing that is cerebral and abstract poohpoohs this *concreteness,* but the Bible unabashedly revels in it. Why not? But the taboos should include the-other-one's-nose limitation on my provincial pride and promotion.

10. **Recognition.** "I matter," my sense that *a*) my existence

---

2. The failure to treat unworthy persons of power or wealth with disrespect can have horrendous consequences. Politically, we Americans got off to a good start on this by treating King George III with sufficient disrespect; and we have done a fairly good job on upstart demagogs. But as a plutocratic society we fail to disrespect the unworthy wealthy more than we do the unworthy powerful.

is recognized and *b*) my contribution is appreciated, is a *sine qua non* of dignity. A church that fails to do this for folks is doing nothing significant for the Kingdom of God. Or a school. Or any other institution. The social cost of letting people live with "I don't matter" is unacceptably high.

In biblical religion, human dignity is *derivative* rather than inherent. Only God's dignity is inherent, as is God's goodness: "Only God is good" (Matt. 19:17 and parallels).

11. **Labor.** The old union slogan, "the dignity of labor," is now too little heard in the land. On Cape Cod we have many unemployed because the work available was (the unemployed said) "beneath their dignity"; while many Brazilians, having taken those jobs, are prospering: they understand that dignity is not in the labor but in the laborer.

12. **Sharing.** Formerly meaning two-way giving, the word has been expanded to include one-way giving. The former is the literal meaning of the New Testament's basic word for "community," which provides member-dignity for all. "Charity" is being used less for the latter meaning of sharing, for the word has acquired the pejorative meaning, "to give in a spirit that bloats the dignity of the giver and shrinks the dignity of the receiver" — but such giving is anti-Christian.

13. **Being loved and loving.** Would you have put this section first? The time sequence is that God and our parents loved us into being. This is our only inherent dignity, and it can be realized only as we love — and fully owned only as we love God, our parents, our siblings and other relatives, our neighbors near and far. Church and society should aim to see that every child is loved into dignity and that none of God's children suffers the indignity of neglect. Thinking about what that implies, even if only for ten minutes, is enough to make a revolutionary of you.

14. **Gratitude.** The ingrate can have no dignity worth the

word. A paradox here: Not all "dignitaries" have dignity, which all the grateful have. For the grateful must be low enough, humble enough, to look up and say "thank you."[3]

1995 Supplement

A few remarks about the **pathology of dignity**:

1. I know of a Nazi stormtrooper whose boot crushed a Jew's foot near the Hamburg docks. I don't know whether the Jew had dignity, but the soldier did: he had the sick dignity of knowing himself to be a member of the Master Race (an ideological fiction).

2. When the collapse of the Soviet Union freed Yugoslavia to do its own thing whatever that might be, Yugoslav demagogues raped "the masses" by retribalizing them, reminding them of their pre-Soviet allegiances, prides, and grudges. Under Tito they all had the larger dignity of being Yugoslavs; now what's important, and worth killing and dying for, is the smaller dignities of clashing ethnicities and religions.

3. People are properly called "masses" when, lacking larger, ultimate, intimate, inner dignity, they identify (an act) with tyrants who feed them visions and dreams of an identity (a state) partly remembered and partly promised. Those whose dignity is within themselves are not mass-able. Good religion, the Lord's Prayer, is a bulwark against tyranny.

3. For this, Jesus highly recommends *groveling*, with publican as model: Luke 18:9-14 is a parable of double chiasmus: *a*) the impenitent is grateful for a list of things, but shouldn't be; the penitent expresses no gratitude, but is silently grateful for penitential access to God; *b*) the retributional teeter-totter awaits!

The Christian liturgy contrasts "Lord, I am not worthy" with "Worthy is the Lamb!" But then — another reversal — the Lamb's "slaves" are granted the dignity of the Lamb's "friends."

Sacrament in the common life

Mother
gave us all love
all the love she had, and love to us all each.
    Mother
    gave us each,
        to be had when she was gone,
            a sterling silver candelabrum.
                The same one.
                    In extreme age, Mother had become forgetful.

In her mind,
    Mother had given the candelabrum only to one of us
        but it was really to one and one and . . .

Mother, thinking that one was only one,
    was unaware that one was each one.

No, that cannot be.
    To give it to only one,
        she would have to give it to this one instead of the others.
        But when she gave, there were no others.
            There was only this one,
                this one standing here now.

140

The gift was for one, this one.
   It couldn't have been also not for the others.
      That was not Mother's way of loving.
         There was no arithmetic in her loving.
         When it came to love, she couldn't count.
      Like God,
      she couldn't say 1-2-3 . . .
      she could say only 1-1-1 . . .

Mother,
Through the candelabrum,
  was giving love to each one,
     was continuing to love each one,
       as through family feasts for more than a half-century
         the candelabrum's candles had illumined each one.
  The candelabrum was only one, but how many candles
    it had served, held up!
The candelabrum was and is zero-sum, only one.
The family love-feasts around it were zero-sum
  their unknown number reckoned when we children
    became old orphans.
Mother's love, and Father's, are not zero-sum.
    Love, when it is love, is not zero-sum.
In giving it to each of us and thus increasing love,
  Mother achieved a miraculous multiplication of the
    candelabrum and (she would have been shocked to think
    of it!) set us up for a probate fight. Instead, the
    candelabrum's miraculous multiplication of love, and laughter.
      Or what else is a sacrament?

But who got the candelabrum?
I can't remember. I'm getting old, and forgetful.
But we all received the sacrament.

141

Sense-making: "the *connexion* man"

Primal sense (such as the "hot" a child senses when he or she touches a hot stove) requires no interposition of human mentation, but *secondal sense* is the seeing or knowing that "thinking" produces. In this secondal sense, "I see" means "I make the **connection**." Riddley Walker, in the novel by the same name,[1] becomes "the connexion man"[2] when his father, who was "the connexion man," dies. He is aided by Lorna, a woman whose connecting power is intuitive: she is their tribe's shaman, always talking about folks' getting "first knowings" and "tels" and "reveals." This human rational/transrational power can be both a bane and a blessing, it can be right/wrong in operation, and it can be driven by fear/faith, or hate/love; it can also be traditional/original — either old/new or present/future.

    1. While reading through the first paragraph, did you look up **secondal** in your dictionary? Since you didn't have to in order to grasp its meaning as formed on "primal" in the same sentence, if you did look it up it was probably to see if the word "exists" (the traditionalist being under the illusion that only those words that are in dictionaries exist). I looked it up for a third reason, to see if the word existed before I used it. It didn't, as far as I can see. I made, from "primal," a simple *extension* or *projection* or *extrapolation* — a connec-

1. Russell Hoban, *Riddley Walker* (New York: Summit Books, 1981).
2. Hoban uses the British spelling, "connexion."

142

tion from existent to new-existent; thus "old/new, present/future." In being thus "original," I was more like Lorna than like Riddley; like a foreteller or oracle or (less close) a biblical prophet.

2. Isabel Venenci, a young Parisienne who lived with us briefly, could be expected to use logic as connector more than most folks do because she was a law graduate of the Sorbonne. So I assumed, when she arrived, that she was beginning many sentences with "Inference: . . ." It seemed stilted, but I accepted it. Then I noticed that not everything following her sentences' first word was an *inference.* She had been saying "Inf'r'nce," that is, "In France, . . ."! I had made a wrong connection! We often mislead ourselves by our expectations. It's sometimes funny, but sometimes tragic.

"The only thing they understand is force." That's a *generalization* (one more kind of connection) based on an *assumption* (another kind of connection); and some chiefs of state, seeking military solutions for economic, social, or political problems, tragically use it for *planning* (a further kind of connection).

3. One of the questions setting us above and beyond the other earth-creatures is this: "What's going to happen?" Futurists (a well-paid breed of connectors) extend "trends" both dismally and optimistically (e.g., Herman Kahn of the Hudson Institute going through his "scenario" stages[3]). In *The Ultimate Resource: The Economics of Population Growth,* Julian L. Simon says that gloom-and-doom demographers/ecologists/conservationists fail to observe the optimistic long-term trends: for humankind generally the cost of the basics has been declining for centuries, and now there's less hunger and starvation. I hope he's right; but because I extrapolate otherwise, I think he's wrong. From the fact that common folk are more survival-resourceful than theorists take into calculation, Simon projects that we're going to make it again this time. I project, from the present flow of flesh and pollution and earth-impoverishment, that we've outrun this adaptive potential and have created

3. Kahn extended this meaning from the arts to futuristics.

for ourselves problems insoluble by us. This is the extrapolation which forms the second assumption of the Lord's Prayer (the first being that God, who is in ultimate charge, loves us). **Malthus**, says Simon, was too short-line as well as two straight-line in his projections. Say I, Malthus needs modification, not rejection.

4. Which is what I say also of **Darwin**, who extrapolated mega-evolution both from micro-evolution and from the explosive changes caused by the Industrial Revolution, whose process-spirit he interpolated into bio-process, then extrapolated from years-changes into eons-changes — three false extrapolations in one! A fourth false extrapolation of Darwin's is this: if we can understand a process, God is not its doer. This atheistic generalization is more than an assumption; it is, in both senses, a presumption. In the sphere of socio-process, **Marx** committed the same atheistical sin using the same false extrapolations. **Freud** was misled into false extrapolations by the same set of mechanistic-materialistic assumptions as Darwin and Marx. Ours is history's most powerful civilization, and we've gone powerfully wrong. The Christian fundamentalists and I say back to the Bible, but how great a difference between them and me!

5. **Prejudice** is another instance of connection, a false one because it adds *a*) inflexible generalization ("All . . . are . . . ") and *b*) malicious arrogance (an evil alliance of false superiority and ill will) to prejudgment (which may be true or false).

Freud's bromide, "Biology is destiny," for example, is true of all us girls and boys, but look to what sexist use he put it! "Women are emotional" is also true (the menstrual cycle subtending an emotional rollercoaster, with no male parallel), but sexism perversely generalizes that all women are equally emotional and extrapolates that "therefore" women are irrational creatures, inferior to "the rational animal," (masculine) "man." How are we going to learn from Lorna if we, even secretly, believe Riddley is the real "connexion man"?

On the other sexual side, we're facing a lot of female arrogance and anti-male prejudice; for example, false extrapolations are made from male arousal (eyeballs toward "sexual objects") in invidious

144

comparison with female arousal (through skin), as though "relationship" were superior to "flesh" (the Manichean-dualistic error) within the created order, "soul" superior to "body." Female prejudice against males is now adding grief and woe to the pile of grief and woe mounded up by male prejudice against females. Thesis, antithesis, (I pray) synthesis?

6. Supply-side **economics** extrapolates (falsely, I fear) from traditional capitalist motivations, a radical swerve away from Keynesian extrapolations in vogue since Franklin D. Roosevelt.

7. **Interpretation** is another type of connection. Chapter 33 of this book has a diagram showing false ("scribal") extrapolation from literature to life, as in "The Bible says . . ." versus true extrapolation from life-then to life-now (the sequence: life to literature to reconstructed life to life).

8. **Integration** is an ultimate term for connecting — meaning connecting everything in sight, in field, or even in existence. I hold integration seminars to help folks connect their life/ministry/feelings/thinking/fearing/loving/hoping/dreaming/relating. I am a "connexion man."

9. **Exegesis-exposition** is connecting **then**; **preaching-teaching-counseling** is helping folks connect **now** (by modeling, confronting, encouraging).

10. **Games** are connection at play. The thirteen-year-old genius who figured out (and made a mint on) the Rubik's Cube says it is "sheer logic": you get the four corners of one side the same color, and you move down on one side if you've just moved up on its opposite. Experience doesn't pay: kids are better than youth and age at the Cube: experience, while enriching, fouls up simple-minded thinking, i.e., reason, i.e., logic. Logical connecting is something, but not much, and it's far better done by computers than by us. But power tends to operate at a simple-minded, humanity-unconscious, age-thirteen level (see Mark 10).

11. One Sunday, my pastor began his sermon by asking, "What saying of Jesus first comes to your mind right now?" For me, it was "Stop being afraid, little children! God wants to *give* you the Kingdom!" *Extrapolate your* **faith**, not your fears! Connect with God in truth and trust and love, not with "the enemy" in fear and violence. Avoid false extrapolations, like "Since we've survived other wars, we could survive a nuclear war" (in spite of the chaos caused by one Trident accident, and the fact of electromagnetic knockout of all computers by one nuke two hundred miles above Lincoln, Nebraska). Or "We've taken care of all our detritus before, so we'll somehow manage nuclear wastes;" or Dives' "I've had it good here, so I'll have it good there" (Luke 16).

12. *True* extrapolations are *a*) Shalom (Hebrew for "total prosperity") out of obedience to God, hell otherwise; *b)* guidance by obedience (Abraham, Moses, Jesus, Paul, we).

13. I've been swimming a number of places where a dolphin could have come up under me and given me a ride, as some are said to have done in ancient Mediterranean stories and modern reports. But the greatest shock I've ever had from my brain's playing a trick on me was the second I realized that in class I'd said a dolphin had so accommodated me! I'm sure the shock was visible and demanded instant penitent, shame-faced retraction. How could such a thing happen to a man who prides himself on his veracity? There may be the *connection*! A false memory pricking a false pride.

Thick-headed Riddley Walker may help us understand ourselves when we discover that our minds have made false connections. He was indeed a connection man, but most of the connections he made were false, contrary to fact, in unwitting violation of reality. The brain files memories by *categories,* which here I'll define as the spheres within and between which connections are made. Poor Riddley was weak in the categories, having almost no invisible means of rational support. But he did have a vigorous imagination. He imagined events, and in his memory they got hopelessly tangled with real events. And the harder he tried to stay in reality and realistic hope, the farther away from reality he got.

We are all, at times, Riddley Walker. Especially under stress and pressure, as in court. And we have learned how to read small children who appear to be lying: their imagined events overwhelm their smaller supply of remembered real events. In the recent rash of child-abuse court cases, we have learned how suggestible children are: an unabused child will, when repeatedly questioned, become self-convinced of abuse. The result is adult abuse: hundreds of innocents imprisoned. Not all abusers are imprisoned, of course: child abuse is tragically common.

Lord, help us become better connection-makers!

1995 Supplement

1. You may have guessed that Riddley Walker got his first name from the fact that he early provided overwhelming evidence that the world was riddle-y, meaning-impenetrable, to him, though his father had been a meaning master, a hot shot at patterned thinking in the present and into the future. So much for dynasticism as a method of smooth leadership-transition.

This dumb guy, like the current film idol Forrest Gump, gives us comic relief: we're all more or less dumb (making stupid connections) and ignorant (missing knowledge we need to make wise decisions). These two plain facts ought to make us *a)* generous toward others and *b)* intolerant of evasions.

2. As a party game but more, ask a group to list the letters of the alphabet and then each one secretly complete each letter with the first word that comes to mind. I completed "m" with "ystery." Thinking about it, I was a bit surprised to find I'd not written "eaning." But then I was surprised that I was surprised; for I believe, and experience, that the wider the diameter of meaning, the longer the circumference of mystery.

Did you notice the NRSV margin on 1 Cor. 13:12? "Now we see in a mirror, [Gk] in a riddle, but then we will see face to face. Now I know only in part; then I will know fully, even as I have been fully known."

147

Providentialists, moralists, empiricists: perpetual trialog

In decision making, human beings as individuals and groups (including states, as political units staking geographical claims) get advice from three clashing/cooperating *ways of* **making sense** *of the world* ("the world" meaning the here-and-now, history, and hereafter-hope). Here's a sketch of each of the three ways:

1. The **Providentialists,** of whom I am one, believe that history is under the personal, direct creation-and-care of the benevolent God. We pray to the One with whom the buck starts, moves, and stops: providence is an intellectual presupposition of prayer; and belief in providence cannot survive the death of prayer.

Modernity, however, has robbed us of the biblical and pre-Renaissance-Enlightenment, bold, prophetic confidence in naming God's action in particular events. New-Evangelical historian Mark Noll puts it this way: "While believers should affirm that God's providence rules over all events, it is nigh unto impossible for Christian historians to discern the purposes of God for any specific event. To attempt to do the latter is to imitate the failure of deductive historians whose infatuations with generalizations blinded them to the causal skein of the contingent world. Christians fare much better when, instead of trying to describe the finger of God in events, they stick to the analysis of motive and character, an effort for which the Bible provides ample and explicit warrant. Scripture promises the church that it will continue the presence

148

of Christ in the world, not that it will be able to discern God's mind as he rules the nations."[1] This qualified providentialism has side-effects, some *specious* (e.g., the temptation to escape responsibility for "declaring the whole counsel of God" *in situ*) and some *authentic* (e.g., responsibly dealing with the "skein" and dialoging with those who see/grant nothing beyond the "skein"). The ploy, however, strikes me as too facile: Christians should be ready to say, "Hear the Word of the Lord," not just in general, but — sometimes — in particular.

2. The **Moralists**, of whom I am one (though less so than I am of the above) believe in (to use an old Stoic phrase) "the moral constitution of the universe," a *lex naturae* discernible by reason/mind (*logos/nous*), and guided by personal and social experience. Every strand of the West's spiritual and intellectual heritage puts more or less weight on this conviction. Resisting the temptation to spell this all out philologically, I allude only to *dik-e* (the inherent morality of "all things") as the root of *dik-aiosyne* ("righteousness," heavy in Paul).

3. The **Empiricists**, of whom I am one (though less so than I am of either of the above), ask us to "sit down before the facts as a little child" (as the Huxley who transposed Darwin into society put it). Have the simplicity and courage and wisdom to let life hit you without the ideological protection of any ontological paradigm, religious or philosophical. This, history's rarest form of spirituality, opens humanity to divine/demonic influences and consequences. How different I would be if I had never known the blessings of (to use a Fosdick title) "the modern use of the Bible"!

All three are in me, and should in me be coworkers today and tomorrow.

1. *Fides et Historia,* fall-winter 1981, p. 36.

Eyeballs for an earhole religion

Imagine a totally black[1] painting of the creation. Better, as you enter the solarium of our home on Cape Cod and arrive at the stair, look up on your right and you will see a totally black painting of the creation: John Locke's "Genesis 1."[2] Why not? There were earholes before there were eyeballs, weren't there?

Before our house was built, we made a small stack of drawings of what we wanted it to look like, and then submitted them to various experts for refinement. But God drew no plans of the universe to show to others or even for himself. Instead, he spoke: "The worlds were framed by the word of God."[3] Into the darkness of primordial chaos "God commanded 'Let there be light!' — and light appeared."[4] Hearing is formative, essential; seeing is appreciative, adjunctive.

When John Locke, Bard College professor of art, came to me to study Bible, I said "We are commanded to love the Lord our God with all, all we've got. You have the gift of seeing and painting. Read through the Bible and record all your visual impressions. Then paint the word of God." Yes, an oxymoron: you can paint what you see with the outer or inner eye, but how can you paint what you hear? In contrast to their neighbors, whose religions were more eye than ear, the Hebrews,

1. Gen. 1:2.
2. As far as I'm aware, nowhere else in Jewish or Christian art is there representation of the precise moment before God said, "Let there be light!"
3. ". . . so that what can be seen was made out of what can't" (Heb. 11:3).
4. Gen. 1:3.

Israelites, Jews, and Christians — "the peoples of the Book" — **heard** their faith at its origins and nurtured their trust in God through the recitation, public reading, and oral exposition of the sacred writings.

"Genesis 1," the first of the thirty paintings in Mr. Locke's biblical series, solved the oxymoronic dilemma by honoring the **ear** over the eye, for the painting is all black; but it subordinately honors the **eye**, for when light strikes the painting at a narrow angle, in raised gesso can be seen a nude woman — Eve? Lilith? Mother Earth? — looking up expectantly in the direction from which the light will come.[5] As she looks up, behind her falls — what? her hair? water? willow branches? — why not all three? And she is pregnant: why not? Is she herself, in addition to being the prototypical worshiper, also the whole creation in process of coming to birth? Arms up in awe, amazement, adoration, as well as expectation. All black, but not all dark! Function precedes form, but form precedes light. "Faith comes from hearing."[6]

1. Now, since the Bible gets off to this dramatic earhole start, we should not be surprised to find the **ear-over-eye** religious style sustained throughout Scripture. Moses' burning bush turns out to be a divine gimmick to get him to slow down, come close, and — curious at the oddity of a bush burning without burning up[7] — give total attention to the Voice speaking from out of the bush. While Moses confronts eyeball-religion Pharaoh with miracles to be *seen*, his persistent appeal to his own people is *"Hear,* Israel . . !"[8] And while

5. To the quiet yet eager expectation as the woman looks up through the upper-left corner of the painting, a storefront-minister student of mine responded "Keep looking up! God is always looking down!" The woman reappears in the thirtieth painting, looking up to receive the *new* creation.

6. Rom. 10:17.

7. Exod. 3:2: "burning . . . not burned-up," three words in Hebrew, appear over the entry of Jewish Theological Seminary in Manhattan. The theophany, the Lord's "Angel" appearance, was the fire itself — a strange, nonconsuming fire. Moses said "That's odd," and that's how we got the Jewish religion: religions, religious experience, corporate and individual, begin with the sense of something odd, mysteriously different, being present and/or going on — in this verse signaled by the exclamation *Hineh!* (Look! Behold!).

8. The *Shema* (Deut. 6:4), Judaism's root utterance: "Hear! Hearken (hear-remember-do)!" Judaism is much more a *Shema* religion than a *Hineh* religion.

151

according to our Christian faith, God appears, becomes visible, in Jesus, the Gospels are more about the Word than about the View.[9]

2. The commandment against "graven images"[10] expresses, as it were, the ear's **suspicion** of the eye. But it's overread if it's taken as a prohibition of the plastic arts in general. What is forbidden is the crafting of statues to be worshiped, that is, idols. Ancient Jewish and Christian architecture used art for teaching and decoration. But because of the eye's power to seduce the ear, throughout the histories of our two religions there have been iconoclastic reactions to purify and simplify religious visuals. Some — for in-

---

When Israel's prophets call the people to attention, they often do so with *Hineh* (cp. German *Achtung!*). But what they almost always are pointing to is a word, not something to see. The force of *Hineh* may be compared to the railroad-crossing sign "Stop! Look! Listen!" with the accent on the last word.

Often when coming upon *Hineh* in reading the Hebrew Bible I remember a street experience worth re-rumination. Walking one day in Jerusalem I came upon two children playing hide-and-seek. So well concealed was one of them, in one of nine covered trash cans, that the other was beginning to lose interest. When the other's back was to the trash cans, I caught a glimpse of a cover rising slightly and heard a small voice cry out *Hineh!* just before the cover gently fell. When God sends a prophet, does it mean he fears his people are losing interest?

The *Shema*, as a call to remembrance and caution against amnesia, visibly appears in the daily experience of going through doors (as the mezuzah, v. 9) and of prayer (as phylacteries, v. 8). It's customary for Hebrew Bibles to make this word in Deut. 6:4 stand out from the text more than any other word.

The *Shema* may be read three ways: (1) "no one else" than the Divinity is Israel's God; (2) "The Lord our God, the Lord is One" (stressing God's unity); (3) "The Lord our God is one Lord" (indivisible, and not to be coupled with other deities). (From W. Gunther Plaut and Bernard J. Bamberger, *The Torah: A Modern Commentary*, [New York: Union of American Hebrew Congregations, 1981], pp. 1366f.)

9. E.g., Jesus' baptism was more an audition (a hearing) than a vision (a seeing). The *bat qol* (Hebrew, "daughter of the Voice" [from heaven]) in Mark and Luke speaks to Jesus only; only in Matthew does it speak to the onlookers (Matt 3:17, Mark 1:11, Luke 3:22). The Gospel of the Ebionites combines *Shema* and *Hineh* with "a great [public] light" dividing between the inner and the outer utterance. The apocryphal Gospels have more Hineh than do the canonical Gospels.

10. Exod. 20:4-6; Deut. 5:8-9. What is ruled out is "a sculptured image" made "with the intent to adore it as a real or surrogate god" (Plaut and Bamberger, *The Torah*, p. 539). . . . and we are completely in the dark about what Jesus looked like: no data.

stance, the New England meetinghouse — have settled into a style of quiet, awesome beauty.

3. After years of college and seminary teaching, including biblical art, I was privileged as a pastor to design, in cooperation with the laity and in consultation with experts in ecclesial architecture and symbolics, a building combining purity, simplicity, and visual richness.[11] One story will speak to the **ear/eye tension** in our religion and to the educational potential of "eyeballs for an earhole religion."

At the east end of the sanctuary, high over the high altar, is a Trinity Cross window, to be read by the worshipers; at the west

11. The symbolism is interpreted in fine detail in *Your Guide to Community Church, Morton, Illinois,* which I had the joy of preparing, including the photography.

end, and to be read by those outside the church, is a ten-foot round window bearing the evangelical-ecumenical message of the congregation: "Jesus is Lord" is central, and the circumference includes — by symbols of the four types of Christianity — all who name him Lord, of whatever tradition, race, nation, or culture.

The symbols? A Spirit *dove* above "Jesus is Lord" represents Pentecostal experience, direct communion with God, and the Pentecostal churches. Moving counterclockwise, the second of the four historical authorities derivative from and therefore subordinate to "Jesus Christ as Son of God, from start to finish Savior and Lord" (the full reading of the words and symbols in the central medallion) is the *Bible*. At the quatrefoil's bottom is my symbol of *tradition* — the tau cross, Jesus' actual cross, in the middle, representing the application of critical scholarship to tradition; the Western or Roman cross on the left; the Eastern or Greek cross on the right. And to the right is the living *church* throughout the world.[12]

Out of remnants we had formed the church as an *ecumenical* congregation, with a polity empowering the laity to their ministries in and beyond the church and with liturgies, changing with the eight seasons of the Christian year, drawn from the churches through the ages and around the world. And I designed this window to "say it all," against sectarian distortion (resulting from overemphasis on particular ones of the four derivative authorities) and for the **balanced "unity** of the Spirit in the bonds of peace."

Now for the story. Throughout the winter of 1951–52, flapping canvas covered the ten-foot hole over the main aisle at the church's west end. The donor, upon seeing my design, which was approved by the church council, refused the promised financial support, insisting that the Bible be the window's center. As spring came on, however, the donor conceded *a*) that my design repre-

---

12. Represented by a ship that looks both like Noah's ark ("the ark of salvation" in early Christian symbolism) and like the logo of the World Council of Churches (noted in *The Christian Century* as probably the first use in a church window).

sented the mind and heart of the congregation and *b*) that to displace "Jesus is Lord" with the Bible would be blasphemous.

For as did the prophets before him, Jesus came as *a mouth for our ears*. And when we heard him, we discerned that he was the Word he spoke. "Before the world was created, the Word already existed. . . . The Word became a human being and, full of grace and truth, lived among us. We *saw* his glory."[13]

1995 Supplement

More on the John Locke biblical series of paintings:

1. Not surprisingly, the first is on the Bible's first chapter and the last is on the Bible's two last chapters. The second, appearing on page 78 as his line-drawing of the painting, is on the Bible's third chapter.

2. This chapter begins with the story of the first painting, which you see as you enter our home. As you move from the solarium into the library, the last painting (mentioned in the fifth footnote) will, with its reds, oranges, and yellows and its considerable size (more than four feet by more than two and one-half feet), grab your attention. Here is what you see, plus some commentary:

(a) The woman who in the first painting looked up to receive the old creation is now looking up to receive the new, which is descending as New Jerusalem in cubic form (Rev. 21:16), on which is superimposed three women merged at the waist.

(b) The three women — the church triumphant, and the Trinity? — have their arms upraised in joy, each playing with her hair.

(c) Alongside the first woman is a woman, in mimesis of the triune woman, playing with her hair. She's a visualization of the joyful-playful spirit of our welcoming woman who now, on behalf of all humanity, completes the Story of creation-fall-redemption-consummation.

13. The beginning of John, the Fourth Gospel.

The biblical way of making sense

It's by story. The Bible makes sense by storytelling, **telling the story of God**. Not the whole story of God, of course — only God knows that — but the story of God's *tangency* to humanity, as a line knows a circle only at the point where the circle touches the line.

Without experiencing this tangency, we human beings would be only flat-liners. But because God has come and touched[1] us through patriarchs, prophets, sages, Jesus, and apostles, the world, life, our life makes sense in its being (the work of the Creator), its sinning (disobeying and forgetting God), its recovery and restoration (the work of the Redeemer), and its open mystery (the shekinah, the presence of the Spirit).

Of course, the world offers many other ways of sense-making. The biblical God is not central for everybody. He's peripheral for some, rejected by others, and some have not even heard of him. As for me, saint is the only thing I've not gotten to be that I've ever wanted to be. A saint steadily centers in God: I do so unsteadily, falteringly. But my Christian prayer and hope is that the day will come when I'll walk strongly and steadily in God, in the practice of God's presence, in awareness of God's will, in obedience to God's voice.

Am I making a high claim for myself? Of course not. Millions of biblical people, Jews and Christians, are fellow pilgrims with me on this

---

1. *Tangency* is from the same Latin root as *Noli me tangere,* in the Vulgate, the resurrected Lord's caution to a particular follower, "Don't touch me" (John 20:17).

spiritual journey. Some of them have, for walking their pilgrimage, gifts I don't have. The rest of this Thinksheet is about one of them: John Lefton, commercial artist and a former student of mine in a course called Midlife Exploration.[2]

In an astonishing tour de force, our artist created, for each Testament, a continuous-line drawing expressing the intent and content of the Testament's story, then followed it up with a playful Jesus-and-the-beasts drawing under the same severe restriction: the minimal lifting of the pen.[3]

Will you come with me on the story-journeys of these drawings? You could make a lot of it out yourself, but I have the advantage of conversations with John, and notes he made for me on copies of the drawings I'd annotated. Here, I give you his explanations. The quoted material is his.

Old Testament: As **Abraham** begins and centers the biblical story of the people of faith, he is central here, and seen in the supreme moment of his faith's testing (Gen. 22). We see the angel of God intervening against the father's sacrifice of his son, and we see the animal substitute for Isaac. John has noted a parallel here: "As Abraham was prepared to sacrifice his son, so God the Father sacrificed his Son Jesus. Isaac gathered wood for the sacrifice; Christ carried his cross."

Now note the central story's line connections. The angel's wing leads to "messianic connections" (which I describe below). The animal about to suffer seems to be smelling suffering Job's foot, thus connecting the central story to the left panel, "the prophets." But the most powerful connection is in the center panel: the fire on Abraham's altar is also the flames in **Moses'** burning bush, and the bush is the altar. How natural to the Bible's sense-making! After Abraham, the next great biblical name (if we let "Abraham" stand for all the patriarchs) is Moses.

In the left panel is Job, who "represents all the prophets" and sages. "Job — the conflict between good and evil. Why do the just

2. A New York Theological Seminary devising of mine. Meeting 4½ hours Monday evenings, participants would bring to each session something representing their past week's experience and/or the theme of the evening. The artist, who was in the 1979 group, did these drawings as his offering in one of the sessions.

3. None of these drawings has been published before.

157

John Clark Lofton

Old Testament

suffer and the wicked flourish?" Then the artist quotes a phrase of mine: "Trust that will not quit, love that will not waver."

And in the right panel we move from Moses to **David**, the next great name in the biblical story. Moses comments about his robe, connected to the burning bush, not being consumed: "That's odd."[4] Exodus 3 continues with "God's directions to Moses to lead the children of Israel out of Egypt." Behind Moses the Decalog appears in the traditional representation of the stone tablets, which are connected to David's city, which is connected both to David's harp ("the Psalms of David — cursings, judgment, praising, second meanings") and to the messianic star. John has quoted Micah 5:2-5 here: "Bethlehem, out of you I will bring a ruler for Israel. . . . So the Lord will abandon his people to their enemies until the one who is to give birth has her son. . . . When he comes, he will rule his people with the strength that comes from the Lord."

"Isaiah" is the one word John wrote on the mountain connected to both the shekinah-angel and the messianic star. Next to the star John has, "The Lord's teaching comes from Jerusalem"; and he indicates a "straight line" running below Jerusalem to its mission, leading the nations in psalming God, and to the star, which bridges the Micah passages and the Christmas star (Matt. 2).

This drawing bridges naturally, as though it were a two-panel cartoon, to the *New Testament* drawing, whose central panel is "The millwork of **Christ**," giver of the "the new law." Moses' sack is marked "old law" ("the law of truth in obscure form — as the flour is hidden in the grain"). John explains, "The Mystic Mill (twelfth-century French) is a visual metaphor in which a man [Moses] pours grain [the law of the Old Testament] into a handmill [Christ]. The man receiving the flour is **Paul**, and the flour is the new law. . . . Paul's mission is to gather the new law and explain and distribute it to people" (his finger being on one loaf, the lowest loaf being continuous with the wine chalice of the Lord's Supper — "bread and Communion").

4. In his note, the artist playfully quotes my saying that these words, though unrecorded, are the first words in the history of Judaism. The experience of oddness is one of the empirical roots of religion.

John Clark Lofton

New Testament

The table over which Jesus is holding the bread has on its top the words "The Communion Connection," from which arrows point to Jesus, who is continuous both with the bread and with the **church** represented by one disciple who is connected to the table, the mill, and the bread. The arrows point also to the bread and to this text: "Luke 24: Road to Emmaus. Two disciples did not recognize Jesus at first. Jesus told them they should have believed what the prophets had to say: the anointed one would enter glory through suffering"; and "Supper at Emmaus: In the prediction of his own passion, he claimed to be the second meaning of Scripture."[5]

In the upper left of the drawing is this: "St. Augustine said, 'The Old Testament is nothing but the New Testament covered with a veil . . . the New is the Old unveiled."[6] The upper register of the left panel is "The **Parables**, 'each a pearl with a thread running through it.'" Standing for all of them is the Prodigal Son (Luke 15:11-32), "Christ's reply to those who criticized him for eating with sinners. To the older son, whose faithful labor is symbolized by the pitchfork, the father says, 'Your brother was dead but now is alive — he was lost and is found.'"

The lower half of the left panel lets the lame man at the healing well (John 5:2-18) stand for all "The **Miracles**." Jesus asks, "Do you want to be whole?" He replies, "I've had no one to put me into the pool these thirty-eight years." Jesus: "Rise, take up your bed, and walk!"

The right panel lets the woman taken in adultery (John 7:53–

5. The phrase "the second [layer of] meaning of Scripture" is mine. Hermeneutics distinguishes "what it means" to us now from "what it meant" to them then. We Christians say the Jesus-rabbit jumped out of the (Hebrew) Bible: Jews have the historical right to say that for Christians, the Jesus-rabbit jumped out of the Bible after we Christians put him in. What we call the higher exegesis, they say, is only eisegesis. Each has a defensible point of view. For our Christian view, read Acts 8:35 and Luke 24:25-27.

6. As sibling religions, Judaism and Christianity began and maintain their self-identities by various devices, one being images. Here the Christian images are the veil and the mill. The divine mystery of our relationship remains, and such images are not to be read harshly, as so often they were in the past. The mill image is not biblical, but the veil image is: see 2 Cor. 3:12-16.

8:11) stand for "The Forgiveness Connection," with arrows pointing to Jesus' hand and to "the [invisible] Cross." By the absence
of the halo (in the drawing's other representation of the Master),
the artist here distinguishes, but does not separate: notice that
continuous lining joins the two figures to Christ the Mill and thus
to each other. "In the old law of Moses, stoning was punishment
for adultery. The new law says, 'Let whoever is without sin cast
the first stone,' and (to the woman) 'Go, and sin no more.'"

The final drawing,[7] which is dealt with in detail in chapter 2,
fills out, in a symbolic way, "the sense the Bible makes" for this
artist. I call it "Jesus and the Beasts of Both Comings," for it
continues and completes the second drawing's Jesus-of-ministry,
Christ-of-resurrection motif. As the central figure, Jesus is the one
who for us Christians centers sense-making in and since the Bible,
in nature as well as in history and hope. Optimistic futurism, the
messianic vision, the Parousia[8] in anticipation, could hardly be
more dynamically and joyfully portrayed. Knowing the artist's profound and joyful Christian spirit, I can testify that in these three
drawings, but especially in this third, he has made his soul visible.

With his pen, John Lefton is shouting to us, "The Bible makes
sense!"[9]

7. Reproduced on p. 8.
8. Greek for "presence," thus for Jesus' re-presencing, sometimes called
the Second Coming or Second Advent.
9. Calvin uses eyeglasses as a figure for this in his *Institutes of the Christian
Religion* I.vi.1 and I.xiv.1.

How life and literature
should be related

A friend of mine has the annoying habit of asking, when he's especially anxious that I not miss what he's about to say, "Are you listening?" Of course I'm listening, but I'd like not to when he pressures me to! But what I want to say in this chapter is so important that I'm tempted to ask you, "Are you listening?" It's important both because so much light and joy can come if the message is heard, and because so much violence can come to truth and to people if it is not.

The message is that literature is a *bridge* from life to life, and it can be abused by *neglect* (that is, by not reading) or by *idolatry* (treating it as though it were itself life, as Isaiah [46:6-7] mocks the pagans for doing to idols which they "open their purses" to buy).

Now, as all Americans should know but don't, the **Bible** is the great literary bridge between the life of Western civilization and our primary[1] spiritual roots. How then can we justify a public-school bus-driver who stops a child from reading the Bible on the bus? Or the teacher who does the same during free time? Or the principal who forbids the teachers to use the Bible in class? Or a community that wants the Bible taught in its schools but doesn't insist on it even though

---

1. We used to say only "our spiritual roots." Now we add "primary" in order to recognize traditions making real though minor cultural contributions. Examples in America are the AmerInd, the African American, and the Asian American. Both facts needs emphasis: these contributions are real, and they are minor. The current academic fad of giving all traditions equal attention is doomed to end in impoverishment and confusion.

the voters are overwhelmingly for it? Or, moving to higher education, what's to be said about a curriculum offering equal attention to all the rest of the world's scriptures alongside the Bible? Or a church that puts personal-and-family Bible reading and group Bible study alongside "many other good things of equal importance we need to be emphasizing"? We all know the reasons for this irrational neglect of our roots, of our religious heritage, of communion between our life and the life that produced the Bible, the life of our founding fathers and mothers. And I do not want to belabor the tragedy. But before I move from neglect to idolatry, please look at this three-stage amoeba diagram on "how life and literature should be related."[2]

2. The "Diagrammatic Representation of the Nine Stages of Production, Interpretation, and Application" is reproduced from my Th.D. dissertation, "'Life' in the Fourth Gospel: An Illustration of a Comprehensive Interpretive Methodology" (Chicago: NBTS, 1943), p. 50. What in that thesis I termed a "comprehensive interpretive methodology" came to be known in certain circles after World War II as "hermeneutic," to distinguish it from the earlier and narrower "hermeneutics."

Diagrammatic Representation of the Nine Stages of Production, Interpretation, and Application

I. Production
Given: Life (solid line)
Task: Literature (broken line)

1. Jesus Christ produces . . .
2. The early Christian community produces . . .
3. The New Testament produces . . .
4. The modern Christian community produces . . .

II. Interpretation
Given: Literature (solid line)
Task: Life (broken line)

5. The New Testament interprets LIFE, reconstructing it.
6. LIFE interprets the New Testament.
7. Environment interprets LIFE-literature.
8. The first-century Christian community then comes alive.

III. Application
Given: LIFE-literature (solid line)
Task: Relation of the first-century LIFE-literature to twentieth-century LIFE (broken line)

9. The use of the first-century LIFE-literature in twentieth-century LIFE is, by this whole process, defined. LIFE and literature together provide two plotting points, enabling lines to be drawn into the twentieth century.

This visual is what during World War II came to be called an exploded diagram, the parts of a whole extended outward for separate study.

The third amoeba, Application, shows "how life and literature should be related," namely, by "a comprehensive interpretive methodology." The entire amoeba, nucleus and body, is shaded, active.

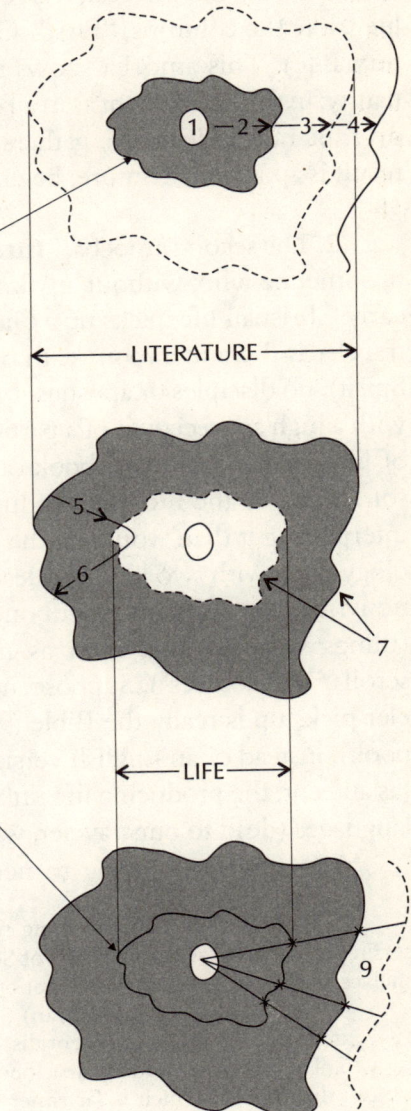

CENTURY

First   Twentieth

LITERATURE

LIFE

1. In the case of the first amoeba, "**Production**," what's exploded upward, as it were, is the nucleus, the life that produced the Bible (here specifically Jesus and the early Christian communities). Literature has not yet come into being, so it is represented by a dotted line; since the life was real, it is represented by a solid line — as is our life (note the columns, "First"-Century Life and "Twentieth"-Century Life). This amoeba shows the oral, preliterary stage of Christianity: in this movement as in all others, life precedes, has precedence over, literature. Jesus (1) gathers disciples (2) around him; and one result is apostolic literature, beginning with the New Testament (3).

2. The second amoeba, "**Interpretation**," pictures the situation of someone who, without any knowledge of the historical Jesus and early Christian life, picks up a Gideon Bible in a hotel or motel. Our traveler is there in a room with only a book. No Jesus (except in the Spirit), no disciples or apostles. Now, a book is not life, though those with a high appreciation of a particular book may refer to it as "words of life." If it's a modern book or magazine, our traveler will know something of the life that produced it and will have an easier time interpreting it than would be the case with an ancient book. Archaeology deals with two kinds of dead things: anepigraphic (things with no writing on them, as most bones and most stones) and epigraphic (things with writing, such as monuments, clay tablets, ostraca,[3] scrolls,[4] and codices[5]). Suppose, now, that the Gideon Bible our traveler picks up is really the Bible (which is a Hebrew-Aramaic-Greek book), instead of an English version or translation of it. A dead book (as ancient, the producing life unknown to the traveler) in three dead languages (dead to our traveler, who knows none of them).

Our traveler is going to need some help. The Gideons have

3. Potsherds, the usual writing material of the common people. In processing many of these, I found bits of Scripture, and can imagine them on lamp shelves as calls to memory and devotion.

4. The Dead Sea (or Qumran) Scrolls, the first of which were found in 1947, are the most dramatic recent discovery in the epigraphic category.

5. The efficient Romans developed, for legal and business purposes, what we call the "book," which is far easier to find a reference in than is a scroll — so early Christians preferred it for Bible-making.

provided a few pretext pages of helps, mainly of the "Where to look when you feel . . ." kind. But this reader is in danger of *literalism,* over-believing the surface of the text, or *poetism,* "finding" in a text a personal meaning that the text will not sustain, or *atheism,* concluding that no such god exists as seems to be portrayed in the text. To avoid these wanderings away from the Book's truth, our reader will need wider and deeper guidance. To use the terms on the middle amoeba, the "task," "given" the literature, will be to recreate the life that produced it (5). Then, almost as though an electric current were begun, the producing life, as the reader begins to understand it, will begin to interpret the Bible (6). And the more our reader knows of the environment of the producing life ("the biblical world" of nature, religion, ethics, customs, politics, the arts, literature, agriculture, business, industry, sports, leisure), the more that environment will illumine both the producing life and its literature (7). "The first-century Christian community then comes alive" (8), the nucleus in I reappearing in III.

To continue with our analogy, the traveler will no longer be alone in the motel room. There, with and in and from the Bible, will be the biblical personages and peoples, helping interpret the Bible: a kind of group Bible study which the biblical scholar experiences whenever opening Scripture.

In hope of making my analogy even more vivid, I'm going to risk being accused of exaggerating. When I pick up a Bible and read anywhere in it, it's not all that much different from when I pick up a magazine or recent book. In both cases the producing life and language are available to me to help me understand what I'm reading. For more than a half century I have read the Bible daily (the Bible, not versions or translations of it) and, in English, newspapers, magazines, and books. A biblical scholar thinks and feels in the biblical languages, his or her native language, and any other languages she or he may have mastered. The biblical scholar knows not only the languages, but also the life of the peoples for whom those languages were mother-speech.

Now suppose our motel guest is a biblical scholar who picks up a newspaper or a Gideon Bible. Can you see and feel that this traveler's interpretive resources in the interplay of life and literature will not greatly differ whether it is the Bible or the newspaper that's getting the attention?

3. This brings us again to the fully shaded amoeba, "**Application**." Now we have "given," for Bible as well as newspaper, both literature and its producing life. And the "task" in the case of the Bible is to move from *exegesis* (the interplay of the Bible and the life that produced it) to *exposition* (9), relating the biblical life-literature to here-and-now life. The biblical life and literature "together provide two plotting points, enabling lines to be drawn into" our life, our time, our world.

How come, then, people have screamed at me, "You don't know anything about the Bible!" And "What makes you think you know what the Bible says?" and "I think you'd better read the Bible to find out what it actually says!"? It's because they are "pro-life" *literalists*. For them, a few biblical phrases are so sacred, inviolable, as to blank out reason and experience — a psychopathological condition I call "**scribism**." Their reading of "Thou shalt not kill" rules out abortion. When I asked one, "Aren't there two sides to the abortion issue?" the reply was, "Yes, God's and yours." Earlier in this chapter I spoke of violence to truth and people. Can anyone doubt what these screamers would have done to me in the age of the Inquisition? These arrogant opponents of us pro-choicers (who believe it's no business of government to try to coerce the pregnant into giving birth) are using the Bible not as a bridge from ancient to modern life but as a bludgeon with which to beat us. That's not "how life and literature should be related"!

4. So you see, I've eased into the other abuse of the Bible. First, neglect; now, *idolatry:* treating the Bible as a divine *Ding an sich,* "thing in itself" without relation to anything else, even the life that produced it. The canon of these bibliolaters is never the whole canon of Scripture but rather a catena of favorite quotations, verses and phrases used in an authoritarian-magical manner, as though the words had a life of their own, self-sanctioning and self-operating as the will of God. It's ironic that this fundamentalist

literalism is more in the spirit of Islam's veneration of the Qur'an than it is of either traditional Jewish or traditional Christian biblical hermeneutics.[6]

God wants to speak to us all through the Bible, but it is *no timeless, placeless word*. The best it can be is a bridge between its imperfect producing life and our imperfect receiving life, both lives time- and place-bound. "We are anchored in history, and no flights of metaphysical speculation or mystical religion [or, I may add, moralistic or legalistic dogma] can be allowed to cut the cable."[7]

5. I mustn't close without a caveat. My dictum that sin is anything extended far enough in a straight line includes hermeneutics. One can so overemphasize the life-to-literature-to-life message that **the biblical text** itself gets lost in historicism, sociologism, anthropologism, and psychologism. Whenever this happens in the history of literature, a *backlash* appears. Instances are the A.D. 1900 founding of the Biblical Seminary of New York (now New York Theological Seminary), to give the closest possible attention to the text by inductive method; the 1941 launching of the New Criticism (with the publication of John Crowe Ransom's *The New Criticism* and his subsequent founding of the *Kenyon Review*) to promote close textual analysis, the text existing as an object in itself, to be explored in its own terms, without much attention to author and originating life; and the post–World War II Canonical Criticism, assuming the biblical canon and the essential structure of its

6. One corrective to literalism is to ask this series of questions on a grid, the verticals being "then" and "now" and the horizontals, "event" and "interpretation." Convert to an interrogative series and we have this: What happened? How did they understand what happened? What is happening? How do we understand what's happening in the light of (1) today and (2) what happened and (3) how they understood what happened?

7. The quotation from W. R. Mathews stands alone on the page after the title page of my Ph.D. dissertation, "Sanctions in the Control-Literature of Postapostolic-Precatholic Christian Leaders" (Chicago: University of Chicago, 1954). The prominence I gave it there reveals my struggles against bibliolatry first in myself, then in others.

sixty-six books as traditionally conceived (though with many differences among the scholars of this movement).

A change of preposition will sum up what I've been saying. When reading Scripture in worship, I never say, "Let us listen *to* the Word of God." Rather, I say, "Let us listen *for* the Word of God." That Word comes to us more easily, more directly through the Bible than through any other book. Not the Bible of oracles floating beyond time and space, but rather, the Bible with hair and skin and blood and dirt and ecstasy and fear and hope and love and hate. God speaks to us on the two-way-traffic *bridge* from that life to this. Let the **bridge** do its double job! That is its glory, and it is our shame if we do not cross it both ways.

Documentary integrity

One of my readers threatens to read "no more Thinksheets on inclusive language." But I can't accommodate him: in religion, the issues clustering around this code-trigger expression are as huge and consequential as the issues surrounding the word "abortion." Neither debate will abate in the foreseeable future.

This Thinksheet's thesis is that **no social movement can justify revisionistic rewritings of historical documents: facticity has priority over utility.**

1. A soft-headed, sentimental language-inclusivist, promoting not just the inclusive-language lectionary but the inclusive-language Bible, asked me, "Don't you care that people are hurting?" My response: "Not really. Not in comparison with my caring that documents are hurting, suffering antihistorical bowdlerization. People come and go, and each new generation's right of access to the documentary past should be honored. *No cause aiming at devictimization has the right to victimize* **truth.**"

2. Why am I so tough-minded on this? Because of my intellectual history of personal, even daily, *involvement* in the textual integrity of the Bible. For example, this morning in the Greek-Latin New Testament I hit upon 2 Corinthians 4:2, Paul's apologia that he was "not handling the word of God deceitfully."[1] Some were accusing

1. KJV. NRSV has "falsify[ing] God's word"; NJB, "falsify the word of

him of tampering with Scripture, tendentiously twisting it to his own purposes. His rejoinder was that God had taught him to read Scripture with Christian eyes, without the veils that were on non-Christian Jews (3:14-15) and on pagans (4:3). But whoever "turns to the Lord" (3:16) becomes unveiled, able to see the word of God openly-clearly (cp. "Lord" in 4:5: for Paul, the precise word to express the dominance [lordship] of the Dominus, to whom Christians submit in obedience, as slave to [masculine] master. Language-inclusivists' hatred of this title for Jesus displays a radical alienation from Paul's gospel and thus radically raises the question of the revelational status of Paul's gospel in general and of 2 Corinthians in particular [the integrity of 2 Corinthians, as from Paul, not being questioned by critical scholarship]).

"Lower" (textual) criticism is the science of searching for *ipsissima verba*, the precise words of a document's autograph (original) or of a person's self-expression. The latter was the aim of the Jesus Seminar, to come as close as possible to Jesus' actual words. I was involved in the earliest stage of the University of Chicago's ten-volume critical edition of the New Testament (involving a score of languages and 250 scholars around the world), a project expensive in hours and dollars justifiable only to those who believe it very important to recover and preserve "the best text." To scholars so minded, the very idea of rewriting Scripture to make its ideas more palatable-communicable is a *nightmare*. (In the past sixteen centuries, nobody has tried to sell a rewrite of the Greek New Testament: the problem today is with loose translations falsely claiming to deal honorably, with scholarly integrity, with the original, but in reality pandering to some ideology, the most serious such ideology being feminist egalitarianism.)

3. Let's look at the degrees of current feminist-egalitarian **violation** of the Bible's textual integrity. And let's use the metaphor of *distance*:

God"; NIV and REB, "distort the word of God"; the Greek may also mean "cheapen"; Vulgate, *adultera[te]*; Zink's German has "falsify or contort-warp-pervert-misrepresent [*verdrehen*]."

172

a) The least violation, the least distance from the text itself, is to **throw in a woman** here and there, to lighten up "patriarchalism." Illustration: "the faith of Abraham [and Sarah]." It may sound-look good till you really think about it. The only thing we know about Sarah's personal faith is that she didn't have any: she laughed at a divine announcement (Gen. 18:12). Abraham's faith is well attested in both Testaments — but Sarah's? As far as we know, her faith was derivative from her husband's: she was in all ways, including spiritually, an obedient wife, and thus a feminist horror. How ironic that the language-inclusivists want to tag her along with her husband by adding mention of her here and there in the Bible!

Another instance of throwing in a woman is in Burton Throckmorton's recent stab at inclusive-language Gospels, John 15:1: The vinegrower is not Jesus' Father (as in the original) but his "Father and Mother." Ludicrously, anachronistically, Mother Mary is sent out into the vineyard (by Burton Throckmorton!) to dress vines! Since the context shows the Father to be Father-Judge, Throckmorton makes Mary the Mother-Judge — a theological anomaly! It can't be too long before such efforts to produce an inclusive-language Bible will be as laughed at as was Thomas Bowdler's expurgated Shakespeare almost two centuries ago. His single contribution was unintended: he contributed to our language the verb "to bowdlerize," meaning to abuse historical literature in order to make it more palatable to a contemporary audience.

Less objectionable, from the viewpoint of textual integrity, is *throwing in women* — for example, "brothers [and sisters]" — to displace a Greek generic, though sometimes it displaces the Greek masculine (i.e., in situations in which the presence of women in the address is impossible or at least improbable). "Sons [and daughters]" is usually even a greater stretch. The text's "Men (the masculine word ἄνδρες, *andres,* not the generic word ἄνθρωποι, *anthropi*), brothers" (e.g., Acts 16:2) is still harder to inclusivize, and there's always the need in trying to do so to ask oneself whether there were women in the audience.

173

Easiest is to eliminate, vis-à-vis earlier English renditions, generics (especially "he-his-him") not in the Hebrew-Aramaic-Greek: the Germanic languages use generics (masculine forms for inclusive [masculine and feminine] meanings) somewhat more extensively than do the biblical languages. There can be *no excuse* for continuing this excessive Germanic/English usage of the generic.

b) A more serious distance from textual purity is **throwing out a man** or men or the masculine. Among the strategems are to move (1) from singular ("he-his-him") to plural ("they-their-them") or (2) from third to second person ("you-your-you" singular and plural). This is frequent even in the otherwise quite conservative New Revised Standard Version (NRSV). Translators working with this as a guideline will in some instances strain or even break the meaning of the original. Better than "people may . . ." as substitute for "a man may . . ." is "one may . . ." ("a person may . . ." usually being too formal). (3) A third strategem is to move from the masculine to the impersonal, but this will usually add an alien abstract-philosophical cast to the translation.

c) More serious still is the **transcendentalizing** of inclusive language, moving it from horizontal (human and human-human) to vertical (divine and intra-divine). Some inclusivists heighten goddess-references (Old Testament), and some even use "she-hers-her" for the Spirit, which in the text is never feminine (though the main Hebrew word is feminine and the main Greek word is neuter). Some, parallel with adding women to men, add Mother (God) to Father (God). And all inclusivists I've encountered face-to-face and in print consider it no crime to convert, for the feminine, similes (God is "like" a mother bird, for example) to metaphors (e.g., God is our Mother) — though the biblical text never uses a feminine metaphor for God, so far and protected is it from goddess devotion. All of this is *positive* transcendentalizing, adding the feminine to the text or heightening the feminine in the text.

174

d) Most serious is the inclusivists' *negative* transcendentalizing, **throwing out masculine terms-titles for God**. In section 2 I adduced the inclusivists' hatred for "Lord," the Bible's dominance-title for YHWH/Jesus. Feminism's ideological platform includes an anti-dominance (pro-partnership) plank, so all terms signaling dominance — especially "Lord," "King," and "Father" — are taboo. The internal logic of the movement is that since men should not have dominion over women (and children), the gods or divine personages should not domineer over people (note the equivalency of "domineer," "have dominion," "dominate," all on the Latin root for "Lord").

Women's "equality" redefines the bio-role of the androgens vis-à-vis the estrogens: the estrogens remain free to do their (pre)historic thing, but testosterone is no longer free to lead, though that freedom must be provided for if in the future all the hormones are to be free to be and to do, in mutual cooperation — yes, in partnership. Bruce Metzger's introduction to the NRSV does not even mention transcendentalized inclusive language but states the version's horizontal inclusive-language policy. Since I agree on both, I consider the NRSV as "way to go." (The English translation of the new Roman Catholic Church's catechism is more conservative: no inclusive language.)

1995 Supplement

In some mainline churches, censoring the way the Bible speaks of God has taken the form of a verbal hit-list (e.g., never use "he" for God) rigidly imposed on all publication. From that it's only a short step to cleaning up the Bible, a process which indeed is far advanced, without regard for documentary integrity. Pressure on their clergy to conform — despite these churches' preaching of freedom and tolerance! — is becoming ever tighter.

On being free through, in, with, and from the Bible

"Is the Bible any longer of any use — and if so, what?" A highly sophisticated group of Christians in professions other than religion had asked me to lead them in a weekend retreat, and as preparation for them and for me I had asked them to present me with a short list of concerns they'd like to work on, rated in order of perplexity. This question, variously worded, was at the top of almost everybody's list.

Most mainline Christians would not put the Bible problem so bluntly. But except for fundamentalists, who are bibliolatrous,[1] most Protestants have a vague persistent unease, verging on guilt, that they know so little of and about the Bible and make so little use of it in the living of their days.

For many years in beginning public lecture series I've met this mentality head on by detailing the **four freedoms** that an intelligent and world-engaged Christian needs today regarding Scripture:[2]

1. Bibliolatry is the slavish, idolatrous dependence on the text of Scripture as the frozen revelation of God. "Scribism" is my shorthand for this mindset. Scribes, authorities on the text, have their place; I am one of them. But the letter is to be servant, not master, of the spirit. In this sense, Jesus' authority was "not as the scribes" (Mark 1:22; "their scribes," Matt. 7:29). Institution, including sacred text, grows out of experience of the Spirit and is ever in danger of resisting fresh experience of the Spirit.

2. The freedoms prefaced five National Council of Churches lectures (July 29–August 4, 1967, Green Lake, Wis.) on "Conversion, Today, to God and His Kingdom." My lectures sketched "a style of life appropriate to the Christian in this new age . . . how the new Christian, responsive to the new age now being born, can

1. *Freedom **through** the Bible,* to experience it as one's literary liberator. More than any other book in the world's library of sacred writings, the Bible deserves to be called Freedom's Book. It's about freedom from the dead weight and destiny of one's wanderings

---

achieve a **a new freedom to respond to the Word of God,** to what God in each situation is asking." The preface concluded with ten *clues* as to "how the Bible is to be used today in discerning and doing the will of God." As they are pertinent to this chapter, and the intervening twenty-seven years have only deepened my convictions on them, here they are in summary, from the text issued by NCC:

(1) The Bible is worthy of, and should get, the convert's daily attention, so as to be a continuous instrument of the Lord in the formation of the convert's inner and outer life.

(2) More than any other book, the Bible is worthy of, and should get, both minimal and maximal interpretation — i.e., both critical objectivity and devotional subjectivity — so that the convert will be free in, from, and through the Bible.

(3) The convert should give a fair hearing to biblical scholars at points where, for factual reasons, the Bible is wrong or at least wrong for our time: converts, absolutely bound to Jesus Christ as their Lord, are only relatively bound to the Bible, that is, bound to the Bible relative to (a) Jesus Christ, (b) facts as the converts apprehend them, and (c) the existential Word of God — i.e., converts' decisions as to God's will for them in specific situations.

(4) When the converts diverge from Scripture at points where they believe God is asking them to — and humbly but firmly admit their divergence — they may be wrong but they are honest. Where they stick with Scripture, they may be right or wrong and honest or dishonest.

(5) On the Christian way, the Bible is not a lord but a God-given companion and pedagogue that leads us, in each situation, both to the Lord and to the world. (Call this "depth Bible," the daily living of Scripture.)

(6) For purity of Christian willing, profundity of Christian service, and power of Christian witnessing, the Bible is the one book which should and must be used regularly for self-examination and for mutual criticism and reproof.

(7) Because the Bible is a future-oriented book, we enter its heart only through our own eschatology, our own hopes and fears for ourselves, for others, for the world, handling past and present truthfully as we hear and answer the call of Jesus Christ, the Lord of the future.

(8) Since the Bible is primarily a guide for pilgrim feet rather than a mine for the speculations of philosophers and the propositions of theologians, the converts as pilgrims should be wary of the pitfall of using the Bible as an idol rather than only as a pilgrim's aid intended to help them on their way.

(9) The convert can rejoice that the new age of the wrap-around psyche, the total sensorium, is better able to perceive and apprehend the import of the Bible

177

from God, truth, loyalty, honor (the book of Forgiveness); freedom from human oppressions (the book of Exodus); freedom from trans-human malign powers, and from death (the book of Resurrection).

It should surprise no one that America's most innovative, free-wheeling university, Chicago, was started by a Bible teacher who invented Bible study by correspondence and had thousands of Americans studying Hebrew and Greek by mail! The early presidents succeeding William Rainey Harper were, as he was, all professionals in Bible, all biblical scholars, all Bible teachers. But it does surprise almost everyone I mention it to, almost everyone I hear from when I tell it in print.[3]

Why? Because a permissive culture views Scripture not as progressive, which it is, but as oppressive. And because many Bible pushers give the public the impression that the Bible is more worried about control than eager for liberation, for total human freeing from "sin, death, and the devil."[4]

The corrective for these misimpressions is Christians whose lives and words witness to the continual coming of Christ the Liberator through Scripture, Christians who in the way they use the Bible, the way they let God use them through the Bible, "stand fast in the freedom with which Christ has set us free, and refuse to permit themselves to become slaves again" (Gal. 5:1).

2. *Freedom* **in** *the Bible,* to know it. Stop being intimidated by your ignorance! Stop concealing, or flaunting it! You became com-

---

than was the intermediate lineal age of Gutenberg, when people were too impressed with print. Television as a medium, apart from the question of program content, is more a friend than an enemy of biblical understanding.

(10) In the new age our new sophistication about language and communication are freeing us to feel the force of the Bible's truth and the function of the Bible's details as servants of that truth, servants that are not to be allowed to lord it over the truth.

3. As recently in the *University of Chicago Magazine.*

4. This ancient liturgical summation of what the gospel delivers us from appears still in many churches' baptismal rites.

puter-friendly; you can become Bible-friendly. Don't be ashamed to use the "contents" page to find not just little Obadiah but even big John. Join, or form, a Bible group that's serious about a first-level mastery of what's in the Bible, serious and committed to a sound process that both lets the Bible speak for itself and teaches the skill of bridging from then to now.

3. *Freedom* **with** *the Bible,* to live and use it. Must you be a biblical scholar for this? Of course not! You could even be illiterate.[5] And, Lord help us, you might be a biblical scholar free in the Bible (knowing it) but not free with it (not intending to live it, to use its way of seeing the world as your paradigm, your life model).

At a surprise party for my sixtieth birthday, Rabbi Chaim Stern[6] spoke "On *being* Torah, instead of only knowing it." This beloved brother of mine in God could not have been more Jewish. Or more Christian, for at our best and truest, we Christians share the Jewish passion for the Word of God in and through the biblical words. The Bible is an action book, meant by the Spirit and the spirits of its authors and redactors to be lived instead of only studied and thought.

Jesus was that Word, come among us "with hair and skin."[7] In a lesser but not less real sense, we are to be that Word, to be God's teaching, to be Torah. We are to be, according to our various measures by nature and grace, the living Word, "so everybody can know and read it."[8]

In the mid-1930s, before electricity came to rural New York State, I preached morning and evening in many rural churches.

---

5. As was great-grandfather Frederick Elliott, an orphan farmboy, who married Maryette Burton, who read the Bible to him all the way through 33 times until it killed him (i.e., until his heart stopped). Their only child, Almon Burdette, was a lifelong atheist, possibly from aural overexposure to Scripture.

6. The editor of the official prayerbook of Reform Judaism, *Gates of Prayer: The New Union Prayerbook* (New York: Central Conference of American Rabbis, 1975), which has gained astonishing popularity among Christian clergy. This is the centerpiece of a small library of liturgical works he has authored and edited.

7. A typically gutsy expression of Martin Luther.

8. 2 Cor. 3:2. Compare Phillips Brooks's definition of preaching as "the communication of truth through personality."

On the central "pulpit" (i.e., ambo) were two lamps on movable arms, one on each side of the reading desk. For the evening services, the saints soon taught me how to use these contraptions. One lamp I was to swing around so I could read the Bible: I could figure that out for myself. But the other? It was to adjust so the worshipers could best see my face. Word of print, Word of flesh, Word made flesh.[9]

4. *Freedom from the Bible,* to move beyond it without abandoning it. We are not, and never will be, beyond it in the "purity of heart to will one thing,"[10] the Kingdom-Reign-Rule of God "on earth as it is in heaven."[11] But we are milleniums beyond it in time, in cumulative human experience and knowledge, in critical methods of investigation,[12] in multicultural dialogue and global consciousness, in the arts, philosophy, economics, technology, government. What a weird book it would have been to its contemporaries if the Holy Spirit had, to use a phrase the inerrantists love, "preserved it from error" in light of later developments in knowledge!

As for the dogma that infallibility implies inerrancy, it's a latter-day fundamentalist myth, a myth that, ironically, imprisoned me in connection with my liberating conversion experience. Breaking out of that prison was painful for me, and expensive for my career. But the more I became a biblical scholar, the less tenable became the claim of inerrancy and the less logical its lock-in with infallibility. The option of stonewalling, leaving my brains and my honesty outside the issue, died, as did the slippery-slope false argument that giving up inerrancy dooms faith in infallibility. Gradu-

9. Jesus' incarnation, a once-for-all divine event, is honored, not blasphemed, when taken as an image-model for Christian living.

10. A devotional classic, the best-known work of Søren Kierkegaard.

11. The Lord's Prayer couldn't be more Jewish, or more Christian.

12. Not that the earliest Christians knew nothing of the hermeneutics of suspicion. The "open-minded" Bereans applied their critical consciousness to Paul's preaching, daily studying Scripture "to see if what Paul was saying was really true" (Acts 17:11).

ally, the freed prisoner became a joyful basher of the myth of inerrancy. The gloomy prophecy that my faith in the Bible's infallibility would weaken proved the opposite of the truth. Stronger grew my faith that the Bible *infallibly* teaches me about God and leads me to God and the doing of his will.

A homely analogy may help. My beloved wife Loree is certainly not inerrant, errorless, without mistakes; but for a half century I have experienced her as infallible, which is Latin for "unable to fail." Of course she's theoretically able to fail; but as I have found her *unfailing*, in practice it amounts to the same thing. She has never failed to love, to love me even when I have had seizures of husbandly inerrancy, to love me until the seizures have passed, and beyond.

As for abandoning the Bible, I am now further from it than ever before: the dismal prophets were false. For me it's all of a piece: being *free* through, in, with, and from the Bible.

This perspective hears the Bible as issuing a clear and ever-useful call to believers to live joyfully to the glory of God and in the service of humanity within the admonition to tend the good earth as the garden of God. To this end, we should **avoid** the following:

- *scribism,* which takes literature more seriously than life;
- *archaism,* which takes the past more seriously than the present;
- *modernism,* which takes the present more seriously than the past;
- *futurism,* which takes tomorrow more seriously than yesterday or today;
- *traditionalism,* which tries to archaize the present;
- *academicism,* which merely studies the past "objectively";
- and *propositionalism,* which uses Scripture as a builder's supply depot for materials to construct a castle of ideas which then, in their articulation, are invested with divine authority.

Much can be *learned* from Scripture, enough for salvation in all its dimensions; little can be *proved* from Scripture, but that little is vital; all should be brought to the bar of Scripture, to be *tested* by the biblical vision, the Word's way of seeing, and living in, the world.

"On the lookout to welcome the Reign of God"

What's wrong? Maybe the model is too small

Each day my ten-minute reading in the Qur'an precedes my ten-minute reading in the history of science.[1] This is having some peculiar effects on my intellectual formation. Time and again Western scientists have had to forsake beloved theories because further data and new-data-caused fresh hypotheses have shown up the former theories-models as *too small*. ("Build thee more stately mansions, O my soul," ever says the chambered nautilus of science.)

For instance? Well, take non-Euclidean geometry, which finally in our time successfully challenged millenia-sacred Euclid for failure to deal with curves: Euclid's plain-and-solid-geometry model was *too small* to encompass curvatures. On the larger scale, straight lines were shown to be circles, and vice versa (about the same time that light waves were shown to behave like particles, and vice versa). Come 1915, Einstein proved gravity to be non-Euclidean, so — despite our impression of it — space itself is non-Euclidean. Our eyes see in straight lines on earth, which looks flat — a double deception, for our eyes seduce us into believing in a video model which "for practical purposes" is adequate but is actually, within the reach of mind, *too small*. The reach of mind, mind itself surmises, is too short to create an adequate mega-model of reality, a scientific conviction that joins with good religion in teaching humility.

---

1. 17 February 1992. My daily-reading shelf always includes a number of great books, each of which gets ten minutes a day. On this regimen one can "do" most of the world's classics in only a few decades.

One more instance? Chaos theory, the baby in the household of the natural sciences, seems to have convinced the majority of theoretical physicists that chaos is an illusion created by working with *too small* a model. Extend (by computer) the field of vision, and thus the model, and chaos fits into a hitherto undreamed of dimension of order.

You wouldn't have guessed it, but this Thinksheet is a meditation on **Mark 15:43,** which I translate thus: "Joseph of Arimathea . . . was **on the lookout to welcome the Reign of God.**" (See vv. 42-46 for context.)

1. Joseph, by his own courageous action in facing Pilate for Jesus' corpse, had the dead Jesus both on his hands and in his arms — a pietá no sculptor, as far as I know, has ever rendered. To his political courage was added his emotional courage in facing the agony of the "deposition" (the technical Latin term for taking Jesus' body down from the cross) and the burial. This was the black background for his bright hope. To see only that Jesus was dead, and so probably also his mission and movement, would have been *too small* a model of what was happening. He had made an anticipatory, prophylactic rejection of that model in favor of continuing to be "on the lookout to welcome the Reign of God." In this he was a proto-martyr, willing to go beyond Z in his witness, himself a model for oncoming Christian martyrs and indeed all Christian sufferers in body, mind, spirit, and relationships. And the resurrection of Jesus rewarded his refusal to accept too small a model.

2. When guests are coming to your house for dinner, you want to be right there, right on the spot, right at the door to welcome them, so you are on the lookout for them. Perhaps another member of the family is the designated lookout, to shout "They're here!" *Two actions,* not one: being on the lookout, and welcoming.

The Reign-Rule-Kingdom of God will come whether or not we're on the lookout for it. But being on the lookout for it is so vital as to constitute a definition of the Christian life — thus, many of Jesus' parables say "Be ready!" This hit me when, looking at an old Bible of mine (a 1935 printing of Moffatt's 1922 translation),

I saw that in Mark 15:43 these words were underlined: "on the outlook for the Reign of God." And in the margin a half century ago I'd written in red, *theme of Bible!* While the Bible is secondarily an ancient book throwing light on present and future, it is primarily a book whose light bathes us both from the future and, as a mirror behind us, from the past. Or rather it does so if we are facing the future, persuaded that the best *a)* has not yet arrived but *b)* is in the process of coming. That, only that, is biblical living. That, only that, is praying the Lord's Prayer with one's being.

3. How can I get from "outlook" to "lookout"? I translated the British idiom into American. Why did Moffatt capitalize *Reign*? To signal that it's a technical term, a metaphor that no one English word can do justice to. "Kingdom" didn't quite do it for him, a Brit living in a *kingdom,* a (highly qualified!) monarchic *realm* — for "-dom" connotes territory. Why didn't he choose *kingship,* then, a meaning closer to the biblical? Probably because it collapses the whole semantic field into a person, the person of the King. Joseph of Arimathea knew that God's kingship, kingness, is an eternal-present fact, not something to be on the lookout for. The trick is to find an English word capable of representing the tension between the eternal-present fact that God is King and the temporal-present fact that for the time being he refuses to function as King over territories with other rules, namely, the hearts-minds of angels and humans who have not submitted to his rule, his dominion, his reign. Thus for Moffatt, "Reign" covers both God's being as King and his functioning as King. This Scottish master of English wanted to re-mint the biblical idea, because "Kingdom" had worn too smooth to feel and read.

My practice varies with context: usually just "Kingdom," sometimes "Rule" or "Realm" or "Kingdom-Rule-Realm" (or some other arrangement of the three). Or "Sovereignty."

4. Where did I get **"welcome"** in my phrase, "on the lookout to welcome"? It's a normal street-meaning of προσ-δεχ = (*pros-dech-* [Vulgate, *expectans*]). So I went on a hunt for it throughout the history of Mark translation, and was astonished to discover that it's never been

used! Instead, we have "look for," "wait for," and (only in the old Catholic Bible, following the Latin) "expect." The NRSV's "waiting expectantly" improves on the RSV's "looking for." The REB's "looked forward to" revises the NEB's "eagerly awaiting" — proof that revisions are sometimes the reverse of improvement.

Another astonishment: no published version or translation uses "ready for." Phillips' "prepared to accept" comes close but is not as good. "Ready for" is in direct line with Jesus' frequent "Be ready!" Let's try it: "Joseph of Arimathea **was ready to welcome the Reign of God.**" But "ready" meaning "prepared" fails to catch the mood of eagerness.

5. Well, what is Joseph's *mood,* the mood he models for us in our dark times when in our arms are the corpses of our hopes? As a disciple of Jesus he's in the shock of grief, the pain of mourning, but our text — instead of mentioning that — directs our attention to his attending to the future, for which each moment (even the moment of his Master's earthly ending) is a new beginning. While attending to, seeing to, the deposition and burial, he was attending to, paying attention toward, God's future. While preparing Jesus' body for burial, he was unwittingly preparing his own soul for Easter and Pentecost.

Conflating the four Gospels, we have Nicodemus (of John 3) helping Joseph: imagine the conversation between these two Jewish leaders who'd been secret disciples of Jesus and now were out of the closet. In the open, they'd been working with a model, the Jewish authority-Sanhedrin-council that was to prove *too small* for the new community they had become a part of in becoming followers of Jesus.

6. For this new community, even the mighty Roman Empire was *too small* a model. Far more than he could have known, Joseph's asking Pilate for Jesus' body was an inchoate religious and political **subversive** activity. "The kingdom of the world has become the kingdom of our Lord and of his Messiah" (Rev. 11:15 NRSV). It took courage to come under the suspicion of Pilate, whose rule of

terror was "When in doubt, crucify" (which he did to five thousand Jews on a single day). But when the political prospect was for Rome's continued brutal tyranny, Joseph's theo-political outlook was for the reign of God to replace the rule of Caesar. To pray the Lord's Prayer with your whole being is to be subversive, on the lookout for a better government, a better world of bread and forgiveness and deliverance from evil.

7. Said a Manhattan Jew to me a few days ago, "How different this city, this country, would be if you Christians took Jesus more seriously!" He understood the essential **radicality** of our faith, which finds actual religious, social, political, economic, and cultural categories and models *too small.*

1995 Supplement

1. Why were the book title, *Your God Is Too Small,* and the play title, "My Arm Too Short to Reach to God," so powerful and memorable? Because both *a)* connected deity and humanity and *b)* used a simple metaphor from everyone's daily experience, viz., **size**. That is the metaphor this chapter rings the changes on.

2. Of the 93 "semantic domains," categories of meaning, in Johannes P. Louw et al., *Greek-English Lexicon of the New Testament Based on Semantic Domains* (New York: United Bible Societies, 1988), vol. 2, six have to do with **space**, and follow close on the subcategory of **size** (viz., "large, small": what's the size of something "relative to the norm for the class of objects in question"?). Size and space are warp and woof: obviously, a penny blocking the sun's light from your eye both is (in the experience of the moment) and (objectively) is not larger than the sun.

3. Our freedom includes the fact that for us, size and distance are *within our power.* For Joseph of Arimathea, the Reign of God was huge and close, the Realm of Caesar small and far.

God prays the Gestalt Prayer

Fritz Perls, father of Gestalt psychotherapy and an atheist, during the time I was studying with him puckishly shaped the original version of what he sardonically, yet plaintively, called "The Gestalt Prayer."[1] At meals with him I picked at it, and finally came up with the lines below, to which I have added Scriptures for your biblical meditation.

You may want to write a personal prayer using my revised Gestalt prayer as a flow-outline.

Gen. 1:31–2:3 John 3:16	I do **My** thing
Gen. 1:26-28 Gal. 5:1	and you do your thing.
Isa. 55:8f Rom. 9:14-21	I am not in this world to fulfill your expectations

---

1. The Perls original: "I do my thing, and you do your thing. I am not in this world to fulfill your expectations, and you are not in this world to fulfill my expectations. I am I and you are you. [While I was with Perls, he added this:] And if perchance we meet, it's beautiful. If not, it can't be helped."

Deut. 11:13-17; 13:1-4 Isa. 1:18-20; 55:6f John 15:10f Acts 4:18-20; 5:27-29	and you **are** in this world to fulfill **My** expectations.
Ex. 3:6, 13-15 John 6:35; 15:1	I am I
Gen. 3:6 Ezek. 2:1 Acts 26:16	and you are you.
1 Sam. 18:1 SS. 8:6f John 14:18-22	And if perchance we meet, it's beautiful.
Amos 7:14f. Isa. 7:14; 9:2-6 Matt. 11:28-30	If not, it **can** be helped.[2]
Hos. 6.3f. Luke 18.23-27	**If you'd rather not, it can't be helped.**[3]

2. Bleary-eyed, chain-smoking **Fritz** was helpful with his *pessimistic* realism: human beings are self-defeating when they make outsize demands on relationships. But in my revision, **God** is more helpful with his *optimistic* realism: grace, on the condition of repentance, offers reconciliation, "meeting," even to "the foremost" of "sinners" (1 Tim. 1:15).

3. Whether or not your home is your castle, your heart is. **Fritz** cannot, and **God** will not, coerce you into letting down your drawbridge for the entry of the Other.

Jacob's ladder: with or without angels?

Metaphors as symbolic ladders to the larger life

IMPETUS: For decades I've eagerly read Owen *Barfield* and Kenneth *Burke,* and this Thinksheet began when a **metaphor** popped into or out of my head as a visual to relate them: Barfield's ladder has angels on it, Burke says we must be satisfied with only the ladder. Some of my thoughts here come from their meeting each other, and others, at Drew University, on "Literature and Religion," as reported in the *Journal of the American Academy of Religion*.[1]

    Kenneth Burke first impressed me in 1945, when I read his *Grammar of Motives,* published that year. He was at work at what later came to be called metalanguage, the reality structures from which language emerges and which language reflects, and how we move and are moved (motivated) by words.

    Owen Barfield was a member of an antipositivist, open-to-the-transcendent Thursday evening group that included C. S. Lewis, J. R. R. Tolkien, and Charles Williams — Christian gentlemen who gave us, respectively, the Narnia tales, the Hobbits, and thin-border novels such as *The Place of the Lion.* Four Englishmen, whether angels or not, running up and down the ladder between literature and religion.

    1. Inevitably, philosophy-theology transposes time-firsts (myth) into mind-firsts (first principles). For example, the first sin

---

1. "On Literature and Religion," *Journal of the American Academy of Religion,* June 1979.

(the apple/apricot, Gen. 3) becomes "original sin." Story precedes proposition The "it" of metaphor precedes its "that" to which it points. So? So be suspicious of the result (Burke), or (Barfield and I agree) view the process as a medium of *God's self-disclosure from within the mind.* Barfield: "Either we accept the real presence of a divine or supernatural agency, or we do not. If we do not, there is not much point in talking about religion."[2] But Burke's logo-logical analysis ("words about words") does sharpen awareness of the fact that mind and spirit operate by symbolic action, in contrast to body-and-matter's nonsymbolic motion. Consider the metaphor of this Thinksheet's title: no metaphor, no ladder — so no "mind" or "spirit." This fact puts a severe limit on deconstruction: a cynicism derivative from it would self-destruct. In a homely figure, the onion has nothing but layers. No tribal language (such as the biblical), no community. No **language-world**, no world. Religion, theology, philosophy, science, art are parallel symbolic modes. I believe the parallels converge in God: that is a faith. Some believe that some of the parallels are unreal: that is another faith — namely, positivism-scientism.

2. Think of metaphors as *dwellings* we live in. I think it was Samuel Johnson who first (!) said we shape our architecture, then it shapes us. I'm sure Coleridge said "language thinks for us," and William Lynch, "images think and are pathways to existence";[3] "Who cares for all the brilliances of the mind if there is no taste of existence in and underneath them?"[4]

3. Our experienced world is a *mix* of perception (by the body's sense) and reflection (by the mind-spirit-soul's "wits" — in the obsolete sense, our inner powers of knowing). Correspondingly, God reveals himself both from without and from within. Take **vision**, for example, a word for what both outer and inner eyes

2. "On Literature and Religion," p. 293.
3. Ibid., p. 302
4. Ibid., p. 295.

do. It's ultimately from the I-E root $\digamma\iota\delta$ (wid), whence also *idea* and (though the dictionaries' eytmologies won't risk saying so) *image,* something you picture to yourself, perhaps then using your body to project into the outer world in forms, sounds, or movements (cp. photo-images, which are chemical or electronic imprints). Here we have a physical-mental pattern that can serve as paradigm for this Thinksheet's first two sections. Our ideas are mental images which easily move into languages as metaphors which easily move back into the inner world as images-visions. I mean this not as physiological reductivism (as materialists who identify mind with brain would "see" it) but as creational reality, the way God "fearfully and wonderfully" has made us. Thought is metaphoric, metaphor is cognition, and the angels are forever climbing up and down the ladders.[5]

4. Notice these **evasions** of religious commitment. Call them "It's onlies":

a) It's only *matter.* Science itself has been progressively weakening the materialists' case, but mind=brain=mind articles continue to appear in the popular press.

b) It's only *story.* The narratological dodge is common among mythologists (Joseph Campbell, not Mircea Eliade) and not uncommon among biblical scholars (but not the National Organization of Bible Storytellers).

c) It's only *history.* The historical-critical method can degenerate into mere historicism.

d) It's only *poetry.* This estheticism substitutes, for devotional transcendence, metaphorical transcendence (poets' power to put halos around words, auras around poems). This springs from, and plays up to, the human urge to merge, the mystical tendency, celebrated in E. E. Aubrey's phrase "ontological continuity in the poetic dimension" (in contrast to "epistemological discontinuity in the prosaic dimension"). While the

5. Not surprisingly, "wis-dom" has the same root.

191

exaggeration that language and knowledge are "only" poetry is illogical, the illusion seems plausible in the light of metaphor's omnipresence in thought-and-language. Take an illustration from biology: the "cell" was so named in 1655 because in a microscope a bunch of them looked to a scientist like monks' cells; and in 1831, somebody called the cell's center a little nut (Latin, "nucleus").

5. In tension with our urge to merge is our urge to **climb**, for which we need ladders (the metaphor of this Thinksheet's title) — to climb *a*) up out of messes we make or fall into, *b*) up into the creative assertion of self, *c*) to God. The first category of climbing often uses, as little ladders, wise sayings (most of which are metaphor-rich) or personal metaphoric illuminations, both often humorous. "Dear Ann Landers: I moved in with a man thinking he'd marry me, but he won't. I get it now: a man won't buy a cow if he can get milk free."

6. As a *parable* is an extended metaphor, an *allegory* is an extended parable. And the point of allegory? It is, said Bunyan of his allegories, to "read thyself" (which George Herbert said is the point of Bible reading; and it's the first point of reading Mel Yosso's "transcultural allegories," the second point being obvious in the adjective). Puritan literature — Bunyan and William Law, for example — is thick with fictional characters functioning as **virtue/vice metaphors**. In his preface to *Pilgrim's Progress* Bunyan asks, Why can't I use metaphors, seeing that God, the prophets, Jesus, and Paul do? "By metaphors I speak. / Were not God's laws in older times held forth / By types, shadows, and metaphors?" (Hos. 12:10 is his prooftext: God says "I have spoken by the prophets, . . . multiplied visions, . . . used similitudes."[6]) In this "characters" Puritan edificatory literature, the reader doesn't climb the hermeneutic ladder upward by allegorizing life's particularities

6. The last phrase is not in the NRSV, but in Tanakh as "spoke parables"; revelation by "similitudes" is frequent in the Qur'an.

into generalizations, but downward to discover the spiritual meaning of life's particularities, as in the Midrashim (in contrast to most
Christian typology, which uses the former style).

7. Maya Angelou's "A Rock, A River, A Tree," written for
President Clinton's inauguration, was a metaphoric ladder up into
a larger life for Americans and America. She'd taken her Bible with
her on a long retreat to write it for the occasion, and it's rich with
biblical power: I count twenty-seven allusions. Clinton's inaugural
address had five biblical allusions and a direct reference, Galations
6:9 (which Hillary held the Bible open to, for the hand-placing):
"The Scripture says, 'And let us not be weary in well-doing, for in
due season, we shall reap, if we faint not.'"[7] Then, alluding to verse
2, he added: "We . . . must care for one another." Bill Safire, a Jew,
looked up the passage and found in verse 5 another Clinton accent:
"all must carry their own loads" (NRSV) but didn't mention verse
2, from which the president extrapolated this: "America cannot and
should not bear the world's burdens alone."

8. *Philosophy-theology* is story rarified into **idea** — such as the
Trinity. *Poetry* is idea or thing intensified into **metaphor** — in
Angelou's poem, thing(s). *Dingedicht* (thing-poem) is a prominent
mode in German literature (and powerfully used, among American
poets, by Wallace Stevens; cp. also Norman Maclean's story-and-
film, *A River Runs Through It*).

Genesis 28:12: May there be angel traffic on our metaphoric
ladders, extending our vision and challenging us to alter our lives
by pondering parallels.

7. NRSV, "do not give up."

The Holy One is more than lover

OCCASION: Two experiences yesterday:[1] a reading, and a conference. The reading was of the adoption, a few days ago, by an Episcopal diocese, of a "Report on Sexuality." The report uses the divine sanction for "love" (undefined), in the hope of smothering the fires of the **homosexuality** conflict; but a theological analysis reveals that the effect is to drag God down into "love": God is so reduced to "love" that, operationally, *Love is god.*

"God measures human relationships by the presence and activity of love in them, and not by whether or not they unite persons of different sexes. . . . The quality of any relationship is determined solely by love. . . . The perceived Scriptural obstacles to such an affirmation rest on incomplete understandings of the meaning and purpose of the pertinent passages." The report pushes its luck too far in condemning heterosexual marriage in a church that does not practice homosexual marriage: "The Church cannot justly bless or celebrate any human relationship while it devalues and denies other relationships in which love is likewise made manifest."

Here is theodynamics prostituted to psychosociodynamics, which first defined and then **divinized "Love,"** and now claims that this idol is the biblical God! The tools used in the crafting of this idol are different from those of the idol-makers Isaiah mocks (Isa. 40:18-31: "trust in the LORD," who "is not like an idol"; cp. Hos. 13:2; Ex. 20:3-5; Hab.

1. 12 November 1993.

194

2:18-20, which ends on this note: "The LORD is in his **holy** Temple; let everyone on earth be silent in his presence").

The report is asking the church to bless homosexual practice, which canonically has a status lower than war: the biblical God is sometimes said to bless war, never homosexuality. The *sanctional range* for churches is to bless, to permit ("accept what cannot be changed"), and to condemn. Here's how it stands with homosexual practice: a) accept scriptural light and it cannot be *blessed* (no matter how disingenuously clever the report's hermeneuts); b) accept modern light and it cannot be *condemned;* c) converge both lights, and it should be *permitted.*

So much for the reading, now for the conference:

Yesterday, some 120 pastoral counselors, psychotherapists, psychologists, chaplains, physicians, and social workers gathered here in Craigville for a conference on "Spiritual Dimensions of Psychotherapy." The key speaker, a professor of pastoral psychology in a theological seminary, performed as I expected him to: *positively,* he praised the biblical God's *tangency* as the **Healing Lover,** to the range of the audience's occupational commitments as people-helpers, care-givers. Nothing wrong with that. In fact, why bother to come if he couldn't show tangency (long-called, in liberal religion, "relevance")? To his credit, he once even mentioned that "Christianity says" that God so intended tangency (though the speaker did not use this geometric image) as to become incarnate in Jesus. Wryly I mused, "Voltaire was right about this speaker: he has made God in his own image."

That dismal musing deepened as the speaker treated *negatively* the non-"love" aspects of the biblical God:

1. God's *power* side as **Lord and King and Father,** God's *dark* side as **Judge,** and God's *hidden* side as **Mystery.** All these join with God's *warm* side as **Savior and Healing Lover** to constitute his holiness, **the Holy One** of this Thinksheet's title.

2. Psychologized theology, sociologized theology, politicized theology are doubly alike. Not only do they expatiate each on its one particular tangency in a manner for which the expression "off on a tangent" is appropriate, but they also *denigrate* the other aspects

195

of the divine, in each case especially the aspect at greatest distance from the emphasized point of tangency.

3. Psychotheologians first translate **theo- into psycho- terms**. Then, as the disease advances, they stand within psychology looking at theology — from, as it were, "Psychotherapeutic Dimensions of Theology" to (the conference title) "Spiritual Dimensions of Psychotherapy." No criticism here of the conference planners: they titled just right to draw the folk they wanted to draw. And their flier used an apt and true quotation from the keynote speaker, Merle R. Jordan of Boston University School of Theology: "If the counselor is not open to hearing theological meanings in the stories of persons who come for personal liberation, then he or she may only be adding to the person's barriers to freedom."

4. Ideas have consequences, and so do their distortions. What happens when theology becomes captive to psychology? The captivity appears as further **alienation** from the biblical God and thus also from church/synagogue, whether the distortions are by amnesia-producing omissions or by anger-producing misrepresentations. (A parallel: children indoctrinated with gender-"correct" language for God are thereby alienated from the biblical God, whom the Bible never represents by any feminine names or even feminine metaphors, though by a few feminine similes.) I was so concerned about what our speaker was doing that I had to remonstrate with him, first privately and then in plenum, that, ironically, in a conference intended to draw psychology and theology closer together, his cheap shots at the non-"love" aspects of God were deepening some participants' alienation from Bible and church. (I saw many heads nod approval when, time and again, he kicked one or another of those aspects.) In plenum I said, "Jesus used the *full reservoir* and circle of biblical God-images (with their appropriate tangencies to human existence private and public)."

5. **"Holy"** (with its cognates) is the central code- or signal-word for biblical religion. To miss it is to miss biblical religion. To misunderstand it is to misunderstand biblical religion. To co-opt it for some extraneous meaning, such as "wholeness," is to pros-

196

titute it (in the instance cited, an error abetted by the fact that the English words "holy" and "whole" share a [Teutonic] root[2]).

In *Diary of a Seducer*, Kierkegaard laughs at the reduction of holiness (theology) to *love* (ethics), the very reduction I railed against yesterday. Kierkegaard profoundly grasped the biblical meaning (as intuition, feeling, idea) of holiness. He was equally adamant against reducing holiness to *righteousness,* the cool side of ethics as love is its warm side. But he saw righteousness as implicit in God's holiness as Judge, whose justice constitutes the divine cosmic and human order and maintains that order jurisprudentially, by revelation and enforcement of his will expressive of his nature.[3] Note that as psychotheology reduces holiness to love, sociopolitical theology reduces it to righteousness. And as love deteriorates into sensuality and sentimentality, righteousness rots into self-righteousness, moralism, legalism (e.g., currently the rigorous enforcement, on some campuses, of politically-correct [PC] speech).

A further characteristic of psychotheology is that it denigrates, as impertinent to an "authentic" image of God, such holiness-associated feelings as *fear, anxiety, guilt,* and *shame.* These are treated as servants of hell rather than of heaven. Scrupulousness against these feelings is characteristic not just of psychotheology but of liberal religion in general, rendering it vulnerable to utopian collapse (as occurred in the 1960s with the death-of-God movement, when, face-to-face with Shoah-Holocaust, liberal theologians found it impossible to continue to believe that "a loving God" rules the world). Mystery, evil, and sin are given too light a reading to sustain the **heaviness** of history and of the human heart.

6. In current liberal religion, the name of God in this Think-sheet's title has a circumlocutory force: to evade gender-referencing of God. In liturgy — prayers, litanies, even some rewritten hymns — **the Holy One** has been replacing "Lord," "Father," "King," "Son of God." If you know what's up, it makes you smile where

2. For an overview, read James Muilenberg's magisterial article, "Holiness," in *Interpreter's Dictionary of the Bible* (Nashville: Abingdon, 1962), 2:616-25.
3. For a distich paralleling justice and righteousness, see Isa. 5:16.

the surrogate phrase does not twist the meaning, and frown where it does. Biblically, this inclusive-language move is a disgrace, for it deludes the unwary into imagining that in Scripture this is a general title for God, whereas the truth is that it's rare and always with special contextual meaning. And sometimes the reference is to Jesus, not to God-in-general. How silly and sad to try to erect firewalls of scruple against the biblical lexicon!

7. An *empiricism* denying revelation will speak, as psychotheology does, of **dysfunction** rather than of sin and evil. The tools for handling "dysfunction" do not include repentance, faith, atonement, incarnation, resurrection, the life eternal.[4]

1995 Supplement

Frequently, of late, in liberal-church liturgies, I've seen the *Nunc dimittis* (Luke 2:29-32) bastardized as "Holy One, now let your servant . . . ." Consider:

1. The owner/slave metaphor is **ruined**. Instead of using the usual NT term regularly translated "Lord," Luke here uses the usual term for slave-owner (which gets transliterated into English as "despot"). Had he used "Lord," the metaphor would still have been intact, for *Kyrios* can mean slave-owner. But "Holy One" here is janglingly ignorant and disruptive.

2. "Holy One" is, in the reader's mind, **polluted**. It's a NT word for the messiah, and thus has Simeon praying to the baby in his arms! Before that, it's more than a dozen times in Isaiah, where no context is slave-owner/slave.

4. Why do so many Thinksheets have an abrupt ending, unlike an essay? Because of their intention as explained in my introduction, and because their thinking ends at page-end or at two-page sheet-end. It's not how I end the Thinksheet, but how you conclude it in your mind as you ponder its message.

"The offended Power"

Lincoln's language in the phrase above was, I'd say, biblical-elevated, or Christian-Stoic-rhetorical. Often I've mulled over the phrase I'm mulling over again in this Thinksheet — this time, in the context of Jesus' question (the title of this year's Craigville Colloquy[1]) "Who do YOU say I am?"

1. The context was Lincoln's call for a national day of prayer during the Civil War: "We have grown in numbers, wealth and power, as no other nation has grown. But we have *forgotten* God. We have forgotten the *gracious* hand which preserved us in peace . . . ; we have *vainly* imagined . . . that all these blessings were produced by some superior wisdom and virtue of our own. *Intoxicated* with unbroken success, we have become too *self-sufficient* to feel the necessity of redeeming and preserving *grace,* too *proud* to pray to the God that made us! It behooves us, then, to *humble* ourselves before the offended Power, to *confess* our national sins, and to pray for clemency and *forgiveness.*" (Italics mine.)

2. "Power" is God's only title in this passage: Lincoln was a man of *power,* driven by the social necessity of using it (abusing it, his assassin shouted), saddened by its easy corruptibility, steady in his sense that all human power is only under-power, power "under God" the **Over-Power**. Our human powers to persuade and coerce, being

1. 1992.

199

modeled on the divine, are gifts we are responsible to use according to the divine nature and commission: we are accountable to God for the proper use, and the nonuse, and the abuse, of both.

3. Lincoln was a master of both *persuasion* and *coercion,* and sensitive to his stewardship of both. He strove mightily to persuade the South, then coerced it into remaining in the Union: he could have avoided the war, but believed that war was less serious than secession. Yet he was not chauvinistic in his theologizing of the crisis: his sense that both sides were under God's judgment was stronger than his conviction that his decision for violent defense of the Union was right.

4. In Lincoln's mind, our nation has *theological standing.* It exists (has ontological substance) under the eye and in the hand of God, Observer-Judge of its political (not just its religious and private) life. In Martin Marty's shocking phrases in the April Fool's issue of *The Christian Century*, he's the Cosmic Snoop, the Gotcha God. (Unfortunately, unlike Lincoln, Marty treats irreverently this dimension in the divine.) In the words of the black spiritual, "He sees all I do, he hears all I say, my Lord's awatchin' all the time." That's the **ominous** sense of the Presence. But another: "Nobody knows like Jesus." That's the **gracious** sense of the Presence. You can have the latter without the former, but yours in that case is not the biblical God.

5. Why ominous? Because *offendable.* But not ominous, threatening, if an offended Weakness. Ominous because "the offended Power" who responds destructively to offense when the offender is impenitent, unhumble. To live in prophetic-biblical fear of the Almighty is to avoid thinking-saying-doing anything that might rile God up, offend him: to live in love of the Algracious is to behave with the design of pleasing God, as one delights to delight the Beloved.

6. The Jesus who asked the question that is the Craigville Colloquy theme — "Who do YOU say I am?" — should get from us this (among other responses): "You are one who steadily lives in the Presence of the **Almighty-Algracious**, the offendable One

200

who destroys but prefers to forgive." Long ago in a Thinksheet I detailed what, in my opinion, we can know of "Jesus' 'Consciousness.'" Because it's postbiblical-Augustinian and modern, the question of Jesus' self-aware interiority can't mine from the Gospels anything like a full answer. But we can say with certainty that Jesus lived, and taught us to live, in fear and love of God. In this, Lincoln was a faithful disciple. "Clemency and forgiveness" are available if we "confess our [personal, interpersonal, collective] national sins," at heart the sin that "we have forgotten God." Otherwise, doom by "the offended Power."

1995 Supplement

Comment on §1 The whole nation, North and South, had a common Enemy, viz., the offended (because forgotten) Power. Both sides were under divine judgment for having committed **amnesia**. Converting Enemy to Friend was simple though not easy: remember (repent of having forgotten), then act appropriately to the character of the Remembered One: "humble ourselves . . . , confess our national sins, . . . pray for . . . forgiveness."

Comment on §2 Lincoln experienced the *United* States as doubly united: theologically (as "under" divine promise and threat) and politically (the states "alongside" one another, in a partnership of equals maintained by a strong central government). The integration of religion and statecraft (a philosophical conviction), not "the separation of church and state" (merely an institutional policy). With our present "one nation under blank," we should not be surprised at a decline of civility and rise of prejudice.

Comment on §3-§6 Living, as did Jesus, "in fear and love of God" fully presses upon us the divine invitation and demand that we live **responsibly** with all our powers in all our relationships personal, economic, social, political. Democracy cannot work without general public awareness of, and obedience to, the Over-Power.

Scrupulous godlessness

When you listen or read intelligently, you use both the hermeneutics of *attention* — asking, "What's here, and why?" — and the hermeneutics of *suspicion* — asking, "What's not here, and why not?" When the children asked Rainer Maria Rilke to tell a story and, for a change, leave God out, they were fulfilling neither canon of interpretation. They had attended to the fact that Rilke mentioned God in all his *Stories of God for Girls and Boys,* but they didn't ask him why; nor did they ask what he was leaving out, and why.[1]

What occasioned this Thinksheet was my attending to the fact that increasingly, **God is left out** of public discourse in our country; and I am asking why. Why should I leave the G-word to the fundamentalists? Further, I've noticed "what's here" instead of, as a surrogate or holophrase for, God — and why. My consciousness is raised on all four questions, so I pass the test of an intelligent hearer/reader on this topic.

1. Even among the religiously committed there's been little consciousness-raising on this topic. Gallup says 97% of Americans think God is the center of reality: I ask, Why then is God seldom even on the periphery of conversations? I answer, Because the populace is taught (in our public schools and by the media) **to leave God out** of conversation (and thus out of consideration: what you don't talk about

---

1. Rilke's response was that God cannot be kept out of the story. If you don't put him in, he'll come in after the last period.

doesn't get your attention, and what doesn't get your attention is **not real** for you). When one's consciousness is not theocentric, something else is central; and if one is passionate about that something else, God will not come in even peripherally, and one will fall under the divine curse along with "the nations[2] that forget God" (Ps. 9:17). But in those who have sentimentalized God, which means almost everybody in our liberal churches, fear of this divine curse has little or no force. As for the psychotheology of God wanting our attention, consider the tragedy of a schoolroom in which the *teacher* fails to get and hold the pupils' attention; consider, too, the tragedy of a *lover* jilted, scorned, forgotten.

2. The **godless** leave God out for the same reason I leave out learning Tibetan: given the vast spread of things I don't know, I can't think of any reason why I should learn Tibetan. Just so, the godless are undermotivated to believe in God, to put God into their thinking and their lives. Thus they are incapable of personal "scrupulous godlessness." (Romans who got *scruples* — small, sharp stones — in their sandals had walking discomfort; ethically, scruples are feelingful ideas that inhibit action [call them also inhibition or qualms].) If the godless have a scruple, or conviction, against hypocrisy, they will scruple to put God in opportunistically, for social-political effects; but the unethical godless will use God-talk to ingratiate themselves with the godly.

The reverse is true of the **godly** (believers in God). They are scrupulous to put God in, to "keep the Lord ever before their eyes" and on their lips and word processors. Their social-political temptation is to leave God out occasionally — they think they or their message will "get further," if they are God-silent — or even to leave God out generally — they make no public God-reference as a matter of policy, arguing that "some might be offended" and even that "it would be unfair in our pluralistic culture." A Christian form of the latter is Christians who leave Jesus out because "there

2. Alternatives for "nations": "pagans" (Moffatt), "heathens" (Knox), "all those" (TEV). . . . The next verse is a warning not to forget the poor.

are or might be Jews present." (Some anti-Semites twist this into an argument for excluding Jews, even for executing them!)

3. *Scrupulosity* is an *ethical* term; psychiatrically it means compulsive, life-crippling behavior (such as perpetual handwashing); popularly, having scruples means you haven't been "liberated": like guilt, scruples are bad and something to be gotten rid of. A **taboo** is a sacrally motivated scruple, or at least a scruple with sacred overtones. What makes the abortion controversy so hairy and even scary is that so many "pro-life" advocates are frenetic, fanatic believers in the sacredness of the fetus. I am attacking here what I consider a life-crippling, or at least life-impoverishing, taboo of some of the godly; namely, leaving God out of public communication if not also of private conversation.

4. Caution! Sin is anything extended far enough in a straight line, and the compulsive God-talker is a case in the psychiatric sense, a public nuisance. Naturally, *compulsive* God-silents and *compulsive* God-talkers use each other as bad examples: "You want me to be like *them*?" Would that the extremes would cancel, instead of thus reinforcing, each other!

Rather, I'm appealing to the godly to be "ready" (1 Pet. 3:15) for God-openings, to be concerned to improve your skills of communicating the Word (narrowly here, the G-word, speaking of God for God), to be prophetic without giving unnecessary offense (but don't imagine that you can be a Christian with your mouth without ever giving *any* offense). The more you practice the presence and purpose of God, the more fire you'll have in your bones (Jer. 20:9), the more **prophetic urge** and urgency to speak of and for God.[3]

5. I'm addressing a cultural phenomenon that amounts to a conspiracy of silence against mentioning God. In the case of *believ-*

3. Remain speechless, says Jesus, and "the stones would shout out" (Luke 19:40). And this from Paul: "Woe to me if I do not proclaim the gospel!" (1 Cor. 9:16).

ers, the reasons are timidity (the fear of confronting, "what would happen if I . . . ?" and "I don't want to seem holier-than-thou"), weak conviction, theological confusion, and lack of communication skills. As for *unbelievers,* **aggressive secularism** is on the rise: the less God is spoken of in the culture, the easier it is to join the partisans who want to quash all God-talk and who use the case of semi-literate televangelists to strengthen their cause. The public, even the believing public, is poorly defended against this anti-God campaign; for almost the entire public, as I cannot tire of saying, learned in our public schools to get along without God-talk.

6. **"Values"** have no persuasive force unless dignified and empowered by ultimacy of roots and reach — by religion.[4] Yet our **public school** establishment continues to prate about "teaching values" without using our civilization's religious undergirding of the selected values. So far, the widest cooperation on addressing this problem is the coalition behind a pamphlet entitled "Religion in the Public School Curriculum: Questions and Answers" (including such divers groups as NCC, NAE, NEA, and AAR[5]). It rules out mentioning creation (which so-called "scientific creationists" wrongly say can be taught without the G-word) in science classes, though "the account of creation found in various

4. Humanist efforts to defend secularism against this claim are persistent but not persuasive. The best such author is Paul Kurtz, who has completed his trilogy with *Living without Religion: Eupraxophy* (Buffalo: Prometheus Books, 1994). The other books were *The Transcendental Temptation* and *Forbidden Fruit.*

Not all who try to support values without specific religious undergirding are, as Kurtz is, hostile to religion. William Bennett's *The Book of Virtues: A Treasury of Great Moral Stories* (New York: Simon & Schuster, 1994) provides traditional materials to move children toward basic moral literacy. But *knowledge* of a virtues list itself cannot motivate the *practice* of those virtues. Goodness, which is virtues-in-action, requires a coherent view of how things are in the universe and in human life. Bennett's selection offers a hodge-podge of world-pictures with their fairies, saints, and gods. Bennett is better than Kurtz, but neither addresses the full range of realities that moral education as induction into the moral life requires.

5. National Council of Churches, National Association of Evangelicals, National Education Association, American Academy of Religion.

scriptures may be discussed in a religious studies class or in any course that considers religious explanations for the origin of life."

Further, "teachers may not invoke religious authority" for the "basic moral values that are recognized by the population at large (e.g., honesty, integrity, justice, compassion)." But the issue is not religious authority: that is to be exercised only in particular religious *institutions.* The issue is religious **grounding,** religious incentives, motives, supports that children need to internalize if the values are to be engendered, to become habitual as character. The selection of the particular values is *culture-particular* no matter how much effort is put forth to represent the selection as culture-general, based on a naturalistic ethic. Why not admit that the supports for the selected values are also culture-particular, Western, ours, and therefore to be passed on to and through America's children (how else can we argue for the use of tax money to support the public schools)?

Radical revisionist history results, retroactively, from this bracketing of the religious underpinnings of values. The children are not told the Pilgrims' religious motivation, or that Johnny Appleseed was a traveling evangelist whose thing was community formation (the seed pitch being, Hang in here till you can harvest the apples), or that Martin Luther King, Jr. was a (Protestant) clergyman. But research psychologist/psychoanalyst/cancer-healer Lawrence LeShan (in *How to Meditate,* and elsewhere) says that values are rooted in "religious, romantic, and compassionate feelings." When he spoke here in Craigville, I referred to Rilke's saying to the children, "Even if I were to leave God out, He would come in after the last sentence." LeShan said, "I'll use that!"

Putting God into conversation is sometimes *divisive,* but leaving God out is always eventually *disastrous.*

206

The public schools' hidden persuaders against God

OCCASION: Monkey Trial II, on PBS's "Nova." The program title: "God, Darwin, and the Dinosaurs."[1] SUBJECT: The current public controversy over teaching evolution(ism) and/or creation(ism) in the public schools. I dreaded watching, knowing how painful the distortions — on both sides — would be to me: spiritually benighted evolutionists, scientifically benighted creationists, and philosophically benighted both. And I wasn't disappointed. I mean I *was* disappointed, though I got what I expected . . . Surprise! The benightedness on the left (evolutionists) was slightly worse than the benightedness on the right (creationists).

1. As I feared, no one spoke for a **religion-neutral** teaching of origins. What do I mean by that? A religion-neutral public-school text would sound something like this:

> What do you think it would be like if, going to a *play*, you missed the first and last acts and saw only act 2? Do you think that, from your narrow experience, you could figure out much of the two acts you missed? That's how it is with us in the universe. We don't know how it began, but both science and religion believe it had a beginning. We don't know how it will end, but again, religion and science generally agree that it will end. But what do "beginning" and "end" mean when we stretch them so far out of our experience?

1. 22 February 1989. This Thinksheet was written the next day.

When we think of universe time as a play, we are using a **picture.** Pictures are what we have to think with when we are thinking big. Often the thinking takes the form of a jump, called an inference. Then we have to decide whether a particular inference is leading us astray or into more knowledge — whether it is invalid or valid, appropriate or inappropriate. For example, would it be proper to infer, from our play, that just as our play had a *playwright,* so the play we call "the universe" has a playwright, a super-author, a designing and supervising intelligence whether or not called God? That is not a question science can help you with. It's a question for philosophy and religion, not for science. This is a course in science, and you should know right off that science doesn't have all the answers; it doesn't even have all the questions. Part of growing up is learning where to go with which questions.

But suppose you ask a scientist the question about God, the universal playwright? Does science require that the scientist say nothing about it? No, science requires only this: whatever the answer the scientist gives, the scientist must not claim that the answer is "scientific." Besides being a scientist, the scientist is a person, and the answer to this question will be personal. Does that mean that the scientist doesn't "know" the answer? No, only that the answer is not a science kind of knowledge. There are many ways of **knowing.**

What, then, is the science kind of knowing? It's a way of checking on ideas (theories) about how things are. But you can check on whether somebody loves you: would that be science? No, because the highly complex reality we call love does not meet the requirement for scientific enquiry — that there be continuity without personal intervention (because science is rational and can explore only areas of logical process).

Yes, there are different ways of knowing; and they depend on different ways of **seeing**: religion, art, philosophy, science. Each way of seeing is important and can help us in the other ways of seeing. This course is on *the science way of seeing.*

Imagine four experts, one in each of the ways of seeing,

discussing among themselves the question, "Why is there something instead of nothing?" Each will present one or more "theories," which comes from the Greek word for a "seeing," a *picture or story* that helps you to say "I see!" No picture or story can say it all, so no one of the experts can free you from the need of hearing the other three. It is in *you* that the four ways of seeing should come together; and formal education is to help you "understand," to put it all together and make of it the sense that seems best to you. This sense-making is a lifelong process to which everything you feel and think and do and experience will contribute. It is your life, and your mind. May you grow in its joy and wisdom.

2. Why don't most public-school science courses begin with such *disclaimers* and *wider contexting?* Because of ignorance and arrogance. The **ignorance** is evident in the public-school pedagogy: our science teachers, instead of being taught to "teach science" in the contexts of all knowledge and all of life, are taught narrowly to be "science teachers" — as other teachers are taught, equally fragmentarily, to teach their specialties.

A doleful accompaniment to this pedagogy, both in teacher training and in the public-school science classroom, is **arrogance:** one who is taught *a* way of seeing will, if not told it's only *a* way of seeing, assume that it is *the* way, and that other claimant ways of seeing are at least useless if not also false. Ancient Roman arrogance destroyed the great public library of Alexandria, Egypt.[2] Centuries later, after the library had been reestablished, the Muslims destroyed it, saying that *a)* where it confirmed the Qur'an it was unnecessary and *b)* where it conflicted with the Qur'an it was evil — the mentality later at work in Khomeini, the murderous tyrant of Iran.

---

2. Almost all of it 'was *pagan*-destroyed in the third century. In the fourth century, a small extension, a pagan temple, was Christian-destroyed when the archbishop burned the temple.

3. Our public schools should serve to deliver the populace from ignorance and arrogance. Both tasks are impossible when "separation of church and state" is over-read as separation of public education from life's *widest context* and *deepest concern,* the realm broadly called religion. The neglect of this realm is educational: the children are being educated negatively, to know what's not important. They learn the syllogism that school teaches what's important (the teachers say so!); school does not teach religion; therefore, religion is not important.

Now note again this Thinksheet's title: "The public school's hidden persuaders against God" are *a*) **negatively,** the absence of God (as a holophrase here for religion), what's left out being un-important, and *b*) **positively,** the answering of nonsecular ques-tions as though the questions were secular, that is, encompassed *within* the secular, God-absent paradigm.

Now, all questions can be answered within any world-picture ("paradigm," "Weltbild," "Weltanschauung," or my just plain "way of seeing the world"). What we the public must press upon the public-school establishment are two questions, one philosophical and the other cultural-political. The **philosophical** question is, Given the historical and contemporary options, is the currently regnant Enlightenment-secular option the most *adequate* for pub-lic-school education in America today? The **cultural-political** question is, Is that paradigm the most *appropriate* to our history and here-and-now (i.e., would it pass the test of being called "the American paradigm"?).

Ironically, the United States is often and rightly called, among the nations (at least of the West), the most religious both in foundation and in life today; yet most of America's children are given no public help to understand the God who is behind, above, and within our national instruments and institutions. And since religion is the motor of morality, our children are publicly taught no coherent moral vision. It would be miraculous if our media and entertainments were not an irreligious and immoral wasteland. The public school's hidden persuaders against God lead to a public that is, albeit unwittingly, persuaded against God. Even droves of churchgoers are intellectual atheists: when pressed, they admit that they don't believe in God with their minds but only with their "hearts."

4. Why is public school science-teaching of **origins** (of universe, life) so crucial here? Because whoever is not in on the takeoff will not be in on the landing: if the origins picture *has no room for God,* how make room later? And how deal with the fact that a later-intruder god would be incompatible with the biblical God? In the first section I showed that it is unnecessary, in teaching science theories of origins, to leave no room for God; indeed, it is necessary to leave room for God if the godless picture is not to become itself a religion (as it is, for example, in the case of Carl Sagan).

5. Those who tell the origins stories in a way that shuts God *out* by nonmention hypocritically accuse the "scientific creationists" (as in the "Nova" documentary) of telling the origins stories in a way to include God *in* by implicative nonmention. Each correctly accuses the other of ignorance and arrogance.

Lord, may the middle way soon emerge and take the field!

1995 Supplement

1. The essentials of public-education reform, in my view, are the **seven Rs**: readin', writin', 'rithmetic, respect, responsibility, religion, and rights.

2. "School prayer" is code for the public's rising concern about the schools' tacit encouragement of religious ignorance by omission, and what the public believes is the moral consequence, viz., amorality, the absence of the sense of right and wrong. Educationism's relativism argues that both religion and morality are private and therefore outside the responsibilities of the public schools. The persuasive counter-argument is that the public schools exist to form children for responsible living in the United States, a society of quite particular religious and moral roots and reach.

211

Prepositions have no religion

Did you know that the preposition was the latest part of speech to develop? That fact explains why it's the least stable part of speech, and most open. That can be an advantage, as the story I'm about to tell you demonstrates.

Ambrose sat in the back row of my Adelphi University evening class in advanced psychology for business managers. A few minutes into the first session, he announced that he was dropping the course!

I had begun by saying what the course was about and who was teaching it, including the fact that I am clergy. "That's enough for me!" said Ambrose. "The catalog didn't say you were clergy. I'm an **atheist** and won't have anything to do with clergy!" But he was polite enough to last out the session.

The assignment for the second session, in addition to the readings, was to make a list of "*changes* I should make in how I treat people," then choose the most important, and write a page — to be read to the class — on the reason for that change. I caught Ambrose at the door and suggested that he might put how he treats clergy on his list, then smiled and said, "See you next time."

Next time, this is what Ambrose read to the class: "I need to be less Scrooge-like to my employees." After each manager-student spoke, I asked, "Would you like to tell us what you intend to do differently?" Ambrose scowled and said nothing. Only a few made an outward commitment to change.

The assignment for the third session was, of course, for each student to report to the class *what happened* when he or she made the change. During the third session, the mood swung from boisterous to solemn, with a steady tone of sympathy and support, the other side of apprehensiveness about one's own vulnerability. Ambrose's report brought his classmates to cheers and tears. My heart recorded what he said, and I'll try to rerun it for you:

"A woman in the bookkeeping department, a good worker who's been with us five years, had irritated me by carrying her left shoulder high. I hadn't wondered why. But to overcome my obviously stupid irritation, I decided to find out why. 'It's been hurting for six years,' she said, 'and nothing I've tried has helped.'"

"I had recently taken a short course in massage, to help my wife. So I asked her, 'Have you tried massage?' 'No,' she said, 'I live alone.' I asked, 'Would you like me to try?' She was startled, and managed to get out, 'Why, yes.' It was Monday, and every morning that week, as she sat at her desk, I spent a few minutes massaging her neck and left shoulder. Now it's Monday again, and she came to work with a big smile as she carried her shoulder at normal height, and her fellow workers gathered around her to share her joy. Me? I was embarrassed, but profoundly gratified. And the atmosphere? A joyful funeral. My employees decided that *Scrooge had died.*

"The other reason for the atmosphere change at the office was what happened to the stock boy, with whom no one spoke: he stammered so severely that you couldn't make out what he was saying, so to speak to him was anguishing to him and to you. In the three years he'd been with us, I'd made no effort to be friendly. I had settled for the fact that he was a social cripple, and for the theory that he would remain so for the rest of his life. But my conscience nagged me about him, so it was an easy decision to try to do something different in relating to him. Eight days ago, instead of going to the executive lunchroom, I brought a brown-bag lunch, pulled up a stool next to him while he was eating his lunch — and said nothing. On Tuesday I did it again, and all through the workweek. On Friday, *he* began to talk to *me*! And without stammering!''

When Ambrose sat down, there was silence, then applause, then cheers and tears. And Ambrose's heart was full of joy, and awe, and humble pride.

After that session, he confided to me that his wife was dying, and it was his bitterness that explained his outburst at me as the course began. I asked, *"Is she dying away from or into?"* He growled, "What the hell's that supposed to mean?" I replied, "Ask her." He did, and wrote about their ensuing conversation in a poem that now is used is some hospices, as my wife Loree, chaplain of Hospice of Cape Cod, has used it and shared it with chaplains of other hospices. Ambrose titled it "**Dying Into**."

```
             Death is to be feared
                 Or revered
        Depending on if you die away from
                 Or die into.
          If you die away from loved ones
              Never to see them again
          If you die away from sunshine
            To dwell entombed in darkness
       If you die away from the scents of seasons
         The churning tides, the rolling hills,
       Death is the awesome pain of hollow void
             Of knowing but not hearing
                 Life's circus shout
           While suffocating below ground

             But if you die into,
          You fuse with essence of all being
             Becoming greenness of leaves
         The purpleness and joyness of peaks
           The thrilling glint of sunspecks
       Reflecting from whitecaps in brisk spring seas
         The breeze filling sails of distant hulls
```

```
                   Gliding sunsetward.
      You become the force that grows the garden
                   Of those you love
                   And become them
                 You become all sunshine
        The sound humming silently in all things
               You become the smile of being
                   Sighing all feeling
                  If you die not away
                       But into
```

I would be eager for a conversation with you, dear reader, on all this. God is listening to your thinking, but I can't. The best I can do is try to stir your thinking with a few thoughts of my own.

1. For Ambrose, and for most of the class, *religious language* was a huge turn-off that I had to avoid if I wanted him and the others to turn on to God.

2. Avoiding religious language is not difficult for me, for I am *bilingual*: I speak secular and I speak religious (specifically, biblical-evangelical-religious, which is my prayer and communion and witness language). But when I am speaking secular, as in that course, those hearing me can have no doubt as to my translation into my preferred tongue. After a student said something in secular, I would often say, "The classical Christian word/phrase for that is . . ."

3. Ambrose could tolerate my religion when he found that it said **yes** both to nature and to his hopes, and even to his suffering. Then, picking up my image of dying *into,* he was able, without traditional language, to say poetically — not prosaically or creedally — this poem's YES to this life and to the beyond. Then, when I said that I experience the poem as a YES to the God of life against death, he could say, "I understand."

4. In this secular world and time, Christians should learn to make an end run around religious language, as well as reinforcing

the fundamental *biblical language,* the langugage of our world-Story, when and wherever possible.

5. Now you know what this Thinksheet's title means. Prepositions have the power to **affirm without defining.** Used intransitively (with no object, as here), they open on the Transcendent instead of closing on doctrine. They are humble servants of the Lord who does not coerce but invites, who does not entrap but frees from the past (*away from*) for the future (*into*).

Where is Ambrose today on his pilgrimage from this world to the next? I don't know. Maybe I should check it out. Maybe I should send him a copy of this book.[1]

Prepositions are spiritual, their objects are religious. Humanity needs both, as the Christian is "in Christ."

1995 Supplement

1. Suppose Ambrose had taken that course by written correspondence or teacher/student computer or even by computer classroom. How would it have turned out differently for him? The more electronics deepens the individual's isolation in cyberspace, the clearer it will be that human beings need, for their surviving and thriving, **human space**. In Ambrose's case, human interaction with teacher and fellow-students.

2. The two prepositions in play, viz., "away from" and "into," are prepositions of motion (e.g., "into," in contrast to the parallel preposition of space, viz., "in"). The students were to be in motion, in **action**, between the course sessions; and language, our talk together, was aimed at, instrumental to, behavioral improvement. Ambrose's behavior improved toward his workers, his wife, his teacher, his fellow-students, and God.

---

1. Ambrose gave me written permission to publish his poem.

"Into the arms of God"

We are *prodigals,* and God waits to hug us when we come home.[1]
We are *pilgrims,* and God waits to hug us when we go home.

Samuel and Rebecca,[2] unlike their families, survived Auschwitz. Long years later, as he was dying, Samuel asked me to come to him in the hope of finding some comfort: "I am going out into darkness, I have *no light.*" But Rebecca didn't want to let me in: "Haven't we had enough trouble from Christians?" Hearing her, he yelled from the bedroom, "Let him in! Would you deny me help if he has any to bring me?" "But" — she struck her fist against the door — "he will talk to you about Jesus!" Samuel insisted: "Let him talk about anything he wants to!"

Of course I did talk to him about Jesus, as my religion requires. I asked him whether he found any comfort in any Jewish words, phrases, or sentences in his memory. No. "Then," said I, "let's go on a hunt for some saying that comes alive and lights up for you." I quoted many before the one that ends "we were not made to pace out our lives behind prison walls but to walk *into the arms of God.*"[3] At those words,

---

1. From a Christmas card of John Oliver Nelson, founder of Kirkridge, Bangor, Pennsylvania. The reference is to Luke 15:11-32, the parable of the lavishly forgiving father but called the parable of the prodigal son because, taking his half of the inheritance, he "squandered [it], with no thought of saving anything" (my translation).

2. Pseudonyms. "Samuel" died in 1987.

3. The complete quotation is printed on p. 251 in this book. Reflecting on

217

Prodigals, all of us...
yet in Christmas each
is divinely discerned
afar, hugged close,
given a party... Glory!

he lifted his head, widened his eyes, and asked, "Quote that again, please!" I did. "Would you send me a copy, please?" I did. Later I learned that he kept the saying rolled up as a scroll in one hand or the other, as though it were a phylactery, and there it was when the prodigal and pilgrim died. The world fell off him,[4] and he walked into God's arms.[5]

Danger! Because hugging is a lifelong hunger, it's easily exploited not only in action but also in words. Fight with me, then, for the real thing, the authentic sentiment, against sentimentality. Fight for **compassion** against bathos. Exercise continuous critical judgment as to the devotional and ethical content of

---

more than a half century in the clergy, and sorting over in mindful prayer what specifically I've done that has incontestably fed souls, nothing rises higher than my use of great quotations, biblical and extrabiblical.

4. In this sentence, the second image is from Aquinas; the first, from Tennyson — as I discovered on the wall while in a meeting in the 1804 Arch Street Friends Meetinghouse, Philadelphia: "For here the habit of the soul / Feels less the outer world's control. / The world that time and sense have known / Falls off and leaves us God alone."

5. The graphic is also from Nelson's Christmas card.

218

feelings and behavior claiming the name "compassion" — because, cut off from worship and integrity, compassion is falsely so called, for it is nothing but sentimentality. God disappears into "Compassion," which then is the highest virtue and value, the central and supreme good. You are extended the cheap and cheapening invitation to come get your hugs without repentance from your unrighteousness and without return to the One who alone is worthy of worship. There are far worse things to make a religion of than compassion; but without worship and integrity, compassion sags into self-righteousness and the conventional behavior of "being nice."[6]

The biblical triad is clear and consistent: God is *holy,* therefore we are called to worship him; God is *righteous,* therefore we are to be righteous; God is *merciful,* therefore we are to be merciful, compassionate, as was the prodigal's father. Draw a triangle with **God** in the center and the three qualities, one at each angle. Now think of some present puzzling situation in your private or public life, and ask how in its light each angle should question the other two — for each should illumine, and serve as a check against the hypertrophy of, the other two.[7]

Now, alongside that triangle, draw another with **church** in its center. Then mark its angles, corresponding to the other triangle's "holy," "righteous," and "merciful," respectively, as follows: **covenant** (which creates the Christian community that its **cult,** or worship, sustains), **creed** (which defines the church, as **canon** defines the limits of its sacred literature), and **code** (Christian **conduct,** whose heart — but not whole body — is **compassion**).

1. While compassion figures in all religions, why is it such a standout in the ideal Christian character as to threaten to become, by

---

6. Making a religion of etiquette is an upperclass temptation, but it's a middleclass temptation to sacrifice *truth* to pleasantness and to behave unpleasantly toward any who introduce awkward truths or outré opinions.

7. God is, and we should be, neither soft (sentimental) nor hard (unforgiving of the penitent). But as appropriate to the situation, God is, and we should be, *kind* or *severe* (Rom. 11:22).

being extended too far in a straight line, a religion in itself? Chiefly because of what the prophets pointed to and what Jesus heightened: the compassionless society as evidence that God's nature and will have been forgotten. For the reverent, righteous compassion Jesus lived, and taught in his radical parables, we Christians use the word **grace**.[8] The prodigal "squandered [everything], without thought of saving anything": his father was prodigal, lavish both in his fullhearted forgiveness and in the coming-home party he threw to welcome his profligate son. If you had law-and-order responsibilities in that society, would not such preaching worry you into thinking that a little more of this will cause things to come unglued?

And if now, in this society and world, we have duties that check our human and Christian eagerness to open our arms and hug everybody, the whole broken church, the whole wounded world, this "irresponsible" Jesus fastens his astonishing parables on us, lest we forget whose we are and thus also who we are. And lest we forget that the bottom-line needs of all of us human beings are, as the Lord's Prayer rightly has it, *bread and grace* (forgiveness in a community in which we are known and loved, and hugged).

2. The parable doesn't say the father was hugged, but can you imagine the ex-prodigal not hugging back? Maybe God doesn't need love,[9] but can you imagine his not enjoying it, wanting it, even enjoining it?[10] As penitents and praisers, weekly we walk into

8. See p. 242 of this book. Of this saying, a woman said to a congregation to whom I'd distributed it, "I didn't get to go to high school, and I don't understand much theology, but this goes on my fridge!" . . . Stages of life, stages of faith — and stages of **grace**: prevenient, justifying, sanctifying. Of the first, after sixty years I can still see the radiant face of a janitor who had his spiritual wits though the community considered him a halfwit — radiant as he said, often, "We love God because he first loved us" (1 John 4:19).

9. The word for this attribute is *aseity*, "God in his eternal and independent being" (*Webster's New International Dictionary*, 2nd ed.; *The Random House Dictionary*, 2nd ed., manages to leave out God and God's independence by referring only to "existence").

10. So begins the Ten Commandments. "God wants us to love him eternally with our whole hearts — not in such a way as to injure or weaken our earthly love, but to provide a kind of *cantus firmus* to which the other melodies

God's arms: *public worship* is being hugged by, and hugging, God. And daily, in private and family[11] *devotion,* we do the same.

"Sorry, I don't do church," said a young man whom I invited to worship recently. "I wouldn't find it interesting." How does he know? And does it have to be "interesting"? God loves us and is interested in what is best for us. That best requires our worship, our attending unto God privately and publicly. If as a lover you are uninterested in showing interest in what your lover is interested in, will not your beloved soon become uninterested in you? But if you show interest, for the sake of love, in what does not interest you, sometimes — surprise! — you become interested.

Grace is surprise, and more. It is *joy* and *peace.* It is always, ever, learning by the cosmic-mystic design of "the Love that moves the worlds."[12]

3. But how can you walk into God's arms as penitent prodigal or pilgrim if you don't believe in God? The question is reversible: how can you believe in one whom you don't love? When a student of mine said in class that "**love**" and "**believe**" are from the same root, I said, "That's too good to be true, but I'll check it out." I checked it out. He was right, as I admitted at the next class session.[13]

---

of life provide the counterpoint" (Dietrich Bonhoeffer, *Letters and Papers from Prison* [New York: Macmillan, 1971], p. 150).

11. Who any longer has family devotions? Strong families. Who any longer has private devotions? Strong souls. For nine years I edited the United Church of Christ's magazine *Family Devotions,* which was discontinued after I left our church's national office: not enough strong families left.

12. From the first line of Dante's *Divine Comedy*.

13. I was proud both of being scholar enough to check it out (an intellectual virtue) and humble enough to admit my ignorance (a moral virtue). But I was more proud of that student, who had learned *etymological meditation*, peering wonderingly into the depths of words, eager to rejoice in, and thank God for, the discoveries you make. Don't miss William Safire's column "On Language." And note with what reverent expectation poets treat words — e.g., in Bill Moyer's six-segment "The Power of Words" (PBS, 1989).

4. The Holy One is both righteous (with base in *truth*) and merciful (with base in *love*). In the beginning, God created the Angel of Truth and the Angel of Love.[14] Said the latter, "Make man to love you, and man will honor me." But the former said, "No! For their own partisan advantage, human beings will weave a woof of lies on the warp of truth, and both you and I will be dishonored!" The Angel of Love won, and the Angel of Truth was right. The moral is, When you lose, being right makes it hurt a little less. But note that God did not do precisely what the Angel of Love wanted. Instead, God made man to love, then set them **free**, male and female, to choose whom and what to love. Their abuse of that freedom has proved as various as the creatures themselves, including love itself — in love with love instead of with God, the Source of love and all the other creatures.

5. In a 1952 debate with me, anthropologist Ashley Montagu argued, "God is love, so love is God." He and a handful of others in various fields were laying the foundations of what was to become the human potential movement.[15] Already by that time I'd bumped into that bit of *crooked thinking* often enough that it felt scriptural, a satanic verse from the garden of original sin. W. H. Auden exhorts us, "You shall love your crooked neighbor/with your crooked heart." But he would not support loving your neighbor's logically or morally crooked thinking. God is love, but love is not God.

Consider this: "A nickel is five cents, *so* five cents is a nickel." Right? Wrong. Why? Aren't they the same thing and thus the statement a reversible proposition? Yes and no. Why no? The "so" is wrong: a nickel and five cents share identity but not logical continuity; you can't conclude either one from the other, so "so" is invalid reasoning. To understand this fallacy, which logicians call circular reasoning, think of this nonsense: "Boston is a city, *so* 'city'

---

14. My version of a talmudic tale.

15. Which now, in some of its versions, has added the occult, to become "New Age" religion and culture.

means Boston" (i.e., "Boston" exhausts the meaning of "city"; "Boston" and "city" are identical). Montagu argued that the proposition is reversible, "God" and "love" being identical, mutually exhaustive of meaning. This twisted logic reappeared in 1988 in a beguiling context[16] in the mouth of mythologian Joseph Campbell: "If God is love, *then* love is God."

6. In secular America, theism is dying not just from malnutrition but also from crooked thinking that **shuts God out** for violating the law of parsimony, minimum hypothesis. If God means love and love means God, God-Love or Love-God is the deity. But — according to this romantic humanism — since "Love" is the content of "God," and tells us what God is, and on independent grounds we are discovering more and more about Love, we can and should dispense with metaphysics, religious traditions and theologies and liturgies and communities. We can and should write our own Ten Commandments and Sermon on the Mount. We can and should relieve ourselves of the burdens and embarrassments of history, of Abraham and Moses and Jesus, for Love religion teaches us to honor only Love and to celebrate it wherever we find it in past and present.[17]

For *Love religionists* who use Scripture, the holiest saying is "God is love" (1 John 4:8, 16), which they use in a fundamentalistic way, ripping it out of context and treating it as an absolute statement (and reversible proposition). But the context is clear: it is not love in general but a particular love, "the love [which the biblical, historical] God has for us" (v. 16a). The generalization is vicious if the distorters are aware of violating the context. As for those who believe "God is love" without benefit of knowing the context, they are only ignorant rather than vicious. But the distortion is no less serious in its cultural effects.

16. Bill Moyer's six-segment interviewing of Campbell, "The Power of Myth" (PBS, 1988).

17. Currently a New York "New Age" Jew is trying to convince me that "universal love" exhausts the "real" meaning of Torah. Decision making is serious: each of us must decide not only what is really important but also what is really real. It's one aspect of the burden and blessing of pluralism.

What cultural **effects**? For one, Love religion in various guises and through a variety of processes and programs is becoming the religion of our *public schools,* more and more grounded in New Age metaphysics. Theism, undefended, is soon defamed: not religion, but biblical (Jewish and Christian) religion, is to be kept out of our schools. The world is too small for anything but love, but it is also too dangerous for anything but *truth.*[18]

7. Back to the debate. To visualize the difference, I drew this diagram:

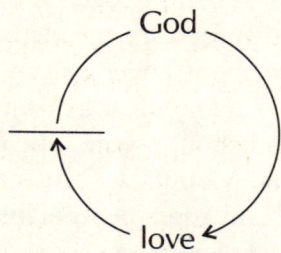

The blocking line means that subject and predicate are not reversible. "God is love," but love is *not* God! To make his counterpoint, Ashley Montagu erased my line and, on the circle's opposite side, put a line of his own, making the circle read "Love is God, but [the historical, biblical] God is *not* love." The deliberate effect was to exclude, from modern thought and life, the God who makes (creation), speaks (revelation), and saves (redemption) — the biblical God.[19] Jesus' story, no longer the capstone of God's *story,* becomes only one among the fading tales of ancient worthies. Since

18. William Sloan Coffin: "The world is too dangerous for anything but *truth* and too small for anything but *love.*"
19. The argument that the fullness of love is available without theism parallels Paul's argument (Rom. 4) that the fullness of faith is available without circumcision. How a Jew feels about the latter is how we biblical believers, Jews and Christians, feel about the former.

biblical *religion* exists as the telling of God's story as the context for telling/hearing our life-stories, concerns, sorrows, joys, fears, and hopes, biblical religion collapses. Where you draw the line on the circle makes "all the difference."[20]

8. "Feel yourself hugged!" concluded a recent letter intended to comfort me. The writer had obeyed the phone company, had reached out and touched me, but felt "frustrated" at not having long-distance arms, and concluded that a letter, which requires hands, would be a little closer to a hug than would a phone call.

"Arms" (as weapons and as limbs) are for protection and attack, defense and offense. They are, in and out of the Bible, metaphors for power, authority, creation, and trust (for deliverance, preservation, and direction). In the New Testament, two Greek words are used for the human "arm," each three times. The arm in action is (as it often is in the Old Testament[21]) an anthropomorphism for God's power; the "bent"[22] arm is for holding and hugging: Simeon holds the baby Jesus (Luke 2:28), and Jesus puts his arms around a child (Matt. 9:36; cf. 10:16). God comes at Christmas, gets hugged, and hugs.

9. "Prodigals, all of us . . . yet in Christmas each is divinely discerned afar, hugged close, given a party . . . Glory!" No longer a profligate, the prodigal is a *pilgrim,* walking through light and darkness into the arms of God.

20. The familiar phrase from Robert Frost's "The Road Not Taken."

21. But for the rich range of meaning, see Deut. 33:27; Isa. 33:2, 40:10-11, 51:5, and 53:1. The three New Testament occurences of the Greek word for the arm in action refer to God's *power* — one, a quotation from the Old Testament; the other two, on the Old Testament model.

22. Your "ankle" is the permanently bent part of your leg, and is derived from the Greek word for your arm when bent, in holding/hugging, for example. We come from the womb of Mother Earth and walk into the arms of God our Father. In between, we are meant to meet One who died for us, to win us from our sins into God's forgiveness, peace, joy, and power to live and love and serve.

Religion projections, A.D./C.E. 2025[1]

"Don't worry: God rules" were the last words of Karl Barth, spoken to a worried friend.[2] That's the long run.[3] But what about the short run?

1. This essay is a severely abbreviated version of "Religion Projections: Early 21st Century," which was part of a project I did for Hudson Institute at the request of its founder and director, Herman Kahn, in 1970. The think tank most influential on President Kennedy and many others, the Institute under Kahn was better known for its work in science and technology than in the humanities. "A.D./C.E." is my way of honoring Christendom ("in the year of our Lord") and of recognizing pluralism ("common era"). Elsewhere in this book, B.C.E./C.E. are not used.

2. *Es wird: regiert.* The free translation is by Mathias Rissi in a conversation with me. Especially as appears in the Gospel of John, said Rissi in dilating on Barth's meaning, "God is ruling in Jesus Christ" as the personal fulfilment of the Kingdom of God (*autobasileia*).

3. Barth's Christian certitude about present and future should not be read as quietism. My teacher Henry Nelson Weiman, one of the two scholars on whom Martin Luther King, Jr. was to write his Ph.D. dissertation, was so afraid of quietism that he proclaimed the future as open, good or evil finally triumphing — depending, partly, on us. God is (as Wieman said many years later in a book title) *The Source of Human Good* but not the hands-down Victor. I disagreed, but his challenge to responsibility remains with me. Our religion, in line with our human condition, is one of *"creative insecurity"* (Peter Bertocci). Andrew T. Lincoln, in "The Promise and the Failure: Mark 16:7, 8," (in *Journal of Biblical Literature* 108, no. 2 [1989]: pp. 283-300) boldy asks "how to understand divine failure to complete the vindication of Christ and his followers" "after Christ's resurrection," failure in the sense of "the failure of the promise" in the sense that the earliest Christians appear to have expected the swift full-coming of the Kingdom of God after the resurrection. All historical promises need *continuous*

"On your knees, for all depends on God; on your feet, for all depends on you."[4]

When in 1969 Herman Kahn, director of the Hudson Institute, asked me to be his religion scenarist, to write what he called **"scenarios"**[5] on the future of religion, his presenting problem was "what will religion look like in South America in 2025?" He'd gotten wind of some young Catholic priests who, inspired by movements for justice elsewhere in the world,[6] were beginning to look at the social darkness around them in a new light. With his genius for imagining oceanic changes evolving from small shifts of attention, producing transformations of consciousness and conscience, he wanted to know whether those priests were stressing the afterlife somewhat less, as they seemed to be becoming more angry and hopeful about *this* life, about the actual lives and living conditions of their flocks.

"Yes," I was able to say after studies and interviews, "your surmise was correct. By the time these priests become monsignors and bishops, the Church will be clashing with the landowners and the military." What came to be called **"liberation theology"** with its "base communities" was not long in coming.

But not all religion-projecting is that straight-line easy. Error, as well as sin, is anything projected far enough in a straight line. History as it emerges is full of surprising turns, unanticipatable emergents, swings

---

reinterpretation as the generations roll, but this one is especially awkward, as the New Testament itself evidences. The Kingdom is now (on which, revisit note 2), and not yet; the Lord's Prayer is for today and every subsequent tomorrow "till Kingdom come."

4. A paraphrase of John Wesley's "Pray as if everything depends on *God*, work as if everything depends on *you*."

5. Recent dictionaries add his meaning — e.g., *Random House Dictionary*, 2nd ed.: "an imagined or prophetic sequence of events, especially any of several detailed plans or possibilities."

6. Especially the U. N. Declaration of Human Rights (1948, with major input by persons connected with the U. S. National Council of Churches), combining social vision with concrete concerns for the common life, and balancing *subjectivity* (the individual) with *community* (the person-in-relationships); and the U. S. civil rights movement.

and reversals. Belief in miracles is realism! Honest futurologists can't afford the luxury of pessimism or optimism.[7] While their primary presupposition is that the future is dynamic within the present, a function of the present, they must be prepared for divine intervention, for what looks like sheer novelty or randomness or chaos alongside of, sometimes canceling, their organismic prophecies. And they must be wary of leading the prescriptive into the predictive and of overweighting, in favor of their personal predilections, the scales of continuity/change, individual/community, subjective/objective,[8] institution/movement, ecopolitical/cultural, and pragmatic/speculative.

What follows is a brief sketch of my now quarter-century-old **projections** toward early twenty-first-century religion on the global schema.[9] I've changed nothing: I'm not interested in looking good, I'm interested in stimulating you to think and pray your own way toward religion's future. The following is written from the time-location perspective of the year A.D. 2025.

7. Not to suggest that writers of utopias, dystopias, and science fiction are dishonest futurologists; they all have what futurologists don't, namely, the poetic license of fiction. Weaned from the religion of progress, and in seminary, I walked all over "The World of Tomorrow" (the 1939 World's Fair), unbeguiled, though impressed, by its melding of futurology and technocratic *utopianism.* Thomas More dreamed of the ideal commonwealth and ironically called his dream *Nowhere* (in Greek, *Utopia,* 1516, the year of the first printing of the New Testament in the original language). Jonathan Swift upped the irony to satire in *Gulliver's Travels,* as did Samuel Butler in spelling "nowhere" backward (Erewhon). Deepening the satire to skepticism, Aldous Huxley (*Brave New World*) and George Orwell (*1984*) produced their *dystopias:* when reality fails to support utopian visions, they rot into cynicism and despair. But the pendulum swings, hope springs eternal, vision returns — with mystical cast when the outer vision fails, as in Hermann Hesse's *The Glass Bead Game* (1943, smack in the center of World War II).

8. For these aspects, I coined the words "*esofuture*" and "*exofuture.*" See, e.g., my "Religion and the Esofuture," *Anglican Theological Review,* autumn 1973, pp. 305-23.

9. The study included a statement of *alternative schemata:* the H. I. Standard World, the human-energy model, issue-orientation, phenomenology of religion, sociology of religion, pedagogy of religion, and the tribal perspective. Each of the twenty-three projects was followed by a supporting essay. For the present purpose, only two of the projections require that I draw from those essays.

1. The major religions have come through the end-of-the-twenty-first-century transition period **weakened** in their negations (and so in their polemic), and **strengthened** both in their tribal and in their global affirmations (and so in their apologetic), with no significant changes in their demographic distribution.

2. Poetic intellectuals and the upper and middle classes have moved massively into **mysticism** and the practice of **meditation.**

3. Religion and statecraft have both profited from **growing political sophistication,** of which the chief components are ideological fatigue and religious pluralism within as well as between nations.

4. Religion in both traditional and emergent forms has participated in and fostered global sensibility, which prefers **richness** (predilection for accretion, tolerance of contradiction) to order, and **spontaneity** (the Dionysiac over the Apollonian) to prearrangement.

5. Beginning two generations ago, **technopsychic events** (nuclear, space, biochemical, genetic) have shocked the promise/threat structures of the tribes, radically pruning their introversion, xenophobia, and (where present) imperial drive — and equally radically fertilizing their subsoil, reinvigorating their roots with global nutrients so that their fruits have come to add to the tribal a global quality, making them salable in the world trade of spirit.

6. In **ethics** and **law,** religion has helped shape the world's responses to technopsychic events. Here religion's effect has been ambiguous, though on balance probably pro-global.

7. The ethical-logical consequences of the appearance of the technopsyche, the global psyche of technetronic humanity now almost universal humanity, were not the only consequences. Con-

comitant, and of equal importance, was **the perceptual shift** in the human "spirit," the domain and energy of the Ultimate Conversation (Thou/I) in tension with the intimate conversation (I/me) and the intermediate conversation (I/you).

8. **East/West religion dialog** has advanced to the point of major concessions: the Eastern hemisphere concedes that it has neglected history and the tactile world; the Western hemisphere concedes that it has neglected meditation and man's agglutinative (accessional) power.

9. The order in which the continents are currently productive of **new religions** is North America, Africa, Asia, Latin America, Europe. Not surprisingly, this is also the speed-of-change descending order.

Turning from those *global* projections, the following are for the *United States:*

10. In the past three generations, **clergy** anxiety in America has crescendoed and is only now beginning to abate.

11. Most U.S. congregations — 7/10 of the 170,000 — **have no salaried resident clergy,** though virtually all of them are under the leadership of ordained personnel, 1/12 of whom are women.

12. **Theological education** has radically changed:[10]

   (a) It has become partitionless (seminarians, clergy, and laity studying together) and wall-less ("class" but not "classroom," the learning site being a function of what is being learned), courseless (the curriculum developing from the needs and commitments of the particular students), and

---

10. This bare statement would have little meaning were the changes not spelled out. Consequently, I draw here from this projection's essay.

communal (the self-teaching group, with theologian as adviser-catalyst; whenever possible, living together).[11]

(b) It revolves around pan-educational centers so that the student will be unavoidably, directly, intimately engaged with sophisticated devotees of other faiths and disciplines as well as of his or her own.

(c) It balances objectivity ("action") with subjectivity ("reflection," "meditation," "prayer") — without falling either into actionism (which leads toward disillusion and then despair) or subjectivism (which leads toward skepticism and then despair).

(d) It seeks to engender image-and-concept control, a unified field theory and praxis in imagination and cognition through simulation games and other interactional artifices using eidomachy/eidofusion (images-ideas battling toward creative resolution).

13. Experience in working together on public issues (human rights, ecology, public education, population control, war control, etc.) has developed a muscled **communication network** of Jewish and Christian (Orthodox, Catholic, Episcopal, Protestant [mainline, evangelical, pentecostal]) composition, both groups and individuals — roughly, "the biblical peoples" (a phrase common for this action-alliance).

14. We have become a **values-conscious** society, aware of the values options within cultural pluralism on this polyhermeneutic[12] globe.

11. By 1970, all four of these conditions obtained at New York Theological Seminary because of our 1969 decision that we must educate for the future, which [I believe] will roughly approximate the religion profile I'm detailing in these projections.

12. Interpretations of reality (nature, history, humanity, images, ideas, institutions) vary with cultures, governments, schools, movements, individuals. When Robert MacNeil (on the MacNeil-Lehrer Hour, 18 September 1989) asked Poland's President Jeruzelski, "Has communism failed?" he smiled as he replied, "Define communism and I'll tell you." *Hermeneutics* is sense-making within a

15. What was roughly called the "**underground church**" in the 1960s because ecclesiastics sniffed at its activities and even its existence, became before century's end the respectable R and D (research and development) department of the ecclesial establishments.

16. Late twentieth-century "**secular religion**" or "religionless Christianity" did not prove durable (any more than had the liberalism, neobiblicism, and existentialism that had preceded it in that century), but the rhetorical contradiction within each phrase did achieve its goal: the oxymorons shocked the old sacreds into "relevance."

17. **Judaism** has once again become missionary with its distinctive offer of a middle way between tribalism and globalism, and exists in an astonishing variety of manifestations.

18. The **decline of xenophobic ethnicity** in America has been "bad" and "good" for (Eastern) Orthodoxy and for (Roman) Catholicism.

19. **Nonethnic Catholicism and nonethnic Protestantism** (there being virtually no ethnic Protestantism left in the U.S.) are still distinguishable in faith and order, but hardly at all in life, work, action.

20. The Protestant **conciliar movement** (councils of churches in concentric circles: local, area, county, urban, state, national, world) presaged the present **coalition movement** (for

---

paradigm or world-picture; *polyhermeneutics* adds the efforts to make sense across and among paradigms; and *epistemology* is systematic looking at the process of sense-making itself. When an ecopolitical theory is tried and fails, it's sometimes abandoned, but more often reinterpreted. Said Jeruzelski, relieving MacNeil of the challenge to define communism, "As an idea," the Marx-Engels *Communist Manifesto* of 1848 "is still beautiful"; but it was corrupted by "Stalinist utopianism" and one-party government, which has proved "ineffective." And four days earlier, Lehrer interviewed the USSR's *enfant terrible* Boris Yelsin who, when asked what communism is, lifted his eyes heavenward and said "Clouds" (a reference to Aristophanes' play spoofing Socrates?).

greater commitment to, and responsibility for, each other — compare the difference, in American history, between the Continental Congress and the Constitutional Convention).

21. American civil life has become more secular in the sense that religious institutions have less political weight than ever before, and religion itself has become a **boundary phenomenon.** This, however, needs *qualifying*:[13]

(a) The sector-cathedrals and metro-church (the latter being the federation of sector-cathedrals in a metropolis) carry less political clout than the old chanceries and episcopal/ecclesial bureaucracies, yet they are *more effective* both in institutional maintenance and in services to persons: they are providing more specialized clergy for service in the general community than ever before.

(b) Indirectly, through instigating the formation of ad hoc task forces (actional coalitions of "the secular ecumene"), the churches have a potential for *more political influence* than at any time in the past century.

(c) Religion has become *more skillful* in translating its doctrines into human values in the public domain. Values education is universal in the public school system, and local clergy participate in this on a nonproselytizing basis.[14]

(d) The primitive centrality of priestcraft in the community (the holy tree with its shaman in the center of the village) has yielded to the continuous *participatory process* of the community's defining its values and its identity. While this process is secular in the sense of nonsectarian and nonecclesial, the churches and their clergy are essential boundary phenomena to the process. The sacred communities and their sacral

13. This is the other projection that calls for some exposition from its essay.
14. My 1969-70 Chappaqua adult-education course, with radio and television parallels, "Suburban Man and the Values Revolution," was aimed toward this goal, namely, values education in New York State public education.

functionaries influence the process through the citizens' participating in the sacred communities and/or in action coalitions generated by them.

(e) The Israelite "true" prophet was archetypal of this boundary location in one of its functions, namely, to *criticize* the Establishment's self-understanding (controlling images, etc.) and behavior in both public and private life.[15] This contribution of Christian and Jewish thinkers to the public life has not diminished.

(f) *Transcendence,* religion's traditional function of pointing to the beyond and the Beyond, has not died but has acquired a new form, namely, the encouragement of a humble openness to creative change and uncomfortable encounters that promise human enrichment (as captured in such a phrase as "the praise of God and the joy of the whole creation"). (Tillich's self-description as "a boundary man" was a precursor of this stance and contribution.)

(g) Ever and always in human affairs, the total or partial nonparticipant is suspected of deviance and either (passively) ostracized or (actively) persecuted (though perhaps later honored[16]). The irony is that while the spiritually convinced nonparticipant individual or movement is a *boundary phenomenon,* as religion generally now is, the witness challenge may eventually affect society at its center. In these past two generations, persecution has been declining (1) because of the mellowing effect emerging globalism has had on the tribes (nations and churches) and (2) because of the widening and deepening recognition that without the deviants' and dissidents' contribution we simply would not have survived as the

---

15. Considering it ominous that President Nixon's control-sociomodel for domestic politics and foreign relations was *football,* I made frequent references to it in national church gatherings and the media and received numerous cartoons of it (though doubtless others were disseminating the same thought) including one from the *New York Times* OpEd, 22 January 1973.

16. Jesus: "Your ancestors . . . murdered the prophets, and you build their tombs" (Luke 11:47f; cf. 13:34 and Matthew 23:37).

human race. But the present persecution-danger is more subtle: ideological globalists (antitribalists) attack, in the name of "man," all efforts of tribes, and subcultures within tribes, to maintain their roots. Ideology impoverishes and dehumanizes, and this one threatens to define global man narrowly as homogenized man, lacking in historical and personal depth and variety because he lacks any short-radius we-feeling. The chief social function of religion in our time is, accordingly, to defend and strengthen the tribe for *peoplehood* and the individual for *personhood*.

22. Because "the person" is both individual and collective, religion promotes both **soft revolution** (radical personal change) and **hard revolution** (radical sociopolitical change). Almost all the religious theory (i.e., theology) of any influence today sees the two as a single process (called by Teilhard "hominization" and by ecumenical-movement theology, beginning in the mid-1960s, "humanization").

23. **Religious tension** today, cutting across all former dividing lines, exists chiefly in the vectors of a **trialog** among tribal, global, and tribal-global man.

1995 Supplement a quarter-century later

1. Haiti's President Aristide more than fulfilled my projection that young Roman Catholic priests would *a*) become liberationists and *b*) come to power — though he came to power in the state rather than in the church, which continued to side with the rich and the military against Aristide and the poor.

2. I underestimated the force of the woman's movement. Projection 11 has only $\frac{1}{12}$ of congregations with ordained women leaders by A.D./C.E. 2025. Revised projection: $\frac{1}{3}$ of all 170,000 Christian congregations in the U.S.

3. I foresaw only glimmers of the electronics revolution, e.g., in Projection 12d. But much of what I wrote of the "technopsyche" anticipated the computer, "technetronic" mentality.

4. In 21g, "man" the species was the word then being used; today we would say "humanity." As for 23, we still have no good replacement for "man" in the three phrases. "Humanity" won't do; three particular character-types are indicated. "Type of person" is close, but clumsy.

5. Part of the cost and joy of building your own home, as Loree and I did, is that you live in it; the other part is that *it* lives in *you*. By "technopsyche" I meant, and mean, that the late-industrial, cybernetic world we've built and live in lives in us, shaping our consciousness, conscience, and concerns. This new reality splits religion into a **conformity** wing (instance the Glass Cathedral) and a **resistance** wing (instance the rise of pentecostalism, non-Christian charismatic cults, and disciplined synergistic mysticism).

For the canonical-critical Christian, the emerging question is this: which will receive the greater investment of energy, the new technopsyche or the biblical-historical **theopsyche**, the mind of Christ (Phil. 2:5-11), which "do[es] everything for the glory of God" (1 Cor. 10:31)?

6. I'm now less inclined to predict (§1) "no significant changes in their [the major religions'] demographic distribution." We seem to be entering a period of intensified Christian and Muslim missionary activity, both of these the largest religions making inroads on the other traditional religions (even Buddhism) and on secularism.

7. What's that I said (§21[g]) about "the mellowing effect emerging globalism has had on the tribes"? Not so as you'd notice it, at least yet. Right now, the tribes are digging in against transnational and global winds.

236

Hell, the Canadian Brass, and
the Christian religions

Recently, our host and hostess in Fort Lauderdale took us to a secular concert, the famous "Canadian Brass," in a sacred space, Coral Ridge Presbyterian Church. At the intermission, the senior minister, James Kennedy (whose late Sunday worship has many hundreds of television outlets), strode forth and quoth in substance thus:

> While we are all enjoying this splendid performance, I am saddened at the thought that some of you who are here tonight will go to hell. It's entirely unnecessary, but you will do it. It's unnecessary because God in Jesus Christ has made it unnecessary by providing forgiveness of sins through the blood of the Cross. But while you don't have to go to hell, some of you will because you will, until the day you die, continue to reject God's offer of salvation. I'm here to plead with you to repent, and accept God's offer, and leave this place tonight not just with happiness over having heard a good concert, but with joy because you have been forgiven and are bound for heaven. . . .

1. That eight-thousand-member church is, in Fort Lauderdale, the place to go for culture and that Christian religion, which is one of the authentic, New Testament-supportable Christian religions that together make up "Christianity." Likewise, all the Jewish religions together make up "Judaism." Why the variety? Because of the Bible's **open paradigm,** many stories interwoven

within one Story, many ways — then and through the ages and now — of telling the one Story. (And even different narratologies. For example, Mircea Eliade tells the story as medium for experiencing awareness of the sacred, heaven touching earth. And Hans Frei is for letting the meanings emerge without too much cogitation about truth in the abstract or in metaphysics. And Paul Ricoeur sees the biblical stories as making truth claims, and uses them to challenge philosophers working within nonbiblical paradigms.)

2. Now, doubtless many nontraditionally religious in Kennedy's concert audience had no afterlife problem in their heads when he told them they had one. Some of them believed there's no afterlife, period; others, that "you go to a better place" (a sentimental notion strengthened, of late, by pseudoscientific discursi on "near-death experiences"). But a recent issue of *U. S. News and World Report* gives some support to Kennedy's religion (that is, his version of Christianity). On the cover, the word "HELL" is almost as large as the word "GOD" was on *Life*'s last 1990 issue. And the subtitle suggests the possibility of going to a *worse* place when you die.

3. Can we say what's happening? **Ethics** is back, so hell — *afterlife ethics* — is back. The eudemonistic (happiness oriented) time we've been living through is, as are all such times, nonethical — or, to use one of its favorite words, "nonjudgmental." The nonjudgmental attitude comports with nondiscriminatory behavior. To eudemonistic ethics, the only thing wrong/bad/evil is to call anything/anybody wrong/bad/evil. "Everything is permitted," as Dostoyevsky says in *The Brothers Karamazov.* Using tax money to exhibit a crucifix in urine is not to be complained about to National Endowment for the Arts or any other branch of government. A thirteen-year-old child with the child she's given birth to constitutes "a family," no euphemism intended. The sadistic denigration of women in movies is protected by artistic license. But now, throughout our culture, we've entered a *revolt against the revolt against ethics.* Even the afterlife is being re-ethicized: moral responsi-

238

bility/consequences for our this-life behavior continue into the afterlife. There's a *moral continuum* between this world and the next. This adds **solemnity and dignity** to human life here and now.

4. While I'm happy about the return of hell, I must point out these *dangers:*

a) The *narcissistic* danger: A few Sundays ago, somebody put a $100,000 check in the collection plate in that church in Fort Lauderdale: the congregation is decidedly upper-income, full of folks who've made it by taking care of themselves, looking out for number one. Avoiding hell and gaining heaven requires no shift in mentality. The biblical concept of conversion is far richer than this.

b) The *orphic* danger. Excessive otherworldliness trivializes this world, diminishing the significance of its concerns, relativizing the woes of the oppressed in body and mind, rejoicing in the soul's wealth to the neglect of the wellness of society.[1]

5. Do you think the preacher's *intrusion* into a secular situation was unfair, inappropriate, perhaps even counter-productive? Revelation, God's inbreaking, is a shocking intrusion. And God's incarnation in Jesus is even more: an *invasion* in the process of becoming an *occupation*.

---

1. In 1966, at the World Congress on Evangelism (Berlin) and in my National Council of Churches debate with Billy Graham (Miami Beach), I warned evangelicals of the orphic danger. (Because of him Orpheus' wife got stuck in the underworld; I analogized to a religion stuck in the afterlife.) Subsequently, evangelicals have come to stress the social and political implications of conversion without losing afterlife concern. Note the "liberation theology" parallel in Latin American Catholicism (chapter 45).

Index of Subjects

This is **less than** a concordance: you won't find here all words, biblical references or names, or extrabiblical names. But it's **more than** a listing of major topics with their main references: it's enough for <u>reflection</u> on topics in numerous contexts.

240

242

Lead, kindly Light. . . . One step enough for me.[1]

I am the way, the truth, and the life.[2]

The road
that stretches before our feet
is a challenge to our hearts
long before it tests the strength of our legs.
Our destiny
is to run to the edge of the world and beyond,
off into the darkness:
sure in spite of all our blindness,
secure in spite of all our helplessness,
strong in spite of all our weakness,
joyfully in love in spite of all
the pressures on our hearts.
In that darkness beyond the world
we can begin to know the world and ourselves —
and to understand
that we were not made to pace out our lives behind prison walls
but to walk into the arms of God.[3]

God
is the light in my darkness, the voice in my silence.[4]

1. The enduring hymn of John Henry Newman.
2. Jesus in the Fourth Gospel (14:6). Translating the Hebraism, we get "I am the true and living way."
3. Thomas Aquinas, my adaptation of the beginning of *My Way of Life: Pocket Edition of St. Thomas,* ed Walter Farrell and Martin J. Healy (Brooklyn, N.Y.: Confraternity of the Precious Blood, 1952).
4. Helen Keller, to me when — her hands on my lips — I asked her who God was to her. I was eleven years old.

Grace,

God's caring Presence,
    supervenes over and interpenetrates the common day.
It is the food within all food,
    the comfort and strength within all assurance,
    the song that sings itself within all our moods.
To know this is light,
    to live it is life eternal.
The Love that will not let us go
    will not let us down.[5]

5. My *Readings and Intentions* (Kirkridge Community, Bangor, Penn.) for the first week in August, 1987. This calligraph was by order of Sally Bailey, Hospice Connecticut, as a gift at my surprise seventieth birthday party.